By Agnes Newton Keith

LAND BELOW THE WIND

THREE CAME HOME

WHITE MAN RETURNS

White Man Returns

White Man Returns

by AGNES NEWTON KEITH

Sketches by the Author

AN ATLANTIC MONTHLY PRESS BOOK
LITTLE, BROWN AND COMPANY · BOSTON
1951

FIRST EDITION

ATLANTIC–LITTLE, BROWN BOOKS
ARE PUBLISHED BY
LITTLE, BROWN AND COMPANY
IN ASSOCIATION WITH
THE ATLANTIC MONTHLY PRESS

Published simultaneously
in Canada by McClelland and Stewart Limited

PRINTED IN THE UNITED STATES OF AMERICA

To my children, George and Jean

The Island of Borneo . . . is counted the biggest Island . . . in the whole world, except perhaps California. . . .

A Voyage To And From The Island Of Borneo In The East Indies.
— Daniel Beekman
London, 1718

Contents

Contents

PART FOUR — *Golden Rain*

PART FIVE — *Lightning in a Luminous Sky*

PART ONE

We Return

I. Rendezvous

"WHY doesn't he come, Mum?"

George on the top deck of the steamer stares anxiously down at the wharf, his gray-blue eyes squinted with intensity of purpose to find his father, his wide forehead puckered, his fawn-colored hair askew, his skin gone pale. It is a very important day when you are going to meet your father who has been away for a year, and whom you do not know well anyhow because of the war which has been all of your short lifetime of seven years.

Looking anxiously to where the stranger-parent may appear, George sighs patiently, sniffles a bit with the heat and catarrh, and picks nervously with his forefinger at the corner of his small, tough, well-scrubbed thumb. His face, which was never round in babyhood because his nursery was a prison, is rounder now with advancing youth, and his cheeks are soft and downy and touched with pink as they never were in prison. His nose is small and upturned, his mouth wide and mischievous, and his bearing is both bold and pathetic, with that terrible capacity which small boys have for heartbreak and defiance in one breath, making you want to reach out and touch their rounded cheeks and stroke their skinny shins which end in such big feet.

"But why doesn't he come, Mum?" he wonders, picking his thumbs. His hands are really sore, I see, and I reach down and take them, hot, sticky, calloused, in mine.

"He will come, dear. Just be patient," squeezing his hand, and trying to soothe, although I don't feel patient myself.

"Is that my dad?" Thumb-picking ceases, and hand is pulled from mine to point at a tall, thin, respectable-looking clerical Chinese dressed in starched white shorts who strolls on the pier far below.

"No, dear, that's not Dad. Just wait."

"But you said my dad would be tall and thin and yellow from taking Atabrine, and that man is," he argues belligerently, as if fighting me would bring his dad.

"But not everybody tall, thin and yellow is Dad," I try to explain to a son who scarcely knows his father; whose father was imprisoned almost four years, while George and I shared another imprisonment with women and children. Through those years Harry had only met us for an occasional fifteen minutes under Japanese guard, outside the barbed wire of prison camps in North Borneo, and then while Harry and I stared hungrily at each other, George would run like a wild thing outside the wire, not noticing his father in his mad moments of freedom. It was no wonder that when Harry went East again five months after reunion, he left a son who scarcely knew him.

Very swiftly now the rising sun awakens the harbor of Hong Kong and breaks through the sodden mist above the city coloring the hills with light and shade, but George and I have been up long before, looking for Harry who promised to be here to meet us. Our ship entered the harbor in the stifling dawn, and now as it docks by the sun-stored warehouses, hot even before the sun strikes them, I search the wharf impatiently with my eyes. Dear

God, I silently pray, if you are on the side of those in desperate need, please get a man here quick to meet his son!

"Well, is that my dad?" George abandons thumb-picking to point again, his round forehead wrinkled with worry. "Is it, Ma?"

"Darling, don't you remember at all what Dad looked like? It was only a year ago that he left us in Canada to come back to the East."

"No, Mum, I don't remember – not much."

A tall Chinese coolie with a straw suitcase swinging on the

end of his carrying pole pushes up the gangway from the wharf below.

"Is that Dad?"

"No, George, that's not Dad!"

"Oh. Oh, well — I suppose he'll never come!" His hand drops listlessly from mine, accepting fate again.

"Now, George — just wait."

Don't disappoint my son, Dear God, I pray. This is terribly important. He's had so little yet.

By now the other ten passengers on our transpacific freight ship are on the deck with us trying to help me find a husband, and each steamship and freight agent, porter and port official who comes on board in the next hour is offered to me as a matrimonial possibility — but Harry doesn't come.

What if he shouldn't come at all? I remind myself of his words on the telephone when he spoke to me from London, where he had arrived by plane from Borneo for a conference with the British Colonial Office on the very day George and I sailed from Tacoma, "I'll be on the Hong Kong pier to meet you!" Yes, he'll be here . . . unless something dreadful has happened! Then I recall the nightmare I had the night before we docked at Manila about his airplane having a crash. The next day I went to every travel agency in Manila to see if they had any word of an air accident over India, but nobody in Manila could check with the B.O.A.C. I went back on board ship and didn't sleep for two nights.

Suddenly June calls, "Come quickly, Mrs. Keith! I think I see your husband. I'm sure this is an Englishman! Now — *that* one — that one, Mrs. Keith! That man with the white suit and the little reddish mustache? He's English, I just know he's English!"

Yes, he's English — but not all Englishmen are Harry. Desperately I search the wharf to the entrance, half a mile away. Oh God, bring him, bring him! You know I do have a husband, and it really is so very important to get him here. Here's George standing beside me so cold and numb — he doesn't understand, he's given up.

My eye is caught — yes! This time, YES! I can't see the features, scarcely even the figure, but I know that walk and carriage, erect, brisk, determined, sure-footed, quick – and impatient. Impatient at me for being early (I have never been so in my life before), at himself for being late (he has never been so before), at the wharf for being too long and the people for being too slow.

I watch him secretly, knowing that he's mine. I won't even tell June that I've found him. It's so wonderful to have a husband again! The sunlight strikes his sandy hair – or is it ginger? And certainly there is gray there now. He looks quite well, but thin. And so much smarter, neater, brisker, cleaner-cut than those about him, so energetic, and his eyes so blue, but squinting still because he won't wear a hat. Such a nice, weather-beaten color on his face, too. Now what is there about him that I love so much? I wish he'd look up and see me. How awful to have a wife who describes you!

"George! George! There's Daddy coming now!"

"Hi, Ma! There he is! I *do* know him! Oh, yes, now I remember him! Hi! Dad! Dad! Dad!"

And Harry looks up . . .

So may it always be when people who love each other meet. You look at the person you love and there is nothing to say – except, I love you. There is nothing to do – except touch the hand that is flesh, touch the lips that will die, and be filled for that second with a love which is greater than your bodies which bear it. And then the moment passes, and again you are mortal and man.

Those were hot nights – incredibly hot in the Hong Kong hotel in August. No breeze stirred, no curtain swayed, no flame flickered, no paper twitched, and the only movement in our room high above Des Voeux Road on the dark hotel alley was the flash and flicker of reflected lights from the street below. The red and green neon glow from the advertisements on the blazing thoroughfare reflected in our windows and mirror, making the walls of the room flare and grow dim, with the rival attractions of Glaxo for mother's milk, or Wincarnis for woman's weakness. In the thoroughfare below hawkers shouted their wares, wooden clogs clacked on cement, taxis hooted, girls laughed, beggars whined, and the smell of garlic, musk, firecrackers and human waste arose like stale incense from steaming roads and sweating people.

On the edge of confusion, in the darkness and seclusion of our room, alone at last, we talked.

"Do you remember the night before the Japs landed in Sandakan? The last night we were in our house together?"

"I remember," I answer.

I remember.

That night I said, "Don't leave me. I am so frightened! *I* need you, too."

He: "I must go. It is government orders, and my job. I have promised."

I: "Is it never your duty to take care of your wife?"

"I must go. But if we live through this – I promise I will not leave you again. Good night. Good-by."

Yes, I remember. Could I ever forget? Has any one of all the men and women who fought this war ever forgotten that last night together before parting? A night when every touch is agony, yet unbearably dear, when every embrace which holds two people close for love is the failing clutch of two drowning people who cling – who cling to life, to love, to each other, and then of their own free wills open their hands and let go. Dear God, let us die before such a night comes again!

And yet, having known this night, it is something I would not give up. Having known the love and pain of it, the crisis seen and feared and met, they are mine forever in full meaning. When other lives know fret and ease and tedium and flaccid times, ours is still lit by intensified pain.

"Yes, Harry, I remember."

"Did you used to think of that night afterwards, when you were alone in camp?"

"I did. But then, after the first year it got too far away, too faint. I tried to bring it back, but I couldn't feel how you felt, and how I felt, because I couldn't feel at all after a while, as a woman. All that came back to me was the awful loneliness of that night, and the fear, and the knowledge of dreadful times ahead of us, just now beginning. That was the most terrible time of all the war – those last hours before the Japanese came."

"It seems queer now to me that we didn't ask ourselves that night – is it worth it to live? Or is it better to die now?"

"Yes. We didn't know enough to – then. How little we knew!"

"But if we had?"

"If we had known the answers – we wouldn't be here now."

"Then it was worth it to live."

Who that has not known death, knows really life, I wondered.

"You know, Harry, I find I have forgotten a great deal of the war – just as everyone said I would – and forgiven it a lot. But there is still one thing that I can't forgive."

"I know."

Neither of us needs to say the thing that we can't forgive – the loss of George's brother when the Japs came in – and no children in those years.

"Is George asleep?"

"Yes. But keep your voice down. What do you think of your son?"

"Not entirely repulsive."

"You mean – he's wonderful?"

"Yes. That's what I mean."

"Sometimes I think I'm sorry for us because fourteen years of our life together is gone. But sometimes I'm sorry for the young ones just married because they don't know what it's all about. Or am I just being philosophical? Just trying to console myself for growing older?"

"It doesn't matter how many years we have behind us – or how many in front – if we have them together."

There are certain times in your life which you know, even as they happen, that you will always keep to remind yourself of when life produces only drudgery, unrest, distrust, and boredom. Times which any life is lucky to have a few of, and which some lives may never have. Times which permit you once and for all always to share in the great emotions of all ages.

The Hong Kong hotel room was hot and sordid and torn-curtained and barren and half-wrecked still from the war, and a rat ran across it and chittered on the window sill and we got up and chased it with table knives, and we went back to bed and sweated on the sheets and drank half-warm boiled water out of old gin bottles, and turned over and over and back again, and pushed off the pillows, and lay awake in the heat until dawn, and then with the first gray streaks of morning we turned to each other again and went to sleep, and it had been one of those nights that you will always take with you through all your life to remember when things go wrong.

II. Retrospect

THROUGH four years in Japanese prison camps these were our dreams:

> Just to sit quietly in the long Canadian twilight over a simple meal that we cook for ourselves –
>
> To talk without urgent need to say the important thing before the guard takes you apart, without death hanging over you, without sorrow gripping your heart, without the smile that holds back tears – with life ahead. Or to sit silent, just ourselves and the children and the future before us – without guards, guns, barbed wire, and hunger –
>
> To smell red roses, damp, fresh violets, fragrant lilies of the valley, and sweet hyacinths as they grow at home instead of fermenting tapioca root and prison camp latrines –
>
> Never to be angry again with each other over nothing, or distraught without reason – And never again to say, Goodby – That's how we'll live when the war is done.

Now we were home in Victoria, British Columbia, and we were happy because it was so different from tropical Borneo. Here in our little garden no lush, overgrown streamers of green enveloped the delicate lines of wintering trees and shrubs, no strangling, equatorial vines overpowered the vital traceries of young growing things — here gray trees stood against gray sky bare of all foliage. Here with the new year of 1946 the war was over — our garden, and the world, were clean and fresh and waiting to begin again. Here on this continent, there were peace and sanity, well-being, and health, all we had dreamed of, and our own people.

For some years before the war Harry had been Conservator of Forests and Director of Agriculture for the government of British North Borneo under the Chartered Company, and the conservation of forests, preservation of soil and natural resources, reforestation, study of topography, rotation of crops, and teaching of simplified agriculture to the people of the country had been his work, pleasure and pride, and his only battle had been for a primitive people against their own destruction of their own resources.

I had gone out to North Borneo from the United States as a young bride, I had lived there since 1934, and our only son was born there in 1940. I was a happy enthusiast for Borneo's tropical beauty and charm, I had been captivated by the alien strangeness of a country where elephants roamed free, fish flew, apes almost talked, natives went nearly naked, ladies wore evening dresses every evening, and I had no dishes to do, no clothes or babies to wash. And, going far deeper than this surface Oriental allure, I learned in those years to respect, enjoy, and love a happy people in a happy land.

Then the war had come. Harry, George and I and other government people remained by government order in the country and met the enemy with ourselves, not with guns — a good idea, in theory. We lost our home and all our possessions, we were pauperized and placed in slavery and spent four years in Japanese prison camps there, and when we were flown out of Borneo more dead than alive in September 1945, in a U.S. Catalina, Harry and I agreed that we had finished with the East; its alien, Oriental attraction was a thing of horror to us, we wanted to go home and stay there.

Yet when the North Borneo government, soon to be taken over by the Crown, cabled Harry in February 1946, less than six months after our liberation, asking him to return immediately if he was physically fit to do so, he made the decision to go. He was still suffering from extreme depletion, from four years of semi-starvation, and, worst of all, from the slave complex which makes you expect to be kicked, and cringe when you meet an avenging eye, and dodge to protect your face. I also suffered slave symptoms, and we two had no heart to ask for what free citizens of this continent demanded as their right. For us, the reality was still war, the present and freedom were only a prison camp dream.

While still in the midst of this preoccupation with our personal sufferings, we were informed that a civil administration was being re-established in North Borneo with the primary obligation of feeding, clothing, rehabilitating, making economically free, the Asiatic people of that destroyed country who had been loyal to us and had fought and suffered with us. To accomplish this it was necessary to bring back those who spoke the language and knew the country and its people and their needs, and Harry was one of these.

He went immediately to a doctor and asked for a medical certificate which would pass him as fit. He had just had two serious operations as the result of brutal treatment by the Japanese in prison camp, and he acquired the certificate against the doctor's advice. Then he booked the first available passage to the East.

I asked him not to go. I had been through the war alone; now in peace, I said George and I needed him to reconstruct our lives, and we were not well enough yet to go back to Borneo. But Harry went. A woman is always hurt, yet always proud, when her husband chooses honor, not her. There was no other explanation of Harry's going than that he knew it was right to return and help.

I thought I could never face it – either to go East myself, or to be parted from Harry, both things we had sworn not to do. Three of my ribs had been broken and my shoulder blade and chest seriously injured in Kuching prison camp during interrogation by Japanese authorities, and these injuries which had gone without care for three years now required skilled surgical treatment. George, who was only two years old at the time of imprisonment and six years upon his release, had experienced every possible disadvantage in early childhood, and I had made up my mind that whatever happened he must remain in the Western world with good food and care for at least a year.

So Harry left for Borneo alone, taking a folding cot, two blankets, a mess kit, a bottle of new vitamins, and some borrowed tropical clothes from a neighbor (cotton goods were not yet on the postwar market) to set up housekeeping again in Sandakan. George and I stayed behind in Victoria with Granny, Harry's mother, in the little brown-stained English cottage behind the squeaky garden gate under magnificent oak trees which we loved.

We stayed here a year, and during this time I was looked upon by acquaintances as a combination of war heroine and poor sap. I had suffered—and that experience alone always requires a special tone of voice to discuss—but I must be a fool for punishment if I was going back again! And because I agreed with my friend's comments, I tried to formulate to myself exactly what reasons were going to take me onto a steamer for Asia little more than a year after I had escaped from there. I still felt real terror at the memories of those days, and felt physically ill at the thought of return, but I knew to a certainty that when the boat sailed, I'd be on it, because fundamentally I shared Harry's belief in the necessity to return.

For my own satisfaction, I traced this necessity to the following causes: first, I must go back to say Thank You to those who had saved our lives at the risk of their own by smuggling food and help to us during almost four years in prison camps, the Asiatics of North Borneo. We could not accept our lives from them and leave them to believe we had forgotten.

Next, Harry had gone to help these people with his technical knowledge in the trade of survival; I hoped to be able to help them either by practical material means of which we now had more than they, or by friendship. They had been my friends when friendship meant death; now when it meant life, my friendship was theirs.

Last, Harry had chosen to go; I was following the wife's part and was not to be turned to salt looking back. Which reason came first in my mind, I cannot say, but I know each one was vital.

You always love your son. But to me George was more. He was four years of concentrated effort for survival, he was my food when food was life, my hope when hope was gone, my desire to live when for myself I desired to die. He was the one good thing for us that came out of the war.

And he was the greatest problem. At the age of seven, he had spent more than half his life in captivity, and what mother of my time has not heard that the first five years of a child's life determine his being? If so, what would George be — a slave? A thief? A problem child? Would he ever forget those sore memories? Brought up on secrecy, silence, terror, deceit, as we struggled grimly through years to endure and outwit and survive, would he ever look the world in the face honestly, openly, and without fear? He would. To that, I was determined. How best to help him was my problem. I had always feared what memories of prison brutalities would do to his mind, as much as I feared what starvation would do to his body. Starvation, I had at least been able to see and fight against.

The ills of his body, I could see now, were vanishing; his cheeks were red, his eyes bright, his colds lessening, his lungs were strong again, and his body was building up, but I could not see into his mind — although it seemed to me that he had suffered much less psychological effect than Harry and I. This was astonishing to me, but reassuring. I could only attribute it to the fact that I did the worrying for him. His one security in camp was me, and as long as I could keep up, he had security. A young child's world is very small, wherever he is. George's six square feet of living space in camp, with me as its walls and roof, was his world, and it was isolated from many terrors that our adult prison camp knew. George's world knew only the things that really happened, only the deaths that were died. Our adult world knew all that might have been, and still might be, besides the pains that were.

During this year in North America I wanted George to forget. We never talked of Borneo, nor of the invasion of the enemy into our home in Sandakan, nor of George's first prison nursery on a small tropical island. We never talked of the Batu Lintang camps in Sarawak to which we were next taken, nor of the brutal and terrifying things we saw there, scenes which I still saw to desperation when I closed my eyes at night. Nor of our relief by parachuted food and drugs, and our final liberation from Kuching by the 9th Australian Division and the U.S. Navy. All this we tried to drop from our lives, and when George and I talked, we began and ended our history with return to America.

Now return to America was ended and return to Borneo must begin, and George must go with me if he was to know his father. I began to wonder if I had done right in trying to make him forget. Would return to the scene of our struggle bring to the surface of his being subconscious hurts which I had tried, perhaps wrongly, to blot from his life by ignoring? Was George going to suffer the nervous fears which already made my stomach turn at thought of the East? I knew just enough psychology to suspect myself of being ridden by every complex, and to fear that George might be.

"George, do you remember Borneo?"

"Sure, Mum. You mean prison?"

"No, I mean Sandakan, North Borneo, the town where we lived before the war, when you were very small?"

"No, Mum, I don't remember."

"Don't you remember Sandakan at all?"

"No . . . Oh, yes . . . I dunno, Mum, I dunno. Say, can I go out and buy a comic before supper?"

"We'll see. Don't you remember when you and Daddy and I lived in a white house on a hill with Arusap, and two Chinese amahs, Ah Kau and Ah Yin? And Ah Yin took care of you?"

George wonders, "Ah Yin? . . . Yes, I remember Ah Yin! . . . Ma . . . Ma . . ." His face changes, and suddenly he is telling me, not asking me, as he recalls something that Harry has written from Borneo, and there is no doubt now of what he remembers, for it is there on his face to see.

"The Japs killed Ah Yin, Ma! The Japs killed her!" Incredulity, horror, and remembered indignation turn him pale.

"Yes, indirectly, they killed her, George."

"Then I hate the Japs!"

"Not alone the Japanese killed her, but the war, and bad treatment, and hunger and anxiety and suffering killed her. Just as those same things killed Japanese people, too!"

"Well, I hate the Japanese anyway – for killing her! How did they kill her? Did it hurt when they killed her? It hurts I guess, Ma?"

"I don't know how – I hope not. Perhaps not – she was weak and sick by then I know. What else do you remember about Sandakan besides Ah Yin? Try to think, dear."

"I remember a night when you and Daddy and Ah Yin took me to somebody's house, and I remember a lot of people there talking and drinking, and pretty soon you forgot about me. I went around and drank a little bit out of everybody's glass until I couldn't stand up any more, and I fell down in the middle of the floor. Then Daddy picked me up and carried me home."

"Do you know why we were drinking that night?"

"Yes, the Japs were coming! Ma, will there still be Japs in Sandakan? If there are – I'm not going back. I hate the Japs!"

George has only learned to express hatred of the Japanese since we have come home. When we were in prison camp, this emotion was something we never dared to express before our children for fear that they might accidentally carry the words to the guards.

"It's silly to be afraid of the Japanese now, when you weren't afraid of them in the war. You must remember that some of the guards in camp were kind to you. Why are you afraid?"

"I'm not afraid! I just don't want to go."

"But you'll have a good time, George. You'll go in the jungle with Daddy, and go hunting and shooting and fishing – and maybe shoot an elephant like Dad."

"And have a pooch, Ma? My own pooch?"

"Of course, your own pooch. Now hurry up and get ready for bed."

"Oh, Ma! How about that comic, Ma? You promised I could get one."

"I didn't promise. I said I'd see. But it's too late now – it's almost seven."

"It's only down to the corner drugstore, Mum! And probably they won't have any comics in Borneo."

"Yes, that might be one thing that the starving natives can live without!"

My practical problem now was to decide what material help to take to Borneo from the plenty of the North American continent. On Harry's report in his letters that drugs were still almost unobtainable in the East I packed many bottles of multiple vitamin capsules, an ample stock of sulfa drugs, all forms of penicillin, oral and for injection, and new penicillin ointment, a variety of malaria preventives, salts, cascara, aspirin, and gauze, bandages, and elastic plaster, all of which were unobtainable in Borneo, and any other medical supplies I thought might meet some need.

I took dark cotton cloth suitable for Chinese trousers and garments, and white cotton for blouses, strips of bright silks and flowered cottons for dresses, pipes and cigarette lighters as gifts.

As clothing for myself I took whatever I could most easily buy in early 1947 in Canada, and, as war restrictions were just coming off, this wasn't fancy, and nylon was not procurable. I took sports dresses, and no shorts or slacks as I had had enough of those during the war, and no evening dresses because it was inconceivable to me that, going to live in palm leaf shacks, women would wear evening dresses again. (I found I was wrong. In a hot country, a woman always needs shorts, and evening dresses are the easiest way to stay moderately cool and attractive, no matter what the housing is.)

To make our temporary house more livable, I took curtain material of a pale buff with delft-blue and lime-green leaves twining upwards in the pattern of a swaying rattan, although no one else recognized it as such. I have found that a safe color scheme in the tropics always blends with the trees or the morning sky in cool, pale shades, and never attempts to rival the sunsets or flowers. As crockery, I took California-made Gliden stoneware in oyster gray with an etched fish design, and extra plates of imitation majolica ware in grape colors of purple, muscatel and green, satisfying to the eye, and likely to improve even buffalo meat.

Our silverware was the combined discards from Harry's and my families for several generations back, and boasted every initial except our own.

A radio was also sold me on the assumption that it was adapted to Far East electrical currents, when such currents might be resumed in Borneo (but proved not to be). I took a gramophone and records, most of which broke on the way. I packed blankets and a few sheets I could buy at the time, and a third-hand standard typewriter, and a new portable for Harry. George packed his scooter, wagon, toys, stones, sea shells, polished sticks, petrified chewing gum, broken marbles, and everything else that I didn't find first and throw out.

Injections, I have learned, come in four categories. There is (*a*) the guaranteed harmless one which forms an abscess the size of a walnut on your rear, and must be operated on the day you are sailing, and dressed and bandaged throughout the trip. There is (*b*) the painless one (all are painless, but some more so!) which keeps you tossing sleeplessly for the last four nights before the voyage. There is (*c*) the nontoxic injection which you accept in the right thigh, which transfers itself to the left foot so you can't get your shoe on, and you limp onto the boat in one shoe, leaving the other shoe ashore, to be without it throughout the journey. And there is (*d*) the injection which surprises you by being just as it is guaranteed, painless, harmless, nontoxic, at time of injecting – but three days later in time for your farewell parties you break out in boils.

All these injections I knew, but when we sailed for Borneo this time I discovered a fifth type (*e*), the cholera injection George had before we left Victoria, and in a class of its own.

The first night after the injection he was feverish and his arm was sore, but he was consoled by the thought that he would be better tomorrow. The next day he was more feverish, and his arm more sore, but he was philosophical because I could promise him that his suffering would be over the following day. The third night he was still ill, with a higher temperature, and to hope for tomorrow brought him no comfort. The fourth night his temperature was 105° and I was frightened; I determined that if the next day ever dawned, I would tell the doctor what I thought.

The next day did dawn, and in the morning light I studied George with alarm, which suddenly changed to relief. His nose and eyes were running, he was covered with bright red spots, and he had the measles.

Two weeks later with measles behind and Borneo ahead, we sailed from Tacoma, Washington. Leaving the Aleutian Islands, we felt the last of cold spray and clean wind, and as we traveled west, the East bore down. Soon the refrigerators ceased to freeze, the water coolers didn't cool, the butter was hot, and the toast cold, the milk condensed and the prunes stewed, and the charm of the Orient appeared. There were brilliant skies and oily seas, twilight nights hot with heat lightning, a stupefying sun and monstrous moon poured down white light, and the long, hot days were followed by longer, hotter, steeping, sweating, sleepless nights.

Now heat, humidity, and lethargy became the protagonists, and even George lay sweating, tossing, sleepless on the rolling sea outside Hong Kong the night before we met his father.

III. Entrance to Asia

This is the entrance to Asia. Here in the secret, land-encircled harbor of Hong Kong are the scents of garbage and urine, of salt fish, coal smoke, bilge water and brine, every wind is garrulous with the story of diet, the journey of food from the earth to the esophagus, through the alimentary canal, and back to the soil and the sea.

The waters of the harbor shine luminously, rose streaked by lovely dawn, shimmering with rising sun, most lovely of all harbors, jewel of Asia set in a Western crown. Against this radiant setting takes place the story of Asia—to produce food, obtain it, absorb it, eliminate it, and grow it again—this is the epic of Asia. It is little, it is everything; it is all a man asks, it is more than he gets.

Where then is dignity, freedom? Does a hungry man choose between bread and a slogan? Does a dead man salute any flag?

Does a child owe loyalty to the boot which kicks it? A prostitute to a patron?

Here then is Asia. Let us of the West carry the four, seven or eleven freedoms to Asia! Let us sing them sweetly to the coolies lying frozen in the street, croon them with gentle emotion to the blue bodies of drowned, abandoned babies, whistle them melodiously to the children and women of famine, and the farmers without any farms. And then wait for the dead to arise and say Thank You, and go in leisurely, orderly fashion to the nearest polls and vote Yes on democracy.

This is the entrance to Asia, this is the coast of China. Into these waters empty Chinese rivers and up these rivers go Western trade. Here at the mouth of Asia the silt of its rivers' slowing once dumped mud. This mud turned to gold.

Here is British territory, the Island of Hong Kong. Small, perfect, colorful, contained, elegant, well groomed, well governed, prosperous for all merchants of any color, impoverished for all poor, but less so than China, this is Hong Kong. Jagged peaks behind tall buildings drip down gray fog over the veiled city where the dawn just reddens the windows.

Behind the island are Kowloon and the mainland reaching back to meet the blue hills of China, prehistoric folds of sandstone and mud, praised by generations of poets and travelers, despoiled and laid bare by those who live in them. Blue hills, blue no longer but eroded to rust-red clay, naked of trees, cropped clean to hungry outlines, yet splendid, magnificent still. No Westerner looks on them without feeling their agelessness, their indifference and calm. Here is absolute China. Man has done all that he can here of evil and good; the contour of earth remains the same.

I first saw these blue hills fourteen years ago. Since then they have watched through the latest chapter in the story of man's destruction of the things he makes and loves. They have watched through the heat of summers and the cold of winters while the captured city, fallen like a jewel from its setting, becomes a place of haggard, suffering mortals, fighting hunger and each other to survive, fighting to eat dogs and cats and human flesh sold on the streets in soup stewed from the bones and skulls and marrow of infants and ill and aged, a city of the yellow man's victory, with victory for none.

Four years pass while the blue hills wait. Again Empire displaces Empire, defeat gives place to victory, colors of flesh change with colors of faith, and the puny gestures of man return the white man's flag to Hong Kong. Again we cheer, again we win, the hills remain the same. Against them the life of man is as nothing; they are the power of stolid survival, the lesson that we are trivial, flesh rots, mountains remain.

Harry and I saw a great change in Hong Kong from prewar days. The place was overflowing with Chinese gold and jewels, and the Asiatic class which these possessions now represented looked confident and opulent in contrast to the threadbare Anglo-Saxons who had only their white skins left. We had little money, the cost of living having quadrupled, and British incomes having dropped; it was a bad time for us to see a new aristocracy of cash replace the old one of class and color, an aristocracy of which we who had been top dogs before by virtue of race were now slightly scornful and slightly envious.

The Hong Kong hot spots which Harry and I remembered from before the war, then filled exclusively with Europeans, were now filled with expensively dressed and beautifully groomed Chinese women, and opulent, well-tailored Chinese men. When we asked where all this wealth came from, we were told that the wealthy ones divided themselves into two groups: (1) those who had been clever enough to keep ahead of a bullet through ten years of warfare in China, and had now taken their wealth into British protection, and (2) those who had profiteered under the Japanese regime, presumably as collaborators.

The most attractive women in every gathering were Chinese. These were graceful, dainty, beautifully formed women, with porcelain skins and sparkling eyes, exquisitely gowned, carefully tinted, tastefully jeweled. Although by cinema standards they lacked the two movie-marks of female pulchritude, the remedy for this lack was displayed in all the shop windows which now offered in profusion foam-rubber busts, falsies and uplift brassières. But the best-dressed women still remained as flat as centuries of breast binding had made them, and only women of questionable class, or blue-jeaned bobby-soxers, pushed pointing prides before them.

The once magnificent Peak homes which had been the pride of prewar English householders stood like specters of the past, as empty as motion picture sets. They had survived the war but not the peace, and during the interval after the surrender of Hong Kong and the reoccupation by the Allies, these homes had been stripped bare by Chinese looters who removed fittings, furnishings, and all woodwork, including floors and walls. These fittings could now be bought back by former owners if they had money enough, on black market at high prices. In most cases the owners of the homes could not afford to make them livable, and sold them to wealthy Asiatics and themselves moved into crowded downtown hotels to live.

Prewar conditions were reversed, the Europeans were now living in herds while the Asiatics sought the pure air of the hills; we searched the menus for cheap dishes and sat in inconspicuous corners, while Chinese occupied the biggest tables under the brightest lights with wine and laughter flowing freely, although the restaurant owners said that money did not flow so freely. A table full of young Chinese in a prominent position in a popular restaurant frequently meant only the sale of a sandwich and a Coca-Cola, while friends surrounding the paying guest at the table smoked their own cigarettes, drank free restaurant ice water, scrawled pictures on the tablecloth, wore out the chairs, and withdrew without profit to the establishment.

Major crime was under control, but petty theft flourished. Harry's pocket was picked twice in the first two days while he was walking down Des Voeux Road, and my wedding ring, one of the few pieces of jewelry I had saved through internment, disappeared during my stay, without my knowing when or how.

Across the hotel corridor from us dwelled a charming pair, eight and six years old, Arthur and Evelyn from Shanghai, whom George met by the simple process of staring at them. Evelyn was

small and exquisite and ordered her meals from French menus with appropriate drinks sent up to the room herself, and Arthur was large and exquisite and settled all arguments by proving that his was bigger and better and cost more, as it did. They had a beautiful electric train and a room with a balcony overlooking Des Voeux Road, and here they and George played happily together until one afternoon the hotel housekeeper knocked on the door and asked who was pouring water onto passers-by. Standing behind her was Exhibit A, a dripping merchant. Investigation revealed the three children leaning far out over the balcony to choose their prey, with a water jug carefully balanced. They had been pouring water all week, it seems, but this was the first victim who had thought a deluge of water in a Hong Kong thoroughfare was worth commenting on.

Then George met Roger, a contemporary from two floors up, and a hotel dweller for all eight years of his life. Roger introduced the elevator game in which the children wait on different floors to ring for the elevator and disappear before it comes; he sponsored indoor football with the glass chandeliers as goals; he introduced the custom of ringing for room boys and climbing out of the window before they arrived to hide on the narrow ledge along the wall six floors above the street. Roger knew hotel lore, and this taught him that stairs were to slide down, stair wells were to spit down, elevator shafts were to throw things down, overripe fruit was to throw, servants were to trip, and old gentlemen were to annoy. It took him three days to pass on to George his eight years of learning.

A new George developed, one who tried hard for half an hour to not-do the things that I told him to not-do, but for the remaining waking hours did them with gusto and glee. I saw that he couldn't help it; he had to be hellish because there was nothing in the cement sepulcher of a hotel he could do for fun that wasn't hellish.

I tried to explain this to Harry, who I was afraid would think I had made a bad job of bringing up our son. But Harry doesn't like to listen to explanations at any time, and he always interrupted me with irrelevant questions on other subjects which showed he wasn't listening. Finally he said, Oh well, George had to do something, didn't he?

So we borrowed a motorcar and drove out of town every day to the bathing beaches. Here we stayed in sand and sun, with flies and banana peelings and dried melon seeds and Chinese bathing beauties and plastic beach balls bouncing over us, laving our hot bodies in the equally hot waters of Repulse, Deep Water, Half-moon, Stanley and every other popular bay into which we could push our way through warm floating bodies, one of us staying behind on the beach to sit on our clothes and keep them from being pinched. Only when typhoon signals warned us in and the winds tore up the tents were we and the other nature lovers released from the need to keep cool in the hottest way.

IV. Borneo Family

In Hong Kong we had been looking for a Chinese cook to take with us to Sandakan. When Ah San said he had cooked for French in Saigon, for Americans in Burma, for Portuguese in Hong Kong, and Russians in China, Harry insisted we must have him – anything was better than British cooking. He was a sad, clean, wan-looking man, who said he was very strong, and his passport gave his age as fifty-five. Ah ha, we thought, no woman trouble! Or at least in diminishing form.

He had no dependents, not having seen his wife and children since the fall of Canton where he feared they had been killed by the Japs. Yes, he would like to go to Borneo; yes, he would like to cook for us, we were very kind people! As he had never seen us before, we didn't know from what he drew conclusions, but as we secretly suspected that we were kind people, we did not argue. And when he agreed without bargaining to the salary we named, which was top wage in Borneo but not high in Hong Kong, we assumed the police were after him – but we needed a cook.

During the two weeks before sailing from Hong Kong, I asked him to supply us with the necessary culinary implements for kitchen use in Borneo, and gave him money to buy them. Each day he visited our hotel room bringing up some new fancy item, a frosting squeezer for making rosebuds on cakes, a meat grinder for "mincie," a fruit squeezer, a fancy biscuit cutter, variegated types of graters, and various artistic molds for agar-agar which we never ate. But he bought no pots and pans.

When I commented on this shortage, he said, "Bimeby." Then one day I went out and bought them myself. When I brought them back he asked, "How much money?"

I told him the price. He shook his head, "Too much money!"

Next day he took my selections back to the shop, and returned with a new assortment at reduced prices, and handed me the difference in cash. This time I shook my head; I had never met anything like this. I became more certain than ever that he was a fugitive from justice, and all I asked was to get him safely out of Hong Kong before the police came.

The day before we sailed, he came to our room accompanied by a bright-eyed Chinese girl only slightly taller than George, with a straight black fringe of hair above her eyes, a bright, unwinking gaze, and four inches of pigtail tied with cerise string. I judged her to be about sixteen years.

"This my wife," said Ah San simply. "His name Ah Min. He like come too. Can do?"

We did not remind him that his wife was dead; after all, this was not as difficult to deal with as a pursuing policeman. It was too late now to arrange for passports, permissions, and passages for the next day's journey, but Harry said that arrangements should be made for the girl to come to Borneo on the steamer a month later.

Next day at the hour of sailing Ah San and Ah Min arrived at the launch which was to take us to the Indo-China steamship, *Hin Sang*, anchored midstream. Ah Min was weeping with the uncompromising completeness of a child, tears washing her cheeks and nose being wiped on sleeve. The launch was delayed half an hour, and during this interval Ah Min said good-by to Ah San three times, and three times disappeared – only to reappear again with a different gift for Ah San, a small bag of sweets, a couple of bananas, a bunch of grapes, and the last time a mess of melting sweets for George.

After a fourth good-by, and much confusion amongst those

who were coming and those staying behind, the launch left the wharf and presumably Ah Min. But none of us was very surprised when upon arriving at the ship's side we found her piled in back with the luggage again. Her tears had stopped, for this time she was sure she had made herself one of the party.

While the luggage was going up the ship's side in the hands of coolies she was cheerfully shouting advice to them in Cantonese, vigorously pushing and shoving huge suitcases, confident of her success. When the moment came for us to go on board, she grabbed George and pulled him on her shoulders, his long legs almost touching the ground behind her, and started up the ship's ladder with him on her back. We forcibly disentangled George, and sent him up the ladder alone, while she attached herself to Ah San. We pulled him from her arms, pushed him up the ladder and her down it, and climbed the ladder ourselves. When we looked down her tears were once more flowing. Ah San looked the other way in noncommittal silence.

"He's got something, all right!" said Harry.

Now it was time to sail for the island of Borneo and the last reprieve was ended. On a small timber steamer we traveled south for six days, swept by tepid winds from the equator and rocked on lukewarm waves which swizzled outward from the Southern Philippines, and on the seventh day the ship dropped its rusty anchor to await the dawn. When I awoke the red cliffs of Berhala Island at the entrance to Sandakan Bay greeted me, and I was back. It was on this island we had first been held as prisoners of the Japanese.

The island's bluffs rise steeply from dark blue waters, the fringe of yellow beach fans out from the shade of coconut palms, pigeon orchids flutter from the scaling cliffs, and green banana trees wave languid plumes against the brightening sky. Here again are the familiar symbols of tropical beauty to beckon the newcomer on, here the same lush, lurid, flamboyant answers to the lure of the Orient, and here all is enchanting — as far as it meets the eye.

On the leeward side of the island, in the stink of swampy mud and the steam of sun and the downpour of rain, I learned as a hungry prisoner to pray for something cold and clean and stark, a bare-leafed tree against a bleak, gray sky. Here I vowed never to look on face or form or expression of exotic charm again, if I could close my eyes in time. Here I dreamed only of going home, and never again coming closer to the Far East than the Far West of the U. S. A.

Quarantine inspection finished, we enter the harbor of Sandakan. Shallow stretches of water on the city side are lined with ruined pilings, submerged hulks, charred wreckage and abandoned, corroded, unsalvaged war supplies, but the far side of the bay is still lush and green, heavily wooded with mangrove and timber and jungle. As we approach the destroyed town which was for years our home, we see that the green hills around it are spotted anew by small dwellings, while on the level land below, town shops come down again to meet the Sulu Sea, but shops built now of palm leaves instead of wood, and roofed with palm thatch instead of corrugated iron. The narrow city streets are already smelly and hot, trembling with flies and mosquitoes, stinking with fish and drains, and again under the iridescent skies against the verdant hills, the sewers of Sandakan flow slowly to the sea.

Here the odor of death was still on the breezes, and ghosts wafted along with the scents of dried fish, human excreta, jungle rot, and night-flowering trees, and corpses came out of the midtown drain, old victims of the Japanese Military Police. Hand grenades, bombs, and incendiaries were collected from every square foot of living space, to be buried or exploded by children and gardeners and all who dug. The soil of all the land enclosed the secrets of war, forests shrouded the ghosts of the dead, tracks were blazed through hidden jungles with white bones of prisoners, and the air strip, hewn out of the jungle by Australian prisoners, was paved with mortal clay.

The white population of the town was again about eighty British, with myself still the only American, but the Asiatic population had almost doubled to twenty-five thousand with refugees sweeping in from China and other revolution-torn parts of Asia to seek the peace, security, and better living conditions of British rule. Many of these brought gold, but our own Asiatics were a hundred per cent poor, having survived the process of slaughter by hiding in the jungle or retreating to the interior.

Our fourteen miles of paved roads had all been bombed, our shopping center filled only four lanes, our places of amusement were as before – the football field, a club, and two palm-leaf cinema houses which represented the apex of civilization and regularly showed *Tarzan of the Apes* in a country of apes to full houses. The nadir was the sewer system which is simply the Sulu Sea, and visitors as usual asked what those cute little houses over the water were.

We went to live on top of our old hill with the same magnificent view as before the war, in a very small house Harry had occupied for the past year, which was to be our home until a permanent timber house could be rebuilt on the nearby gutted foundations of the one the Japs had destroyed. Here on bare red soil this swaying palm-leaf shack drifted in a blast of sun. When the midday sky undulated with heat waves we dropped our palm-leaf shutters and half squinted our eyes and pulled the new green and blue curtains across the windows, and the house floated in blue sky, blue bay and heat. Bright pink oleanders in pots surrounded the house, transplanted from our old garden by Harry during his year here alone, and frangipani trees, some with white, egg-centered blooms, and some of a rare, shaded, cherry red, brought by us ten years before from Malaya and now transplanted, were doing well. A huge, cup-shaped, lemon-colored allamanda climbed in the windows, and a tiny pink rose bush was blooming profusely and really smelled. Lavender-shaded Vanda orchids lined the handmade walk constructed by Harry from fragments of bombed bricks, and a small formal garden of purple ground orchids between house and tumbling latrine was fertilized by human bones. A Japanese skull stared out from orchid blossoms and a Japanese sword stuck tip down in the red earth beside it, and these Harry refused to move. Our only amenities and only adornments were the bay, the Sulu Sea, tropical islands, trees and flowers.

Up here it was drier, hotter, windier than in town, and very isolated. By day we went almost naked, and at night, we did. On starlight nights we looked out through broken window shutters into warm, windy blackness and owned the shining sky, and on moonlight nights we looked entranced on a sea of cool, white loveliness – and slowly again on a Borneo hill, the scented, sensual, primitive beauty seduced me, and here in the ruins of war, for the first time since the war, my memories of it became bearable.

Our house was built of palm leaves tied together in a nonchalant, non-wind-resistant fashion, with a nearby cook shed of the same material for the preparation of food, with dirt floor, open wood fire, and plentiful rats and cockroaches, and an openwork, hand-knit latrine some distance from the house for the final disposal of what was prepared in the cook shed, and a Chinese lady known as the Labatrine Lady who whisked away the end products to return them to the garden again.

Ah San, who had recommended himself to us by his cosmopolitan references, had a taste for the niceties, and he himself was scrupulously clean and neat, and tropical beauties did not seduce him. Perhaps I should have known better than to bring him to Borneo – but we needed a cook. Cooks were practically nonexistent, having either been killed in the war or driven inland to settle on their own bits of land.

For the first few days Ah San brought all his Borneo problems to me as he uncovered them: the flour with weevils, the tinned butter that was rancid, the refrigerator that didn't freeze, the lamps that didn't burn, the fire that didn't cook, and the stove that wouldn't bake – that was the worst.

"Misiter" – this means me – "no can bake fine fancy cake with fancy flosting with fancy flower, if no oven for bake cake."

"We don't eat cakes."

He looked at me without believing, telling himself I had said something else.

"No oven, Misiter," he explained carefully, "for making Misiter fancy cake with fancy flosting . . ."

"Oh, all right, we do eat cake, then! You can use a kerosene tin for baking."

"But no oven, Misiter, for make fancy cake with fancy flosting – "

"Now listen, Ah San! I know this is a horrible kitchen and an impossible stove and Sandakan is a dirty, stinking little town, and you'll hate it! But I'm paying you top cook's wages in Borneo. I don't care what we eat, or how you cook it – that's your job – but just don't tell me about it!"

It was the sort of thing I never said to servants, so having said it, I felt like a signer of the Declaration of Independence. My servants could worry for me this time, not me for them!

"Yes, Misiter. But Misiter, no oven for make fancy cake for Misiter with fine fancy flosting. . . ."

I left – fled is the word.

Meanwhile Harry had resumed the most griping of all struggles, the making of bricks without straw. North Borneo was about to become a British Colony by purchase by the Colonial Office from the Chartered Company; thus the Company would not reinvest, yet the Colony which had not yet paid for itself was in the red in an Empire which was in the red. Meanwhile the small, equatorial state of North Borneo was both destroyed and bankrupt. It needed American dollars to rebuild it – and it had bankrupt sterling. The official answer to every request was No money, or Wait – and Harry could never wait.

It wasn't enough now to plant trees in order to conserve land to grow crops to feed people to survive on a long-term policy. The hungry people had to be fed now. And they had to be fed rice, the greatest local postwar shortage and the mainstay of local Asiatic diet.

Sandakan district, on the northern tip of the east coast of Borneo, was not self-supporting in rice. Tapioca and various tubers were being unsuccessfully promoted as substitutes, and expert dietitians said they were better for the health than rice. The Asiatic answer was simple; no rice, no work!

This coast was not suited to the production of rice, an uneconomic crop and one tending to keep the standard of living low. The import of rice was regulated by international food agreements based on European ideas of rice-sufficiency, ideas not concurred with by the Asiatics who in the long run had the final word. Other food might have vitamins and vim, but without rice their bellies were empty and they felt hungry.

I sympathized with their view, having lived for years on tapioca root in prison camp. One may re-educate the digestive tract with pain and wind in a lifetime, but not the psychological attitude of generations which decrees to the Asiatic that rice is the staff of life, as much as it decrees to us that bread is. The rice ration at this time was only one half what the Asiatic laborer was satisfied to work on, and if there was no rice to work for, what was the object of working? The entire economy of the state was tied up in solving the rice problem.

Immediately upon the return of civil administration in North Borneo steps were taken not only to assist native farmers in planting more rice, but to require the planting of all suitable areas with rice, and in time, government itself purchased all locally grown unmilled rice and distributed it by ration. Government also imported rice and distributed it at cost price, and ultimately negotiated successfully for an increase in the international import agreement.

Large imports of wheat flour were also made for distribution at cost. Rice seed was sent to inland villages where it was not available, and an agricultural census of food crops and livestock was put under way with a view to taking from the less depleted areas to assist the most needy. Local Indian cattle and pigs for breeding stock were moved to the more impoverished areas.

Closely connected with food shortage was another problem — there was no place for anyone to live, villagers, workers, or administration. When Harry arrived in 1946 people were living under old pieces of corrugated iron, in zinc vats, or under any scrap of noninflammable material which remained from the holocaust of the town. One family was living in the old cement strong room of the Secretariat, the only part of the government buildings left, and another family occupied the bullet-shattered base of the town clock.

The emergency answer to the housing problem was to use

palm-leaf shingles, as the natives themselves did, supported on round mangrove poles and tied into temporary, very temporary, houses, until sawmill machinery could be obtained and put into operation to cut down trees and to mill lumber on a large scale. Soon shops, small dwellings, best residences were all alike made of palm-leaf shingles, the only difference being in roofs, some of which leaked, while others blew away.

There was no sanitation of any sort, and both food and water supplies were threatened with contamination, as the reservoirs had been partially destroyed and the catchment areas polluted. The wonder is great that the survivors of war were not wiped out by epidemic disease, but surprisingly, no new epidemics swept the place; instead, old enemies, malaria and dysentery, fastened on the weakened victims of starvation with more deadly grip than ever, and the war's death toll continued to grow during the first year of peace.

Shipping was almost nonexistent because of lack of vessels, and land transport was nonexistent because of complete destruction of motor vehicles and slaughter for food of transport animals, and until shipping resumed, land transport replacements could not arrive.

Fishing, the main native and Asiatic industry on the east coast, had practically ceased owing to destruction by the Japanese of junks and native boats. To re-establish this industry the Administration was importing and distributing materials necessary for fishing and making of nets, and establishing temporary sawmills for production of boat-building timber.

No matter what the specific task, rehabilitation of the country was the one job that every man in the Administration had come back to do, and for once departments worked without jealousy or friction. There was no longer any discussion as to whose department a job came under; the task was completed first, and then indexed under the proper heading, a most unusual government attitude. It is a tribute to the spirit of the service that these men, themselves war victims who had lost their own worldly goods and might well have claimed the need to rehabilitate themselves, devoted their first and best efforts to helping others. But they all showed the strain in their private lives, and even Harry was both tireless and cranky.

In our own household, we had problems. Packing and unpacking always becomes a crisis in the family because Harry hates all untidiness except his own, and he cannot rest until everything is either (1) unpacked and in place, or (2) thrown away. Yet living in Borneo, one must hoard – never throw away packing materials, tissue paper, string, empty bottles, or containers. The two systems, Harry's of dynamic disposal, which suited the size of the house, and mine of saving for the next migration, now met in death grips, and food became a minor problem. We ate, but what, I scarcely knew, house-settling nerves carried over to the dinner table, appetites failed, Harry shouted "Take it away!" with every new dish, or else demanded bread and milk instead in a tone that said, "Let him try and spoil *that* one!" Ah San watched through the curtain-hung door, his face completely gone. Yet from our point of view, everything was as expected – and, even going fine!

Until one morning after Harry had thrown out the porridge, and gone off to his office behind a stream of epithets, Ah San stood at the doorway, and said sadly, "I am sick!"

He was only half my size, thin and tubercular looking, and now almost in tears. His whole dejected being accused me of brutality, a quality I loathe.

"Sick! Where are you sick?" I said anxiously. "Where is your pain?"

"Misiter, I am sick. I no can eat. Will you please give lemonade?" In his hand was an old tin of lemon crystals, left behind by the Allied Occupation forces.

"Of course you can have lemonade, Ah San. But what is the matter? How are you sick? Is your stomach sick?"

"No, Misiter. Sick here. My heart sick." He placed his hand on his heart with great dignity, in case I did not comprehend that a cook has a heart. "My heart very sick. Misiter always angry. He no like me, he all time talk angry me. I very sorry, I very unhappy. My heart sick. Cannot eat. Maybe I no good cook for you, then more better I go back Hong Kong."

"But I am not angry with you."

"I no mean you, I mean Number One Misiter. Before I come Borneo, I talk my cousin number one boy in Hong Kong hotel. He worked for you in hotel on holiday. He tell me Misiter always very kind heart, very good and happy man. So kind man I think good Misiter. So I come to Borneo with you. But my heart no can stand more trouble. Trouble make me sick. Then no can eat. Now Misiter angry because he no like me. More better I go back Hong Kong."

It came to me as a shock. We had been recommended as good, kind, amiable people – and we were not!

"Ah San, please wait. I talk Master. He like you O.K. Only Master always angry when come new house. And Master work very hard now – very tired. Bimeby everything O.K. I think. Bimeby government build new house for Master. Then Ah San have very fine kitchen for very good cooking. Then everything O.K. I think. Ah San please wait."

That night I told it all to Harry. And Harry interpreted Ah San's collapse from heartsickness as being the proper and worthy tribute to himself as the ruling spirit of the household. Ah San had shown true delicacy of spirit, and here was a cook worth holding.

"We must be more careful, dear, and show less impatience with the poor old boy!"

"Yes, dear."

"The poor old boy must take his cooking seriously or he wouldn't be so upset."

"Yes, dear."

"I'll fix him a better stove and make him an oven to bake in."

"Yes, dear."

"What about that Little Bit of his in Hong Kong? We must get her down here."

"Yes, dear."

A strange calm took over. In the past I had been the one to advise patience with cooks. Now we had a cook with heart-sickness, who had to be spoken to gently, whose feelings had to be thought of, who drank lemonade for his stomach's sake, whose appetite had gone, poor chap, because of our very harshness. An artist, none the less. I was facing something new in the line of Borneo cooks.

And then, although not as easily as it sounds, the refrigerator began to make ice (after I strained the kerosene), the fire to burn (mangrove wood instead of mill ends), the oven to bake (a super kerosene tin), and new flour arrived in town. The man who slaughtered beef turned out to be the friend of a friend of a friend and soon we got beef instead of water buffalo, the vegetable market man used to live in Hong Kong, the steward on the boat knew a steward in Hong Kong and brought us down fresh butter, milk came from the cow of a cousin, and fruit from the tree of a friend. The artist began to function in the hand of a cook, and our appetites returned.

"The best cook we've ever had!" Harry said. "But he wouldn't work for everyone, you know. You have to be patient with him!"

"He come!" Ah San said in excitement, and pointed below us at the harbor where the Hong Kong boat was just dropping anchor. "He come!" It was Chinese New Year, and the boat bore his bride.

"You go down to meet her, Ah San," I agreed.

An hour later they stood before me. Little did Ah Min look like the waif we had left on the Hong Kong wharf. She was dressed now in a new shiny black Chinese suit, with a new red string about her four-inch pigtail, and although her black fringe of hair still shaded her bright black eyes, they shone like wet licorice drops, but with excitement rather than tears.

"He bring presents!" said Ah San triumphantly, and stood back for me to gather the effect.

Ah Min at that moment was a woman of goods. About her feet were grouped a swollen, extendable, Chinese-made suitcase, a bulging Hong Kong wicker basket ("For my friend," said Ah San), a bowl of telescopic-eyed goldfish ("For George"), a pair of mandarin red lacquered Chinese clogs ("For Missee" as I was now called), a basket of mandarin oranges ("For Mister"), and a tin of Chinese cakes ("Ah San"). The value of the presents was probably more than her personal belongings.

"He bring presents!" reminded Ah San again proudly, while Ah Min's face glowed like a Chinese lantern with a candle inside.

Ah Min could speak neither English nor Malay but spoke Cantonese firmly with complete expectation of making herself understood. The first idea that she wished to put over to us was that she belonged with us, that she was delighted to be here, that she had our welfare at heart, that she trusted us and we were to do the same with her, and that she would soon have us all properly organized. This was quite a bit to put over without words, but she did it in twenty-four hours. Her language was the same as that of a stray cat who finds a home and expresses its satisfaction by rubbing fondly against your legs.

It was necessary that she sleep in a small lean-to off the kitchen which her husband shared with Ah Sing, the houseboy. Here in this tiny room, to accommodate three people, was one small cot and a small built-in platform bed like a narrow shelf. Neither one was large enough for two people, but neither was the room large enough for another cot. For privacy, Ah San had hung a blanket between the houseboy's bed and that of himself and wife. I was ashamed to offer any human being such housing, but the Chinese townspeople were sleeping in worse. Ah Min examined the setup without dismay, and that fact alone was sad; she was accustomed to such things. I determined that when the new house we all so longed for was built, this house that was to be the answer to everybody's dreams, which was soon to be under construction as promised on the foundations of the war-destroyed one, the first thing I would specify for it would be decent servants' quarters and a good kitchen.

Ah Kau, the Cantonese woman we had imported twelve years before from China, occupied a tiny separate room. It was always told to any newcomer: Whatever Ah Kau does is right with us – if you want to stay here, you must get on with Ah Kau.

Ah Kau had a quality that you had to recognize in any language by any standard, Ah Kau was good. And at forty-eight years of age she had acquired a venerable yet ageless calm, a quality much needed in our household. In the first months of the Japanese occupation she had stayed with us and fought for us without pay until we were taken from her and sent to prison camp, and had it been years we needed her, not months, I know she would have done the same. After we were imprisoned she had worked in the town, and then hidden in the jungle, fleeing

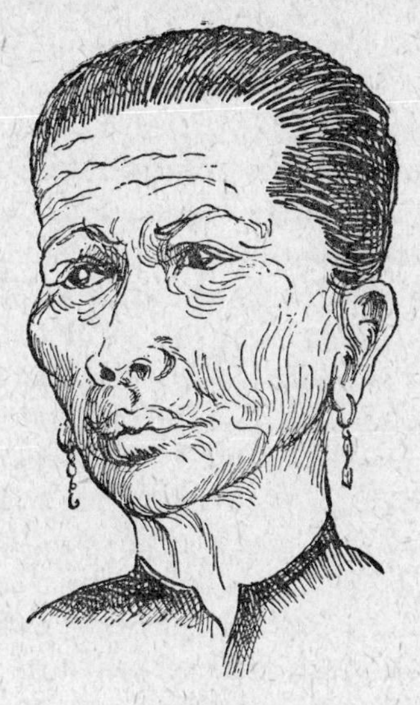

AH KAU

alternately from Japanese persecution and Allied bombs, until with the Armistice and Harry's return, she had come back to our household as servant-matriarch and greatly revered friend.

Ah Kau's small separate sleeping room, a tribute to her esteemed and honorable position in the household was, however, shared by a non-human inmate, Pooch, the black and white Borneo mongrel whom Harry had permitted to adopt him on his return to Borneo, with the excuse that George would need a pooch when he arrived. Pooch was a pup in Sandakan at a time when dogs were legitimate food in a hungry town, and he showed his appreciation of being rescued from the list of market meats by a violent adoration of everyone in the Keith household and a fierce and indiscriminate attack on all visitors whom he classed as bandits and threats to home life, and ferocious and terrifying pursuit and battle with every dog who passed on the road. This ferocity naturally made George adore him, and "See 'em off, Pooch!" would ring from a small boy's throat as a large, thundering, shaggy-coated, half-tailed, black and white monster hurled himself down the steep garden path. The only thing that saved Pooch from being named a killer was the fact that he seldom pursued far from his own place, and in postwar Borneo every dog was within his rights to take a bite at prowlers.

The first day when we arrived at the house Harry had said, "Now you'll have to be very careful with the pup I got for George. He hates strangers, and he bites."

I looked nervously at the thing facing us in the garden, and said, "Is that a pup?"

"Yes, just a pup. I told him you and George were coming, but be careful, dear. Stand by, George. Give Pooch time till he knows you." Harry had us both by the arm, then, "Come on, now, Pooch. These are your friends. This is Agnes and George that I told you about. You remember them, Pooch," he said gently.

The thing tore madly down at us, then came to me and pushed his head against my legs, then went to George and pushed his wet, black nose against George's knees—sniffing gently and looking kindly up at him with—well, affection.

"Look Dad, he does know me!"—a delighted shout from George.

"Why Harry, he does know about us!"

"Good old Pooch! Smart dog!" said Harry proudly—but I'm sure with surprise.

From then on, like all unpurchased pooches of strong stomachs and mixed blood, Pooch was the butt of each of us in times of annoyance because he would put up with abuse and love us still, and the pet of each when times were good. We kicked at him when he barked at night, shoved him out of the way when he threw himself on us in affection, were embarrassed when he had affairs in the front garden, abused him when he chased the wrong friends and bit the wrong people, and loved him fondly when he was ill, or came home torn up after a fight.

Ah Kau, who had taken care of him during Harry's recent conference with the Colonial Office in England, welcomed him as an inmate in her room as a preventative for postwar petty theft. As well as Pooch, her room was jam-packed with the things we threw away, the broken three-quarters mirror, the broken chair she had no time to sit on, the three-legged table that leaned against the wall, and the emblems of her trade, a basketful of well-washed clothes and the ironing board, and a decrepit chest of drawers spread with empty perfume bottles, an old hot water bottle, old Christmas greeting cards, and many snapshots of George.

Now into Ah Kau's parlor this first day, onto the decrepit chest of drawers in front of the broken mirror crept Ah Min's beauty kit. This consisted of a red plastic comb, a jar of jade-green, gardenia-scented hair pomade, and a set of ivory ear-cleaning instruments. Here beside this altar to art, squatting on the broken chair, I found George the first afternoon. Ah Min was bending over him with concentrated gaze, and scooping wax from inside his ears with a tiny spoon.

"She's cleaning my ears," George said in a hypnotized voice. "Sssssh! Don't disturb her. Go away."

"You shouldn't put anything inside an ear, Ah Min," I said educationally.

Ah Min smiled, and continued her work.

"Ssssh! Go away, Mum. She knows what she's doing, she's done this for lots of folks. She used to work in a place like that."

"A place like what?"

"I dunno, Mum. Go away."

"I can clean your ears myself, but you always make such a fuss about it!"

"She does it better than you, and that spoon tickles nice. Chinese all clean their ears this way—they're smarter about some things than us."

"Well," I said doubtfully, but reminding myself, When in Rome . . . "Come in the house when she finishes."

"Oh no, Mum. She's going to manicure my fingernails and toenails, and then do my hair."

Some time later, when a very strong scent of gardenia jade hair pomade became present in the house, that was George.

It was three months since Ah Min had come down from Hong Kong, and she now occupied the position of houseboy. How we loved her—and hated her!

"When she is good she is very very good, and when she is bad she is bloody! Why in God's name can't she ever shut up! Natter, natter, natter! But these Asiatic women never do behave when they once get the upper hand!"

"Well, we never had any houseboy do the work she does," I suggest. "If only she wouldn't fight with everybody. And she is wonderful to George—she really dotes on him—maternal instinct gone wild. Look at her."

At the table in the center of the room George dawdles as usual over his dinner. Ah Min stands patiently near him, pressing his glass of powdered milk on him.

"*M'oi!*" he says firmly. "*Sudah!* I have had enough!" pushing it away.

"Finish *sik-faan*, Jorr," insists Ah Min, who now uses Cantonese with a few key words in English thrown in, as George does vice versa.

"*M'oi!*"

"Finish milk, Jorr." She places the glass to his lips.

"*M'oi!!*" But the milk goes down.

"Take medicine, Jorr." She pours dark liquid from the bottle of mineral tonic on the table.

"*M'oi!* Not taking medicine tonight!"

"Take medicine, Jorr." The spoonful is advanced under his nose. "Medicine very good, Jorr. Take medicine, Jorr."

"*M'oi!*" The medicine goes down.

"Jorr" wipes his mouth in disgust, and snatches at Ah Min's short braid, calling over to me, "Hi, Mum, make this woman leave me alone! She's not my mum!"

"Jorr! Here Jorr!" Now Ah Min surreptitiously produces a

huge, blue-white bun stuffed with red bean curd and places it in front of him. It is his favorite, and she has purchased it for him at the Chinese coffee shop in town this afternoon, and has been withholding it until his proper meal was finished. She stands back to see his delight.

"Oh, Ah Min! Thaaaank you!" Jorr's appetite miraculously returns. "Thank you, Ah Min!"

Dinner over, now Jorr brings me *Uncle Remus*. This is my one parlor stunt—I can read *Uncle Remus* out loud just fine! Even Harry likes it.

"Some folks travel fancy. Some folks travel plain . . ." we sing together. "But when I goes to a party I travels on old Brer Fox!"

Ah Min listens at the door, smiling.

Now we go through the Whipme-Whopme pudding made of Winniannimus grass, and it is eight o'clock.

"Time to go to bed, George."

"No, Mum, just a little longer, please!"

"Bed, George."

Ah Min advances from the doorway. "Bed, Jorr!"

"No, Mum. Ah Min go way."

"Bed, Jorr! Bed, Jorr." Ah Min offers her back to him, then pulls him on it piggyback fashion. George accepts.

"No, Ah Min! He's too big for you!" I protest. But Ah Min canters off, with George singing from her back, "When I goes to a party I travels on old Brer Fox!"

The phone rings. Harry answers. "My God, really, Chuck?" Harry swears. Chuck is our only neighbor on this sliced-off hill-top. Harry turns to me with a groan. "It's Ah Min again, Agnes!" Then back to the phone. "You say she emptied the coffeepot into your drain? . . . Threw our garbage in your rose bed! . . . Threw dishwater on your cook? . . . Spat at you when you bawled her out for it! . . . Well, I'm terribly sorry, Chuck, I'll see what I can do."

Chuck's voice crackles over the wire, "I just thought I'd let you know before she puts ground glass in my food!"

Harry turns from the phone. "She's been fighting again!"

"Hello the dinner, Misiter," now announces Ah Min.

"Well, it can't always be her fault, Harry. Anyway the servants' quarters are impossible – built right up against Chuck's kitchen! There is bound to be trouble. When we get in the new house she'll be all right. What did Chuck say?"

"Mostly – that she was a bitch!"

"Hello the dinner, Misiter," Ah Min insists gently, smiling at us.

"Come on, dear, let's eat before it gets cold."

"Hello the dinner, Misiter." Tenderly she draws us towards the table.

After an almost juicy cut of buffalo has gentled Harry's heart, I venture, "Why don't you talk to Ah Min? I can't talk enough Cantonese. Or talk to Ah San, and find out what's making her fight with everybody?"

"They always fight. And whoever makes most noise and shouts loudest is right in a Chinese fight."

"Ah Kau doesn't fight."

"She did at Ah Min's age, probably."

Ah Min smiles politely at sound of her name, and places a very fine *soufflé* in front of Harry. She waits outside the door to see that this is consumed. Then she shuffles in again and says urgently, "Hello the dog! Hello the dog! Misiter!" showing by gestures that she wishes us to accompany her outside.

On the back steps we find Pooch lying in a mournful attitude beside an untouched bowl of food, with one ear almost chewed off. Ah Min has placed a bowl of warm water ready, in which I smell my disinfectant, for us to bathe him. Ah San stands by.

"Who has he been fighting?" Harry asks, as he sets to work.

"He fight Misiter Resident dog. Too much he like to fight!" mourns Ah San.

"Like Ah Min!" says Harry grimly. "Ah San, you must tell her she's got to stop it. We've had enough of it. Tell her, shut up or get out."

Ah San looks gloomy. "Plenty time I tell him! He no good. He too much trouble. He bad girl." Now he directs a fire of

Cantonese at Ah Min, which she returns with machine-gun rapidity and increased volume with gestures. While this battle rages we complete the doctoring of Pooch, and retire to the house.

"I wonder what Ah Min did with that book I was reading before dinner?" Harry wonders. "Ah Min! What-the-hell . . ."

But Ah Min is beside him smiling amiably, always ready to serve. "Hello Misiter?"

"Book, Ah Min! My book, *book*, BOOK! What the hell did you do with my BOOK?" shaking a book at her as a sample. "For God's sake leave my things alone, Ah Min! BOOK! Where is it? My BOOK?"

"She doesn't know what you're talking about, Harry. Do stop shouting and get another book to read tonight. It'll turn up tomorrow."

"Hello, Misiter, hello, Misiter," begs Ah Min urgently, beckoning Harry towards the bedroom. There on his side of the bed, with a mark at the page he has been reading, placed ready for the final five minutes in bed, is his book.

"Hello thank you good night Misiter. Hello, bye-bye!" reminds Ah Min.

"Let's go to bed. It seems obvious we are intended to," I suggest.

"Hello, bye-bye, Misiter," Ah Min urges me.

"Hello bye-bye!" I repeat, fascinated by the new farewell. "Hello bye-bye!"

Ah Min disappears, and I hear the lean-to shutters dropped down for the night, before I discover something.

"Damn! Now my book has disappeared, *The Razor's Edge* – I know I put it there ready for tonight, where I thought she couldn't find it and 'put it away.' "

"There's a book just under your pillow. What's that?"

"Oh – *Roget's Thesaurus* – well, I'm not going to read *that* in bed!"

"Why not? It's red, same color as *Razor's Edge*. No doubt Ah Min reckons that red's your reading-in-bed color," says Harry, settling contentedly into bed with his own book. "Well,

Mum, when you combine bed, love and literature you've really got something!"

"Well, I guess I'm too tired to read, anyway. But I wish I knew what to do about Ah Min. She's too good to lose. Anyway, I'm fond of her – but I get so sick of her eternal rowing!"

"Ma, did you know that Ah Min's going to have a baby!"

"Who said so?"

"Ah Min. It's going to be a boy, too. If it isn't they give it away. That's a good idea, isn't it?"

"Is Ah Min glad?"

"Sure is!"

"What does Ah San say to another baby?"

"He says 'No want! Too much money!'"

"Well, I guess if Ah Min is going to have a baby she'll be stopping work by and by."

"No, Mum. Ah San says she has to work and earn money to take care of the baby. Because Ah Min wants a baby, and Ah San doesn't."

And as Ah Min's pregnancy grew there became apparent in the backquarters two opposing schools of thought. Ah San reckoned that he had made a fool of himself again in allowing reproductive capacity to outwit judgment and that he would have nothing to do with the matter, Ah Min's bulging belly could be her own affair, he had finished with such nonsense. Ah Min, however, showed a bright-eyed joy and blooming fertility which gave proud testimony that she felt she was about to enter at last into the blessed circle of legitimate mothers of men. And old maid Ah Kau, seeming to swell sympathetically in her enthusiasm, soon became almost as pregnant as Ah Min with the importance of being best friend to the bearer of the seed.

One day when Ah Min had grown large beyond disregard, I called her and Ah San for a three-cornered conversation.

"When is the baby due, Ah San?"

"Baby do, Missee?"

"When baby come? Get born?"

"Yes, baby come."

"I know that, but when? What day? What month? Suppose nine months for make baby – then how many months now before baby come?"

Consultation takes place between Ah San and Ah Min, before he answers, "Maybe three moons, maybe four."

"When baby come, Ah Min go English doctor? Or Chinese doctor?"

Consultation. "English doctor."

I hide my pleased surprise at having no argument, and press my advantage with the suggestion, "Ah Min go Government Hospital for baby I think very good."

Consultation. "Yes, Missee."

"More better Ah Min go hospital doctor now for examination. Then we know everything all right before baby come."

"Yes, Missee."

"Tell Ah Min I go with her this week to see doctor. More better go now. Next week Mister and I go away for one month."

Consultation. "Ah Min say, maybe this week too soon. Ah Min say later more better. She go next week when Missee away. No work to do then."

Knowing that an Asiatic in a European household usually prefers a personal introduction to an English doctor in the belief that this may bring preferential treatment, it momentarily crossed my mind that there might be something behind Ah Min's refusal to go with me. But I answer, "All right, Ah San. But tell her to be sure to go."

"He go."

"Here is a bottle of calcium and vitamin D tablets. Tell her to take two tablets three times a day. These make baby very strong. I take this medicine before George is born. Tell her now."

Ah San presents the bottle with explicit directions to Ah Min.

"Ah Min say thank you, Missee."

"You see that she takes them, Ah San!"

"He take."

"Tell me when the bottle is empty, and I buy more."

When we returned from our trip a month later the bottle was empty and I replenished it. The nurse-matron from the hospital telephoned to say that my amah had been in for a prenatal examination and her condition was satisfactory. It was all too easy.

Now as the Mister and I begin to observe Ah Min with an abstract form of satisfaction, and as Ah Min and I establish the bond which is common between women who have children, and as a friendly bustle of preparation becomes evident, Ah San grows less noncommittal. Ah Min's liability gives promise of turning into an asset.

"Ah Min have got cloth for baby's clothes?" I ask.

"Have got, Missee."

"Have got these things?" I draw the diagram of a diaper, knowing that the town Chinese babies don't use them.

Consultation. "Not have."

"Tell Ah Min I give her cloth for these. Have got basket for baby sleep in? Mosquito net for basket? Baby must not sleep with you and Ah Min."

Consultation. "Not have. Bimeby get Sandakan."

Next day Ah San reports sadly, "Missee, basket have got. Mosquito net have got. Oh, too much money! Too much money!"

Ah Min laughs heartlessly nearby.

Now Ah Min and Ah Kau go regularly to the hospital together for examination, carrying a big black cotton umbrella over their heads and wearing shiny black trousers and their best black flat-heeled Mary Jane shoes, the two of them almost equally pregnant with the oncoming child.

Meanwhile Ah Min arrives at her most gravid, and therefore her Asiatic mightiest. Even after years in the East, I still look with alarm at the feats of strength which pregnant Orientals perform, up to and on the very day of giving birth. Ah Min and Ah Kau were accustomed to chop the cooking firewood fifty yards from the house, then carry it to the kitchen. They would stack it into a four-foot-high pile, rope it tightly, and carry it between them swinging from a stick across their shoulders, always building the pile so high and heavy that they grunted and groaned and laughed hysterically as they struggled along. They could have piled it lighter, or Ah San could have helped them, but of course these two things never happened.

In tribute to Ah Min's condition, I now hired a boy to carry firewood. On his second day he was put to the job of potato peeling for Ah San, whisking egg whites for cakes, and beating frosting, and silver polishing – Ah Min continued to carry the firewood. Harry said the baby would be born between the woodpile and the kitchen, and Ah Min would pick it up and place it on top of the firewood and carry it in.

Now Ah Min looked like a tip-over toy, swollen to great proportions around the middle and miraculously kept upright by concealed weights in her feet. She became the alarm of bachelor neighbor Chuck, who forecast a situation in which Harry and I would be away for a few hours, Ah Min would indulge in weight-lifting, and he, Chuck, would be called on to deliver the baby. Harry assured him that the situation was quite probable.

However, the estimated birth date came – and passed, and no baby appeared. I told Ah San he must count dates again. This time the three of us did so together, and I found that when Ah Min and Ah San had named a date "nine months" from the time of conception they had counted by moons, or Chinese lunar months of 28 days each, instead of calendar months of 31 days. This had given a computed birth cycle of 252 days, instead of the true gestation cycle of 280 days, and left Ah Min with a month still to go.

During this month we started to move from the palm-leaf shack to the new but long-anticipated and dreamed-of frame house on the same red hilltop, rebuilt on the cement foundations of our former home which the Japs had destroyed. The new house was too far from the road for a lorry to be of much assistance, and we carried most of our possessions from house to house. Every bone in my body ached with the setting sun of the first day, but Ah Min carried on energetically, while, "Be careful, don't trip, don't fall, don't stumble!" became a family refrain in three languages.

The second day of moving came, and I ached worse by then, but Ah Min was cheerful and active, carried wood to the new kitchen (and a good kitchen it was), cleaned the servants' rooms (decent ones this time), swept out the new living room (with a beautiful, polished floor), laid the table for breakfast (looking across the blue bay), and then came to me in the garden where I was planting rose cuttings, and promising myself never to move again.

"Baby come! Bye-bye, Misiter!" She patted her stomach urgently, then rolled off to join Ah Kau, who was waiting outside with the black umbrella. The two of them hurried down the hill to the hospital to have their baby.

An hour later the hospital called me. I went to the back-quarters and proudly told Ah San that he had a son, weight seven and three-quarter pounds, and the largest Chinese infant to be born in the Sandakan hospital.

"Son very good!" Ah San said smugly.

"Calcium and vitamin D very good!" I said.

I went immediately to the hospital. The baby was beautiful. That is, to Ah Min and me he was beautiful; he was man born of woman, and our hold on immortality. Ah Min did not consciously think this, and wouldn't have said it this way if she had, but this knowledge is in the heart of every woman when she holds her child in her arms.

"What a huge baby for such a tiny mother!" I said wonderingly to the nurse-matron. "Her first one, too! It's a wonder she had it so quickly!"

The nurse looked at me pityingly. "It's not her first baby – it's her third. She doesn't want her husband to know. She's had two babies in China and lost them – or done away with them. You know what she was, don't you?"

I looked down at Ah Min. She was looking at me with bright, questioning eyes, and smiling confidence, as she waited my approval. I looked at the sleeping infant; I understood more now – but nothing that was at all important compared to the successful and happy birth of this largest and youngest Oriental in Sandakan Hospital.

And then Ah San came, followed by Harry. Yes, it was a fine thing Ah San had done, this having a new son, the two men seemed to say.

"A really beautiful boy, Ah San. What will you call him?"

Ah Min had her eyes glued to Ah San; this baby would have a name!

"My name, Li San," Ah San answered proudly. "Baby's name Li Ping Cheong."

Li Ping Cheong opened his eyes and ogled us.

"Well, the beady-eyed little beggar!" Harry said admiringly. "I think very good *I* call him Gung Ho!"

Gung Ho means More Better. Gung Ho the baby remains to us.

V. Brothers

THANK you, Little Brother!" says Gung Ho, youngest son of our household, to George.

Or such is the sentiment indicated to be his by Ah Min, who, with the babe in her arms, mouths the Chinese words at us on his behalf in a grotesque mimicry of baby voice and manner.

"Thank you, Big Brother! Thank you, Big Sister!" repeats Gung Ho to Harry and me, via Ah Min, as we lay our red paper-wrapped gifts beside him.

This is an occasion: today Gung Ho, more correctly Li Ping Cheong, is forty days old. The practical Chinese reckon that high infant mortality in China make it a wasted gesture to acknowledge an infant's arrival until it has survived forty days, then if the child is still alive there seems a reasonable chance of its becoming a permanent member of the household. On the fortieth day gifts of cloth and food are presented by friends and accepted by the infant, who may at this tender age be permitted to sample a variety of spicy sweets which again imperil its existence.

During his days of probation Gung Ho has never wavered in his determination to be President or War Lord, and now on this day, Ah Min holds open house in the servants' quarters. Before six-thirty this morning we were on our way down the path to the backquarters carrying red-paper-wrapped parcels. Three of these contain two-yard pieces of brightly figured cotton goods for Gung Ho's jumpers, the fourth conceals a ten-dollar bill wrapped in red paper, and the fifth is George's idea of what Gung Ho needs, and probably more to Gung Ho's own taste – a red celluloid elephant with a tinkling bell inside. The elephant has been dangled before Gung Ho's unwinking eyes and tucked gently into his strengthless little hands by George, who hovers over the child in fascination, determined that his gift is to be the best and most loved – as it will be.

Ah Min glows in a halo of reflected glory as she presses Chinese cakes upon us, which we refuse. And I add urgently, "Do *not* give Gung Ho any of this food! Gung Ho, *m'oi sik-faan!*"

Ah Min agrees by nods.

"She will, though!" says Harry.

"I don't think she will. She's very good about him."

"Come here, Little Yellow Peril," invites Harry, holding out his arms towards Gung Ho without really expecting to receive him. But Ah Min promptly places the child in them, where Gung Ho performs the first tactful act of his life and curls up without a cry.

"Well! The little beggar! He knows me!" says Harry.

"Not really," I say accurately, "he's just too young to notice at all! As soon as he's old enough to take things in he'll discriminate between people, then he'll probably yell when you hold him!"

Now the most important interest in the household becomes bringing up Gung Ho. Warned by past experience, I had feared an unceasing struggle to prevent foreign bodies and highly spiced foods from entering Gung Ho's diet, a fight to keep him from sucking tinned milk through dirty rubber nipples out of unboiled bottles rather than fresh milk from his own mother's breast, and countless other food irregularities which might crop up. But I was wrong. Ah Min placed him regularly at her breasts and gave him nothing else, bathed him according to hospital instructions and used only antiseptic baby powder which I provided, rather than the heavy-scented Chinese talc with which Chinese babies are usually encased until they look like chickens floured for frying.

Gung Ho's infancy was made noteworthy by the diseases which he didn't have; he had no prickly heat, no diarrhea, no malaria, no scabies, no septic sores, and no enteritis. Constipation was once treated by milk of magnesia, and a cold on the chest was rubbed away with camphorated oil. I put Ah Min on Haliveroil; she had sufficient milk for the baby, and the setup seemed ideal.

"But it's ruining him for China," Harry complains, as he holds Gung Ho on his lap one day. "No natural immunity or resistance to disease being developed! No dirt, flies, famine, flood, infection, plagues and pestilences! He'll pass out in the first epidemic in China!"

"Perhaps he'll not go back to China."

"Then he's even more of a problem. Here he's taking the food of this country from the people it belongs to – besides destroying economic equilibrium by forcing them to compete against Chinese business methods, which the natives cannot do."

"Why hang the economic problem of all Asia around the neck of one baby? Gung Ho didn't cause it, and he can't solve it. Babies are born, and the natural impulse of decent beings is to preserve them. And the opposite pole of that impulse is not a thing to play with. It produced the ovens of Buchenwald and Auschwitz, fed with living human beings. If I have to choose, I'd rather be destroyed by the Yellow Peril than take to burning up babies like Gung Ho!"

"Well, just as you say, my dear!" says Harry amicably, pinching Gung Ho's fat legs. "Gung Ho, my boy, you have just escaped being thrown into the kitchen stove – as has always been my custom with Chinese babies!"

At this time we had a guest staying in the house for ten days, a representative of 20th Century-Fox Film Company, who had flown out from Hollywood to discuss details of the filming of *Three Came Home*. Bob was a quiet, courteous, dignified person, the guest for whom one instinctively desired one's household to appear sane and well ordered. On this day Bob was sitting in the living room making notes for the coming film, and the household was quiet with the soundlessness which means the servants are all asleep and if you want anything done you'd better do it yourself. I left this peaceful scene to drive to the office and fetch Harry for tiffin.

Coming up the road twenty minutes later we heard screams, sobs, wails, and Ah Min's full vocabulary, before we could see the house. Coming in view we saw Ah Min marching up and down on the front lawn sobbing and yelling, and combining the gestures of a professional mourner with those of a less respectable professional service. Thinking that something awful must have happened to Gung Ho, I called out anxiously, "The baby? Is something the matter with Gung Ho?"

Instead of answering me, Ah Min increased the volume of sound, and with tears, sobs and screams pouring forth she paced as close to the open house doors as she could, and then back to the road again. Meanwhile noonday traffic came up the road taking it all in. The Keiths' amah again! Mrs. Keith just doesn't know how to handle the servants; of course, she's American!

But Harry knew. He shouted angrily, "Shut up, Ah Min! Stop it! Shut up, I say! Go to the back of the house and keep quiet!"

Ah Min paid no attention. Neither did Bob, who sat like a perfect gentleman just inside the door making notes, and ignoring the nasty scene; perhaps Hollywood had trained him.

There was a time when I would have been badly upset, or at least painfully embarrassed in this situation. But all I thought now was, Well, here we are in the new house which was to solve our servant problems—and Ah Min is still making scenes! I went quietly around to the cooking shed where Ah San was getting lunch ready, and asked, "Is the baby sick?"

"Baby O.K." And there was Gung Ho in Ah Kau's arms.

"What *is* the matter with Ah Min? You must make her stop this noise."

"No can! Ah Min very bad woman. No want him stay here any more. More better he go away. I keep baby."

"But Ah San, what is the trouble? Mister very angry all this noise."

"Ah Min bad woman. Trouble? I dunno. I tie chicken outside for Misiter's dinner. Chicken go away. Ah Min say boy take. Boy say Ah Min let loose. I dunno. I no like trouble. More better Ah Min go. Too much noise."

"But why does Ah Min want Mister's chicken?"

"Ah Min not want chicken – he want make trouble for boy. Ah Min want boy go away. Ah Min he want work houseboy again."

"Oh!" Perhaps not a bad idea, I thought! Still . . .

"Well, for goodness' sake make her shut up, Ah San. At least, get her away from the front. Mister very angry."

"Yes, Missee," walking toward the front garden.

We joined Bob in the living room then, and sat down to talk about how fortunate it was to have the servant problem solved in the East, and how inscrutable, silent, and wonderfully trained Oriental servants were.

Ah Min continued to howl. I could see Ah San standing modestly at the corner of the house, making mild gestures towards her which she disregarded.

Ah Min knew exactly what she was about; this was her May Day and she was picketing to prove her point; she was going on record as being a hundred per cent for – or was it against? – something. Perhaps Ah San was right that she wanted the boy's job. Anyway, whatever she wanted, the fact that we had a guest made the occasion especially favorable for her to make her point, as it occasioned us loss of face before more people.

We finished tiffin. Ah Min was still picketing.

"If her milk doesn't turn sour," I said, "there can't be much in the theory that nursing mothers should avoid emotional upsets! Gung Ho will have a belly-ache tonight!"

After lunch Harry and Bob left the house and I went upstairs to work. There was little incentive for Ah Min to continue her patrol, and she disappeared towards the back. At four o'clock, the time the men come home for tea, she reappeared with Gung Ho in her arms, and slogging up and down the beat again, wailing and calling, she pulled one breast free from her Chinese coat and popped it into his mouth. Gung Ho quickly satisfied his first hunger, and then joined his howls to hers, one of the few times I ever heard him cry. They stayed in front until after Harry and Bob had come home and then left again for a drive, then the pair disappeared.

Later I heard her belligerent, now tearless, voice in the kitchen, and knew the row had passed its climax. Neither Ah San's voice nor that of the houseboy was heard.

That night Gung Ho cried loudly. The next morning Ah San came to me.

"Baby's stomach no good! Can have medicine?"

I said, "What way no good? Food come up? Or food go down?"

"He want w.c. too much. And he milk comes into mouth."

I took down the milk of magnesia bottle.

The next day Gung Ho was in control of his food, Ah San was silent, Ah Min was smiling, and the boy resigned.

When Ah San called me into the kitchen one day and said, "Missee, I tell you surprise!" I didn't think he could surprise me; I was prepared for anything from a request to finance an import-export scheme to giving the baby a dose.

"Missee, yesterday Hong Kong boat bring letter from Number One son!"

"But you tell me Number One dead! You say Japanese kill!"

"Yes, Missee. Before I think dead, but now he send letter. Japs no kill him!" Ah San's thin yellow face now glows with pleasure and pride. "Now he say he escape from Canton and join American Army in China all same Number Two son. Finish war he go back Canton. Now he write cousin, Ho Quan, in Hong Kong, and Ho Quan send letter here."

"I am very glad for you. That is very good news."

"Yes, Missee. Now I tell you more. Number One son say Number One wife alive Canton side. Japs no kill him." Ah San's expression is less delighted this time.

"Oh!" . . . Then cautiously, "How interesting!" This is the man with no dependents! Suddenly Ah San catches my eye, and we both laugh, then look guiltily over our shoulders to see how much Ah Min is understanding. She is listening attentively nearby, knowing that something is afoot.

"Missee, I like ask Mister one thing." This is the point of Ah San's conversation.

"Yes, Ah San?"

"I like Number One son come Sandakan side. You think Mister can fix?"

There's a lot in that word "fix."

"I don't know. Very difficult for Chinese come to Borneo now. Plenty Chinese try to leave China, go Hong Kong. But Hong Kong have too much people, not enough food, no firewood, cost too much money. So plenty Chinese want to come to Borneo. But first must ask Government for permit to enter, much trouble to get now. More better you talk Mister." Which meant that I must talk to Mister first.

After discussion, "fixing it" for Number One son developed into writing a letter to the Commissioner of Immigration on Ah San's behalf, giving his son's name, age, birthplace, parents, scholastic qualifications, vocation and avocation, religious and political affiliations, and anything else he could think of, and requesting that the nineteen-year-old boy be permitted to enter North Borneo as the charge of his father, who was employed and earned a sufficient wage, and would act as sponsor for the boy in combination with H. G. Keith, Conservator of Forests.

Two weeks later the letter came back enclosing five duplicate forms to be filled in in Chinese and in English. Then Harry, with a typewriter and a Parker 51, with Ah San on one side of him and me on the other, and five duplicate forms, transferred the necessary information to the proper forms, with the additional promises on the part of himself and Ah San to pay for the deportation of Number One son if at any time he should prove undesirable in Government eyes.

To these quintuplet forms were then attached two copies each of an old photograph of Number One son which had been cherished for years by Ah San. This bulk of vital statistics was then addressed to what we hoped was the proper channel although experience led me to doubt it. By then the three of us were mentally exhausted: It seemed obvious that only college graduates, or people with high I.Q.'s, were expected to make application for entry into Borneo.

"George, don't eat like that!"

"Why not? That's the way Americans eat. They paw things apart with a fork instead of using a knife."

"Certainly not in the way you are doing! You never saw me eat like that."

"Another olive and pickle, please, Ma."

"Finish your fish first."

"Enough fish. Another olive, please."

"Finish your fish! I'm not going to have you waste food. If we lived cheaply and you didn't have good food to eat, I'd say, Well, it's too bad but that's all we can afford! But we spend a lot on food; Ah San buys the best there is and it costs a lot out here. And then you complain all the time, and Daddy sits and looks slightly nauseated no matter what comes on the table."

"Why, no, dear!" Harry protests. "I'm just not hungry. One gets so tired of tropical stuff. Now if I had a good crisp green apple . . ."

"Ah San got some cold-storage apples from the Hong Kong boat yesterday," I answer joyfully, feeling, for once, a good provider. "Ah Min! Bring apple! *Ping kwa*, Ah Min."

"*Ping kwa*, Ah Min!" George takes up with enthusiasm. "*Ping kwa!*"

Ah Min disappears, and a flow of Cantonese is heard outside.

Ah Min returns. "*Ping kwa m'oi!*"

"*M'oi?* Why?"

"Misiter no like!"

"What do you mean, Ah Min?"

Ah Min and George exchange mongrel Cantonese, and start to shake with laughter.

"What is she saying, George? Do stop that roaring. Ah Min will break another glass any minute!"

"Minnnnna!" exclaims George. "*Ping kwa* Gung Ho *awsee! Awsee!* Baby *awsee!*"

"George, stop it! What's it all about?"

"*M'oi! M'oi!*" denies Ah Min, shaking with laughter. "Gung Ho *m'ho awsee hai koh shi!* Not wash yet."

"George, will you stop talking at her across my body! What is she saying?"

"Ah San told her Gung Ho did *awsee* on the apples in godown. She says it's only wee-wee so never mind – by and by she'll wash the apples!"

As Gung Ho grew and flourished it was impossible for me not to compare his robust figure favorably with that of the small Chinese infants who were perpetually attending to their sanitary duties in the gutters of the town. Gung Ho himself had no sterilized nursery to live in, and he was not above the use of our own drains; what kept him healthy was mother's milk, fresh air which is free, very moderate cleanliness, and escape from the fetish of Chinese medical practice. These conditions cost little in cash or skill, their greatest price was common sense. Many babies in the town could have had such conditions, had the mothers been willing to accept them. The thing to be wondered at in Gung Ho's life was not that such conditions were made possible for him, but that a Chinese woman of Ah Min's class had the open mind to adopt them, and respect Western advice.

I do not know what to thank for this receptivity to our ideas – unless it is that for the first time in Ah Min's life she had found a home, and had placed her trust, and when the final reward of an infant son came, it crowned all our words with meaning.

"Who's that?" asks Harry, pointing to the smallest, shyest, sloppiest and newest Chinese small-girl who scuttles up from the backquarters like a bird roused from the bush to whir across the front lawn.

"Oh! . . . That? Well – I guess she must be new, I hadn't noticed her before. Let's see – she must be the amah to take care of the amah who takes care of the baby's amah."

"More fleas to feed on other fleas!"

"Well, somebody has to support them. The best way to justify our high standard of living is by the fact that a household of our size and expenditure supports a dozen or so lesser households, and that means there's no waste."

"I suppose that you and George and I only eat about a third of the food that we pay for?" hazards Harry.

"Well, it all comes on the table for us to have first choice, and after that it goes to the backquarters. In that way we can set a good table, which you like to do, and not eat leftovers which you don't like to do, and not have waste, which I don't like to have. And the bulk of the food goes where it's needed most – the backquarters. They know it's intended that way. Anyway, I don't like to have the people who work for us looking starved. It frightens me; makes me conscious of the difference between their living conditions and ours. Makes me remember the Russian peasants rising against the Czarist regime, and episodes in history like that."

"Or the Boxer Rebellion," suggests Harry. "With all those poor, downtrodden Boxers rising against all the nasty, selfish, vicious, high-living old Christian missionaries who had been rubbing Chinese noses in the dust by teaching them Christian religion!"

"Well – that's the first kind word you ever said for missionaries, Harry!"

"Well, here comes somebody to be on my side," says Harry, looking across the garden. "The doc's just parked his car on the road down there!"

Before coming to Borneo the doctor has lived for years in China, and reflects its saddest moments; his face, voice and mind are filled with thoughtful melancholy, while his soul is a well of idealism and deep dejection. And who should have more reason for woe than a doctor who has doctored many years in China?

The doctor seats himself on the veranda, and asks moodily, "That baby? That amah's baby? He does well, I suppose?" The tone commiserates with the unhappy fact that no doubt the awful child will live to slay its benefactors.

"Oh, yes, Doctor, he's wonderful, really," I answer, caught off guard by reference to my enthusiasm. "He's the healthiest Chinese baby I've ever seen. You must see him. I'll get him."

"No, no, no! I do not wish to see him!" says the doctor hastily. But not hastily enough, for Gung Ho, who is always hovering near in the arms of the amah's amah's amah, has already come. Now with Gung Ho in my arms and Gung Ho's mouth opening in a handsome grin which exposes his newest teeth, I press my point.

"He really *is* a fine baby, now isn't he, Doctor?" The doctor must admit that there is at least one desirable Chinese infant in the world!

The doctor looks at the child in my arms, and dodges back as if exposed to a venomous snake, while he murmurs dolefully, "The Horror! The little Horror!"

"There she goes, Doc!" says Harry. "Fostering the Yellow Peril that's going to wipe us all out!"

The doctor looks at Gung Ho, then averts his glance and says in a tone of deep dejection, "There are too many of him, too many, too many! They ought to stop doing it. China's trouble is overpopulation. Everybody's trouble is overpopulation. That's why we're fighting all the time. They ought to stop doing it!"

"Yet you doctors go out of your way," I suggest, "to uphold the law of this country which forbids a doctor to perform an abortion, or a dispenser to sell abortive drugs."

"It's the law! It's the law!" says the doc hastily.

"In fact, you won't even help prevent the birth of all those unwanted, illegitimate Eurasian youngsters. They are doomed from the beginning, with the prejudices of two races to fight. You are afraid to keep these children out of the world, although common sense tells anyone they should be aborted on humane grounds alone."

"I have to obey the law," repeats the doctor. "And that's the law."

"But we make the laws. If overpopulation is the cause of wars, why don't we make sensible laws to control it? Sterilize the unfit, make birth control popular and contraceptives cheap. It would cost a lot less than wars!"

"Birth control interferes with religious teachings, so your orthodox clergy will tell you," says Harry, "because it does away with life."

"So does war. Yet no church stands out against the state in the matter of war. By the time a country gets into war the clergy on both sides are giving their blessing to it!"

"To listen to you, anybody would think you were a Communist in favor of giving up God, when you are really a Christian in favor of giving up Communism," Harry suggests.

"I know," I agree. "But it makes me so angry that people don't see, or admit, that there's anything phony about professing Christianity – and then always dropping the biggest bomb, throwing the hottest flames, and shooting the biggest gun. Of course we always say, and believe, that we are fighting a good cause – but do we know what we are fighting for? I'll bet that if we put as much effort into living decently as we do into fighting wars, there'd be less cause for wars."

Harry sighs, "You could be right. But to be practical, how do we start? Do we let the servants move up into this big house, and we move down into the backquarters? Do we give my pension back to the government? Do we give your book royalties away to the poor?"

"The question is, how do we start, and still stay selfishly comfortable, ourselves? Jesus Christ and Mahatma Gandhi had the only answer. They gave themselves and their lives for what they believed, holding back nothing. But they were martyrs to a cause. What we are always trying to do is to live the good life, and still not be martyrs to it. I'm not the martyr stuff. Well, I start with Gung Ho! He's my Yellow Promise." At this Gung Ho suddenly shouts loudly.

"Perhaps the odor of your white skin offends his nostrils, dear," murmurs Harry. "Or are you pinching him?"

"Neither, it's feeding time. Now, Gung Ho, you needn't mouth me in that suggestive manner, it's eight years since George got anything there!"

Meanwhile Ah San's Number One son has made his way to Hong Kong, a British Colony into which by treaty agreement no Chinese may be refused entry. In Hong Kong he acquires a passport, supplied possibly by a cousin who perhaps has several extra ones, or supplied, if all else fails, by legitimate means. There he awaits the arrival of his entry permit to Borneo, and receives a passage to Borneo purchased for him by Harry. Meanwhile Shanghai and Canton, once more in China's history, fall, arise — and reopen for business.

The day comes, and once again Ah San points to the Hong Kong boat in the harbor below.

"He come!"

This time Ah Min, the one-time bride, stands in the background — hungrily, jealously, wonderingly, hugging Gung Ho.

"You go meet him, Ah San," I say.

An hour later father and son stand before me, both quiet-spoken, clean, gentle, slim and long-faced, like and unlike. Number One son at nineteen is alive with the vigor of unlived years that his father has already put behind, slim like a tree limb while his father is thin like a worn cord; son's eyes sparkle with life to come while father's sparkle only with pride in him.

"This Number One son, Ah Kin. He speak English, Missee," introduces Ah San.

"Good morning, Ah Kin."

"Good morning, Missee," and he shakes me strongly by the hand; it is the proper American salute.

"He knows plenty Americans. He bring drinks for American Air Force in China after war," Ah San explains.

In Ah San's market basket I have spotted two magnificent camellia plants, great rarities in Borneo, but the roots of the plants, I see with dismay, are bare of earth as no gardener would let them be.

"Ah Kin bring," Ah San explains. "He bring Misiter two flower plants in very fine garden pot from Canton because Misiter very kind. But Customs man say no can bring dirt in Borneo, must throw dirt. So Ah Kin throw dirt, bring flower, but no can do pot. I think now flower die." Ah San looked sadly at them.

I looked sadly at them also; undoubtedly flower would die, the roots were dry and broken.

"What did he do with the earth?"

"He dump in Customs."

The bare feet of coolies were by now trampling the condemned earth through the Customs barrier onto Borneo soil for wide dissemination – but regulations had been obeyed.

"Can you fix a place for Ah Kin to sleep in the back, Ah San?"

"Can do, Missee, I ask you something. You will ask Misiter please?"

"What is it, Ah San?"

"Ah Kin like be engineer bimeby. You please ask Misiter help him get job Sandakan? Suppose he work in machine shop, he very much like."

"I talk Misiter. Maybe can do."

The following week Harry got him a job as apprentice in a machine shop in Sandakan, where Ah Kin was soon reported to be doing very good work. He started night school to improve his English and continued to live in our backquarters. Between working hours and school hours, he volunteered for various household jobs, and he was skillful at everything he touched. I would have delighted to take him on as houseboy – for Ah Min was giving all her time to the baby, not the house – and would have paid him more than he was earning in town, but this would have limited him; if he continued with his machine training a good future lay before him. Meanwhile he was tireless, doing odd chores in every moment of leisure. After some weeks of volunteer work I attempted to hand him five dollars as pay. He refused to take it. I gave it to George to give to him, and it was returned again.

Then I called Ah San.

"Ah San, you must take this money to help pay for Ah Kin's food. He not yet make much money in shop. He help me – I like to pay him."

"No can do, Missee! If Missee give Ah Kin money, he no can help here. Misiter good to Ah Kin, bring him Borneo. Ah Kin no take money for help this house!"

I did not argue again.

The sun glows hotly in the garden, the air shimmers with the noonday glare, and the leaves of the trees lie still in the heat. Number One son and Number Four, now nine months old, bask companionably together in the shadow of the old African tulip tree on the grass outside my window, while discussing family affairs this Sunday morning.

"Number Four, you are a nice little brat!" approves Ah Kin.

"Unnnnh huh!" Gung Ho's mouth opens in a toothy, amiable grin of assent. "Oooh gooh!"

"Number Four, you have beautiful little brown legs, and a nice round fuzzy head, and a little indelible blue spot on the end of your spine that means you are truly Chinese. Your mother is Ah Min, a yellow bitch with a temper like ginger root and a tongue like a cat's – but your father is my father. Your name is Li Ping Cheong, my name is Li Keng Kin, and we are brothers. Now I will bite your little flat nose with my strong teeth, because you are my brother. . . ."

"Ooh gooh!" Number Four agrees.

Ah Min appears, flouncing out from the back, dressed spotlessly in crisp Chinese white. This child is mine! her attitude says. Come, Gung Ho, your mother will teach you to talk, to laugh, to play! And today your mother will teach you to walk!

She swings Gung Ho up to his little, uncertain feet. Ah Kin lies back with his eyes half closed, half smiling, saying nothing. He knows – these women!

Now Ah Min supports Gung Ho by his soft armpits, bending adoringly over him, pulling his little shirt well up above his wrinkled belly to show his wonderful, naked sex. Ah Min knows, too. Her son, thank heaven! Son, not daughter.

Ah Min is thin now, and strained-looking, and growing bald with the premature age which comes suddenly on Chinese peasant girls with husbands and bearing babies, but when she smiles on Gung Ho her face is beautiful as any madonna.

She has come a long way from the yellow mud of China's rivers, from its crowded brothels, from fright and fear. Whatever terrors she was born to, Gung Ho is born to different things. Whatever she meted out to his predecessors, those other two babies who were to be hidden from us all – whether it was merciful death in a flowing stream, a pressed-down pillow and a smothered moan, or illness and weakness from a secret, shameful struggling birth – whatever it was, Gung Ho is born to love and devotion no different, no less intense, no less human than mine for my son.

Gung Ho's fat legs bulge outward with the weight of his bottom, or else his chest outdistances his feet while his legs swing loosely under him like pendulums. This manner of movement could not be called walking – by any but a mother.

"He walk, Missee! He walk!" Ah Min calls proudly up to me. "He walk!"

Her son walks, and she has taught him, and that is as it should be. Now Gung Ho is returned to Ah Kin for playtime, and Ah Min goes back into the house to finish her work.

"Ah Min had another fight with Ah San today, Ma," George confides to me upstairs.

"You shouldn't poke your nose into the backquarters all the time! Well, what happened?"

"Ah San says that if Ah Min makes any more trouble he'll throw her out."

"What about Gung Ho? Ah San will never throw out Ah Min because he wants Gung Ho."

"Ah San will keep Gung Ho, Mum. Gung Ho belongs to Ah San because he's a boy. Sons always belong to fathers, Ah San says. If it was a girl he'd throw her out with Ah Min. Daughters are no good."

"What about me? I'm a daughter. Do you think I'm no good?'

"Yes, I know – that's all right for English folks, Ma – but not for Chinese. Maybe we know what's good for us, but Ah San knows about Chinese. He says sons O.K., girls throw out!"

"Well, I wouldn't let him throw out Ah Min, and I wouldn't let him take Gung Ho away from her, either – even though she is a damned nuisance sometimes! Anyway, Ah San could never get Gung Ho away from her, I know that. Ah Min would keep coming back and back, and probably cut Ah San's throat in the end. Gung Ho's her whole life."

"You just wait and see, Mum. Ah San will manage it when he's ready."

"And you just wait and see, George. And the first thing you see – Ah Min will be pregnant again – that's her answer."

But George is tired of the subject.

"O.K., Mum! I'm going out now to get Ah Kin to fix the brake on my bike for me. Ah Kin! Ah Kin! I'm coming. . . ."

Ah Kin looks up and smiles agreeably. Soon the three are lying together on the warm lawn under the tree – my son, Ah Min's son, and the other woman's son.

As I watch them, I know that the same deep emotion I feel for my own son goes out to them all three. These children, born of the common experience, all equally children of a human womb, all pulled naked from a birth canal to struggle for breath, to cry for milk from a human breast, to fight for food, to need for love – all three are brothers. The human blood that unites them is a stronger bond than the swords that would come between.

PART TWO

People Who Live in Grass Houses

I. Land of Sabah

SEVENTY years ago this city was known as Elopura, meaning in Sanskrit, Beautiful City. Now it is Sandakan, a huddle of palm-leaf huts built above charred ruins, knowing hunger as it never knew plenty, knowing suffering as it never knew ease, knowing the face of death as closely as the faces of its own brown children.

Yet for all that man can do with implements of large-scale destruction, his work is transient against the timelessness of land. For this country of Borneo is essentially the same lurid, hot, primitive, untracked stretch of humid, sweating jungle green that sprawled across the equator when the first white adventurers came in the 1800's. When, winding on their cholera belts, putting on their chalky sun helmets, pulling up their tall snake-proof knee boots, tucking up their walrus mustaches, they waded ashore through the warm shallows of the Sulu Sea, they must have seen as I see now a chromatic landscape of hills, sky, and bay.

Through swarms of mosquitoes and sand flies, they found islands that sprouted like fungus out of the falling tides, green trees growing in ocean and fish flying on land, and mangrove roots like gnarled old men with the gray color and stench of mud. They saw exotic jungle flowers blooming to the size of a man's arm stretch, and the color of raw flesh and the odor of decomposing bodies, while anthropoid apes that looked like men, and men who looked like — well, the men wore headcloths and the apes didn't — lost themselves silently in the dark, secret shadows of the haggard trees.

It was a land, these men learned in their time, rich in timber, gold, copper and coal, with swift-running waterways, white rapids, heavy jungle, and mountains like sleeping women outlined against the sky, and a moon, on those hot silent nights, like an oversize copper ball floating in blue-ink air, and a sea like a painted picture of a tropical island sea.

But by then these young Britons adventuring in the tropics lay on beds of pain and fever, seeing the sun through yellow malarial eyes, their silky mustaches wet with cold sweat, their bones shaking, their boots off, their cholera belts discarded, their sun helmets gone — but undimmed their enthusiasm for a strange, far land. "This is the Venice of the Orient! This is the new Ceylon!" they wrote home with trembling, feverish, but inspired pens.

It was the northern corner of the island of Borneo they described, and it belonged then to the dark-skinned Sultans of Brunei and Sulu, who were always hard up. The Sultans had country, and they wanted cash — what with opium, women, horses, and gambling, to keep them poor! The young British adventurers wanted land. They arose from their beds of fever to get it. Soon a promotion scheme was under way.

Part of this territory was under lease to the romantic and enterprising Lee Moses, the United States courtesy Consul to Brunei, and a Yankee businessman from Maine named Torrey, who formed the American Trading Company. But the company failed from shortage of capital and surplus of coolies, and the Americans relinquished their claims. The Sultans made final settlement with the Englishmen for annual payments in cash and a few good parties, and the new white sovereigns, now known as the Maharajas of Sabah, were introduced to their dusky subjects (those whom they could catch) over whom they now had complete power (on paper), and Queen Victoria placed the Royal Seal and her blessing on a new British charter.

Three years later, in 1881, the Chartered Company of British North Borneo was born, with governing and administrative rights over the country, and the adventuring Englishmen again wrote triumphantly home, "The happy destiny of this land is now made certain under the enlightened heads and liberal hearts of Englishmen." The country was then called Sabah, and its capital, built by the wind-swept blue silk of the Sulu Sea, was appropriately called Elopura, Beautiful City.

This primitive country was peopled by simple savages and unsophisticated pagan tribes, men who took heads, burned villages, pirated travelers, plundered traders, sank ships and scuppered each other as simply and with as little sophistication as that. Then the white man came. He was English: the country continued to be peopled by simple savages and unsophisticated natives. They were preserved like game and ripe peaches by the colonizing British who pride themselves on kindness to simple savages and preservation of old tribal custom. But the towns along the coast were hungrily settled with Chinese, Javanese, Indians and Malays, who understood trading for food and living, while the natives fished, hunted and killed for theirs.

When I first came to Borneo in 1934 it was the only country in the world still run by a Chartered Company, which was then the modern version of the seventeenth-century synthesis of adventure, piracy, business and government which had at one time been responsible for carrying British commerce and younger sons all over the world. When I came on the scene the anachronistic combination of benevolence and self-profit, the Chartered Company of British North Borneo, was overlord, landlord, war lord and boss to the people I met. And although it required a great number of typewritten pages written in triplicate forms mailed to the London office in order to install new knobs on doors in Borneo or remove keyholes, it was all done in a gentlemanly way and everybody was happy. And as the Chartered Company installed more knobs than it removed keyholes, its operation could not be called exploitation, for signs of which my American heritage had warned me to be on the alert.

At each half-yearly London meeting of the Chartered Company disgruntled shareholders of one share each liked to arise and ask pertinent questions aimed at uncovering something dirty in the dealings of the Board of Directors. These questions were always answered politely by important gentlemen who prided themselves on politeness even to shareholders, who might make their own lunches on bags of large black cherries in dark offices in Leadenhall Street despite the titles before and the initials after their names, but who always replied politely to shareholders because—there really wasn't any dirt to uncover. The Chartered Company, in fact, was honest, and dealt justly with its country and the people.

Every few years the President of the Board of Directors visited North Borneo, and as a visiting potentate he was treated to messes of potage and jugs of wine in company with the leading ladies and gentlemen of the European and Asiatic communities dressed in new gowns and old tails, exotic loincloths and gaudy sarongs. Then, having seen Borneo as it seldom was except when he came, the President returned to London to tell the story of his wilderness adventure and his jungle trek, and to speak with pride of the good feeling which existed between Asiatics and Europeans.

In this he was right; the native peoples of North Borneo expressed no wish to rise against their wrongs, first, because they had no wrongs, and second because they had no rising power. They were better cared for and governed under the administrators of the demoded Chartered Company than they would have been under themselves at this stage, and they were still too primitive in social evolution to have the desire to try.

There was little antagonism between the white people and the Asiatics because publicly they accepted us as what we set up to be – the governing race, although not necessarily a superior one. Private interracial relations were more often determined in bed than in court in a back-door relationship which so long as it stayed at the back door was accepted by both races. This relationship, although supposedly initiated by the white man, was encouraged and cultivated by brown women.

In this country there existed no huge mass of unadministrable laws, and Government did not oppress or exploit. The most unpopular law was one which aimed at making it compulsory for the natives to plant enough rice to feed themselves, and to harvest and eat it, rather than drink it in the form of fermented, fiery rice wine. There was no money in the country, but also no poverty as poverty is known in the Asiatic sense, and the faces of the poor people were happy and cheerful compared to the slum peoples of the West.

It was into this state of benevolent despotism, or dangerous capitalism according to the way you looked at it, of North Borneo under the white man, that the yellow man came in 1942.

With the Japanese came war; and four years of Asiatic rule for Asiatics, of semi-civilization, of moral dissolution, and physical desolation. The country was invaded by Japanese shock troops, occupied by Japanese military police, raped by Japanese bums, burned by Japanese zealots, bombed by Allied enthusiasts, liberated by Australian forces, reoccupied by Important Allied Initials, administered by Tin Hats and Brass, exploited by experts and succored by amateurs.

By the time of the surrender in 1945 the jungle had closed over the charred townsite of Sandakan and few ruins, even, could be seen. The surviving populace had moved to the jungle or to small islands in the bay, their women slept with by all and married by none, their widows left without weeds, their orphans without names.

Then 1945 came, the news went round, the war was over, succor was near. People moved back to the weed-choked ruins, the British returned, the flag flew high, the soldier ruled, relief ships came. Soon bully beef and fur coats, vitamin tablets and pink satin slips, high-heeled slippers and woolly pyjamas, stale blood plasma and fresh tomato juice, white face powder and black sea boots, malaria prophylactics and frostbite medicaments arrived without prejudice to arctic or tropic, sent by relief agencies half the world away with much good will and little knowledge. These were distributed to those who got there first, some stolen, much resold on black market. A town sprang up out of the ashes and jungle, out of the bones and bombs; old mistresses knew what was expected and shifted their beds, and blond-haired, blue-eyed babies joined the black-headed, bowlegged ones. Sandakan, once Beautiful City, came back to the white man's rule.

Two years later this tropical island state, now a new British colony, although surrounded by violence and lawlessness in China, Mayala, Indo-China, Formosa, Java, Sumatra, the East Indies, and the Philippines, had itself regained security. In neighboring countries peacetime was as threatening as war, criminals, agitators, revolutionaries were better armed than armies, and citizens could not walk on streets without being attacked, robbed, murdered. Here in North Borneo the only battle was that of man against bad living conditions and undernourishment in the fight to rebuild a destroyed country. Here on sunbathed shores, under British rule, there was peace.

Five years earlier I had left Sandakan for prison camp a captive in rags, starving and ill-treated under Japanese rule, a position to which my white skin entitled me then. Now I return; my skin is still white, my position enviable, but any faith I may have had in the invincibility of color is dead. Color is certainly important, to look at, but only for that. It is convenient to be white, but not sufficient, and credit for it is due to chromosomes; it is convenient to belong to the ruling race, but is it the ruling race? I can remember when it wasn't.

So I speak without prejudice to color, and certainly without belief in the *Herrenvolk*, when I say that the brown races to whom this country belongs, the aborigines of North Borneo, are not yet ready to govern themselves and are better off under us. We do not do much for them, God knows — a dollop of medicine, a pinch of hygiene, a sniff of education, a whiff of prosperity, large schemes and limited action, an exposition of the theory of Christianity accompanied by feeble practice – but an honest administration of justice, the washout of crime compared to other Eastern places, and the import of rice by international agreement, and assistance in all local planting, for a non-self-supporting and undernourished people. It's not much – but it's more than these people can yet do for themselves. It is not their skins, but their minds and manner of thought and their values which must change, through future years of social evolution.

At present the native of Borneo has no national concept, much less world concept, because he can't think that big; he doesn't know that he has a country because he can't see that far. His farthest horizon is the pig under his house, the outermost tree in his clearing, the footpath over the mountain which he treads twice a year to the nearest village for salt.

The rugged, unmodified topography of this country, its heavy jungle, swift rapids, untraversable swamp land, and untracked hogback mountains, plus the condition of heavy rainfalls averaging 75 to 150 inches a year, result in lack of roads, transport, communications, and this, in turn, results in almost total lack of education among the natives.

Pagan tribes of the interior and plains, and Muslim tribes along the coasts are said to be of Indonesian-Polynesian-Mongoloid origin. The Murut tribes of the Interior are believed to be a basically Mediterranean people with an infusion of Mongoloid blood. All these people keep alive today the description of hundreds of years past of a simple, savage, archaic people, un-co-operative with and ignorant of civilization. An Interior Rundum Murut dressed simply and solely in his cardinal red loincloth, his teeth filed to the gums for beautification, his incisors knocked out to admit his poison-dart blowpipe, his gums dripping red saliva from the juice of the betel nut he chews, his long, lank black hair hanging down to his small-buttocked behind, would occasion comment even in Hollywood.

There are four main divisions of North Borneo Native Tribes, the Dusuns, Muruts, Bajaus, and Suluks, and twice as many subtribes, all representing minor differences, are included under these four broad headings. All these tribes speak different dialects, have no common spoken language, and only the Suluks and Bajaus have a written language. They have no easy means of communication, no literature or books, no newspapers or radios. Each tribe has different tribal customs, and the only things they have in common are dark skins, endemic diseases, a disastrous sense of humor, and bad habits.

They live in groups of twenty-five to a couple of hundred people, in some cases in some tribes all living together in one community long-house. Each group is isolated from the other by days of foot travel over narrow paths or swift rivers, and each person thinks only in terms of his own group.

Government vernacular schools teach Malay, which is the nearest thing to a common language here, and mission schools teach English to those who can and will attend and Chinese schools, for Chinese, teach Chinese ideology. From figures based on the last local education report it appears that only one native child out of every ten goes to school long enough to be registered and estimated among the school population, but observation leads me to say that not one out of one hundred stays to acquire education. The schools are all primary, and no secondary, vocational, or special schools exist. The Chinese in towns conduct their own schools independently, in Chinese for Chinese.

In the East Indies and Malaya before the war, there were excellent educational facilities, natural wealth, and ensuing leisure, a combination which had developed an Asiatic intelligentsia class of high standing. But in North Borneo there never has been and still is not a moneyed class among the natives; a man's wealth is in his personal possessions, and his dogs, pigs, buffalo, blowpipes, weapons, brass, and wives. As there are no secondary schools here and no rich men, no rich men's sons set forth from Borneo to enter foreign universities, and no native of North Borneo has ever to my knowledge acquired a university education or a degree.

Current anthropology suggests that the aborigines here are growing decadent and impotent through interference with tribal customs, lack of heads to take, enemies to murder, ships to sink.

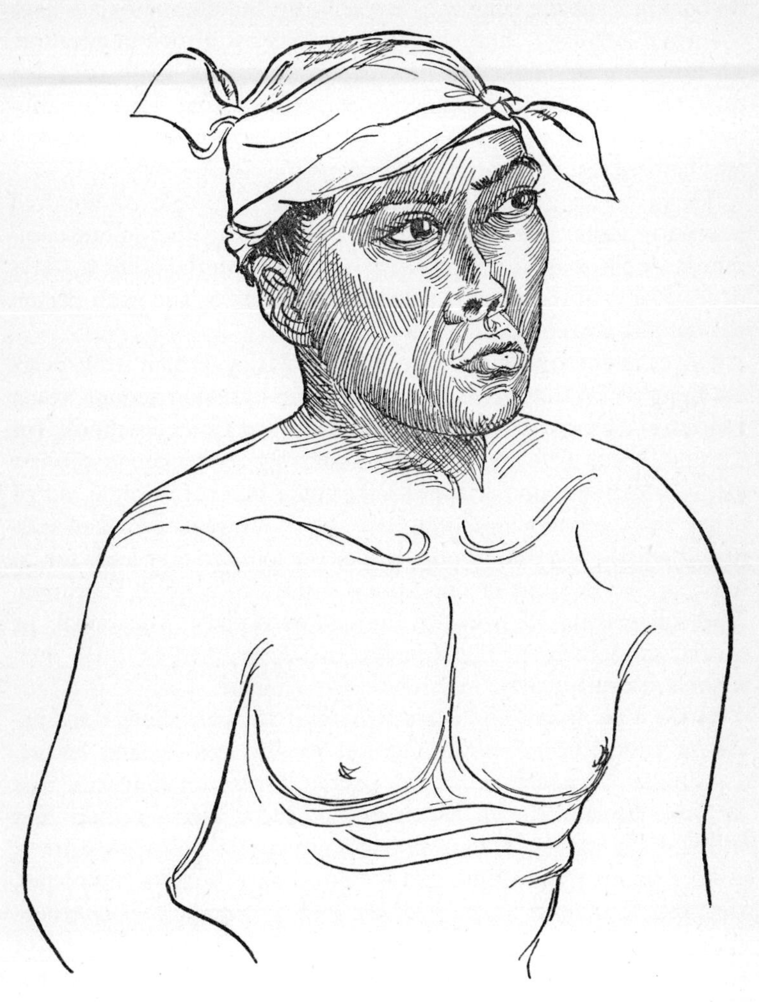

A NORTH BORNEO NATIVE

To this theory current medicine adds a postscript that malaria, dysentery, tuberculosis, and continued malnutrition caused by drinking their rice crop in home brew instead of eating it, and ignorance of hygiene, probably contribute more to infertility and high mortality than do suppressed head-hunting desires or the schizophrenia of balked assassinations.

These people are a link between ourselves and the past, but a link which makes the past seem further. To deal with them, and at the same time in the same world to treat with the atomic theory, modern bacteriology, the United Nations, Trygve Lie and Einstein, is fantastic. The fantasy of it sometimes robs me of the urge to deal in terms of reality, and to elevate, educate, clean teeth, kill germs, and spread welfare. Against me and modern methods, the natives win; they have more germs than I have disinfectant, more lethargy than I have energy. The more I know of aborigines the more I suspect that only time, unhurried, unharassed, unorganized, untiring and unbeatable, will tell on them.

But time will. And meanwhile the factor that the primitive people of Borneo need for civilization is the liberty which alone prepares men for liberty. Whether this liberty comes with the security of British rule, or with that of their own brown and yellow brothers, may be for the future to say.

In Sandakan, formerly the capital city and still the commercial hub, the majority of inhabitants are Chinese with smaller representations of Indians, Javanese, Filipinos, natives of Borneo and Malays. This is the biggest shipping port, being in line with both Hong Kong and Malaya traffic, and the sea is the city's business center, its main traffic artery, its line of communication, its bathtub, its sewer, and much of its food supply, while the city suburbs are built on stilts over it and children fish their breakfasts from it.

Except where it is fiercely hewn back, the jungle meets the shore and gardens' edges, and bananas, coconuts and pineapple ripen all the year, greens and beans flourish and little else, and water buffalo give milk, haul carts and furnish steaks. Local pigs and dogs kept under pagan village houses or in Chinese gardens consume refuse as it drops, and return it threefold to the initial rhythm of life on feast days and Chinese holidays. The Muslim population, shunning both pork and dog, look to the sea and the rice fields for food, and mark their religious festivals by consuming small, bright-colored sweet cakes made from maize flour, and locally grown coffee, and tobacco. Everyone smokes or chews, infants drop their mothers' nipples to pick up cigarettes, native mouths are always red with the juices of well-chewed, well-spat-out sireh, and Chinese teeth click tirelessly on dried watermelon seeds.

A few days' travel from Sandakan, up the Kinabatangan River in the famous Gomantong Caves, swiftlets employ their home-building instincts in the best-paid occupation a Borneo bird can indulge in, the making of nests for birds'-nest soup, which is no joke, but real soup. The sale of the essential gelatinous ingredient of the birds' nests brings annually to North Borneo some ninety thousand dollars.

Now already, the Chinese shopkeepers in the town are beginning to make money again and mahjong tiles clack nightly above palm-leaf shops, while lean-shanked Indians barter with cheap, brilliant silks in the bazaar, and dapper Filipinos pound broken-down, third-hand typewriters at wilted white-collar jobs. Again the Malays laugh, dance, supplicate Allah for heavenly grace and earthly help, and live on love; the sojourning natives with unfading charm laugh, joke, drink, and add local color and extract paternal instincts from responsible Administrators, while smiling, sireh-lipped women toy daintily with temple flowers in dark and shining hair which smells of rancid oil and cheap perfume, and life in Sandakan, which ought to seem sordid, does not.

This is not an easy land to regiment or reform; there is too much to do, too little to do with, and too few who want it done. Rather, it is a place to give freely and expect no return, to cast your bread and ask back no butter. It is a place to give for the reason that when such inequality exists between two ways of life as exists here between our way and that of a native or Asiatic laborer it eases my conscience to give, but not because the recipient will thank me, love me, or cease to defecate in front of my house. It is a place to accept gratitude, if it appears, as a free-will gift to which you have no claim.

Yet I have never found kindness lacking here, nor friends, nor have I found any person of any color who, if you treated him as a human being with human needs and capable of performing human deeds, did not respond as such. When these people had and I had not, in wartime, I existed for three and a half years on the charity of Asiatic friends, but this perilous survival was not vouchsafed me as a return for obligations from the past, but to me as a friend. Today, it is I who owe them.

Take our friend Ah Leong. He is an old Chinese coolie who has carried our luggage up to our house from the Customs wharf all the years we have lived here, back and forth on every home leave, and every local trip we ever made. Ah Leong and we have always discussed each other's children together, our home "villages," our illnesses and our businesses. We have had confidence in each other; we that he would never lose our luggage, even the brown paper parcels; and he that we would never take a younger, swifter coolie.

During the Japanese occupation I saw him just once. This time I was the coolie-prisoner dragging a suitcase, bedding roll, and baby, and trying to lift them to a ship's deck three feet away from the wharf and three feet above it, while Japanese officers stood laughingly by. Seeing me struggling alone, Ah Leong came running up to assist me, and was knocked down by the butt of a Japanese rifle.

When I returned to Sandakan a free woman again, Harry and I were one day walking along the sandy path towards the native village of Keramunting with George running along the beach, when we heard a voice shouting after us in Chinese-Malay, and steps running. We looked behind us and saw a figure in sack-cloth underpants and a frayed straw hat without a crown, and a face under the hat that was glowing with gold teeth and glad greetings. It was Ah Leong, and we were as valued old friends meeting again after long adversity. We learned that an American bullet had shot off his toe, he had rheumatism now and had stopped carrying luggage, he lived at Keramunting and fished for a living, the Japs had been very bad here, the children were growing up, we were all growing older, and then came the important question, "And where is your baby, Mem?" – the baby whom he had last seen tied on my back when I was a prisoner.

I pointed ahead at George's long-legged figure which was loping back towards us now; George had seen us talking and feared he might be missing something. Ah Leong shouted in delight. "Wah! That big strong boy? Wah! Very good, very good!" and he and George stood and stared at each other with flattering interest.

Early one morning a week later when I was driving home from Harry's office, Ah Leong ran out from the side of the road. Brandishing his arms in front of me like a wind-driven scarecrow, he took a stand in the middle of the road, with more confidence in our brakes than I have. I swerved around him and skidded into the drain. He came after me, and leaning informally over the hood of the car he inserted his smiling, gold-toothed face through the open wind screen and carefully scrutinized the interior of the car. Ours is an English made petrol-saver, about the size of George's prewar pram, with ten tubercular horses coughing their lives out under the hood, and Ah Leong's masterful attitude toward it led me to believe that he was going to offer to pick it up and carry it home for me. However, it was only George whom he was trying to locate in some corner.

"Where is that boy, Mem?"

"George is at his father's office. Today is a school holiday, and he is going fishing with the Malay fishermen."

"Wah! That is good! That boy is very big and fine! I have brought him this basket of crayfish to eat," and he emptied a basketful of live fish into the bottom of the motorcar at my feet.

It was a good catch, and worth several dollars, and Ah Leong had walked three miles from his village to waylay me on my homeward route with it. I accepted the crayfish with gratitude and thanks. I was driving the car; he was the coolie on the road.

Ah Leong has no obligation to us for the past, he always gave value for payment received. The only thing we ever gave him in excess of his fee was recognition that he was human.

II. Green Graves

THE new house is haunted by the old one.

Standing on the same hill, on the very foundations, facing in the same direction and built to a similar design, this lovely, new, fresh cream-colored, green-trimmed house, the first permanent timber dwelling in Sandakan, is haunted by the old house, and a ghost.

I don't believe in ghosts. But every day I see a tall, gaunt woman telling her husband good-by, taking her baby and walking down the path alone, standing at the bottom of the path and looking back for the last time in the late afternoon sun at her home and earthly possessions, and crying. I don't believe in ghosts, I say; but this ghost woman doesn't believe in me, or in real people, or real houses. She thinks I am the ghost, and this is her house — and I'm getting confused.

The new house is beautiful. Round-trippers on world boats come up to see it, carrying their cameras and calling, Why look! It's just like a real house! Young Chinese from the town climb up the hill and stand proudly by the front entrance to have their pictures taken to send back to China, themselves resplendent against this splendid, anonymous backdrop of prosperity. And all this, too, without seeing the real plumbing inside, or the polished floors, or the all-cream interior, or the screened sleeping rooms!

The ghost likes the house, too. She says she always *did* like this house, even if it *is* an old one, because of the lovely view! If only she didn't have to keep seeing the Japs down there in the harbor, she says, and hear them singing that Hymn to the Sun!

The long French doors with real glass windowpanes look south over the tops of trees which scatter down the steep slope towards the bay to meet a background of pastel water; the upstairs bedroom windows, wide open to admit sun and wind, gaze languidly across dark jungle tops to the shore of the Sulu Sea, crested with white waves. Crimson flame-of-the-forest covers the hill slope in front of us, and impromptu clouds throw perpetual glamour over the bay which shifts with a breath from peace to a storm.

I don't believe in ghosts. The other day I came down our new stairway to answer an urgent pounding at the door — and Japanese soldiers were framed against the harbor with bayoneted guns waiting to take me away. The ghost woman was there too, and she said, It's no use to be afraid; this is just the beginning. There's much worse to come!

I don't believe in ghosts. Yesterday I walked down the path to the road and turned to wave good-by to Harry, and the ghost woman hurried after me and said, Careful! Don't drop the baby! I said, What baby? She answered, George. He's there in your arms. And I looked down — and he was.

Harry doesn't believe in ghosts either. He asked Government to rebuild the new house here on the site of the old one amongst the overgrown trees and abandoned garden we planted years before. He wanted it that way. Here are the same mauve Vanda orchids we brought once from Singapore, moved to the palm-leaf shack and back again, here the spicy oleanders from Kuala Lumpur, the golden bougainvillea, the crepe myrtle with pale pink bloom, the honeyed cerise lantana, the fringed hybrid apricot hibiscus; and cannas, lipstick red, carmine, daffodil, orange. Here are the forester's pride, trees from far places, the China pine from Hong Kong, the eucalyptus from New Guinea, the porcupinelike Dracaena from the top of Timbun Mata, and the *Brownea grandiceps*, breath-taking in Singapore with downhanging buds like a flaming magnolia which open to a core of fleshy scented blooms – in Singapore – but nonflowering in our garden. Here is the *Saraca declinata* with masses of tiny, smoldering, burnt orange flowers which cling closely in angles between branches and offshoots as if someone had sprayed masses of molten gold against the tree, with a scent like intensified oleander or decayed vegetation – like this in Singapore – but also nonblooming in our garden. All these reminders of past gardening adventures are now sad and scrawny – but we will make them thrive again, Harry says. That is the sensible way to take it. No ghosts allowed!

All day we work at many things and keep busy, and heaven knows there is much to do, with the house to settle, curtains to remake to fit new windows, gardening to do, a book to write, and George to keep occupied. But when I sit at night and read with my bare feet tucked under me, looking across the cool dark space of the bay to the far shore as I used to do, I am listening – listening for something I do not hear – the gongs of native dwellings whose flickering fires once lightened the darkness across the bay where now all is blackness and silence. And that is the foolish way to take it. But sometimes I look up quickly – and Harry is listening, too.

Back in the old house – I mean the new house – it becomes inevitable that we reminisce. Now for the first time we talk freely together of those days after the occupation of the country by the enemy and before our imprisonment. We retrace our steps together, we give up our bluff, we admit now how deep were our fears, how great our fright, and we recognize that to have come through alive is almost too good to be true.

We do not bury our ghosts, we dig them up. We see them for what they are, terrible creatures well worth being frightened at. We bring out our dead, and looking carefully in their friendly, familiar faces, we wonder that we are not among them.

We talk of the lost dwelling places across the bay, and now for the first time I learn their story. It seems that shortly before the end of the war, the village houses and their native occupants were completely destroyed by the Japanese, leaving only one survivor, a Dusun girl child. This small one was left, almost decapitated by a Japanese sword stroke, and abandoned to die with her head nearly severed from her body. The next day she was found still unbelievably alive, and brought to Sandakan and nursed back to survival.

When the Allies reoccupied the country and the English nursing sisters returned, the child was taken into hospital for care.

The cords in her neck which controlled the raising of her head had been cut through, and though she grew stronger she could not lift her head from her chest. As she began to show interest in life, the nurse told her that she might ask for whatever she wished to have, to celebrate her improvement.

The child thought a long time, her head hanging forward on her scarred neck to rest against her meager chest, while she searched her small-girl soul for what, in this strange new life she was in, could bring to a Dusun child the greatest joy, the most power and pride. Then rolling up her shining black eyes for an admiring view of the nurse's well-waved hair, she asked for a permanent wave.

When Harry tells me the story of this small girl, we look at George, our son. We recall how his old English perambulator used to adorn this very same garden, standing out in the sun with a green cotton awning over it when he was a baby. Now it is a bicycle that stands in the garden in the sun, and an air rifle that lies on the grass.

It takes time to bring the oleanders and orchids back to bloom, it takes time to learn to live with them again, everything takes time. So many of the people we used to know have no more time. But we are fortunate, we still have time. I am beginning to believe in ghosts now – but they are friends.

"Poor bastard! Well, that's one that didn't get carried back to the shrine of Yasakuni. It's a nice little bowl, though. Do you want it for flowers, Agnes?"

Harry examines the little mud-caked earthenware pot filled with crumbling brown fragments, as he stands beside the sunken grave. Behind him the murky blue six o'clock sky hangs low over the hills, filled with thunder and violence, and the stormy air sweeping up from the sea carries the smell and feel of rain.

"Do you want it, dear?"

"Uuugh! No! Put it back. I thought these were only token graves!"

"Oh, no. They had to do something with the poor bloody so-and-sos, and they couldn't get any ships out of Sandakan

Bay after '43, so they left the laddies all behind. They're all here with us still – our little brown brothers of the baggy breeches!"

He drops the burial urn back in the mud, and stoops to look at the miniature wooden obelisk marking the head of the grave, translating aloud the Japanese characters which make known to those who pass that this is all that remains of Japanese soldier Number 11,163. That this is all that is left to see of a once jaunty Asiatic warrior who wielded his glittering sword in this subjugated land, who shouted and sang as he marched and hymned to the Sun with his adolescent might, while the land and its people bowed in pain. That this is all that is left of one little Japanese soldier who killed here, and raped, and made love and got drunk here – who suffered and shed tears and finally died here.

Now gone are the great shiny boots from the little sock-clad feet, small feet with big boots that kicked hard; gone are the too-large khaki trousers, the jaunty, laced fatigue cap, the buttons and braid, the flashing gold teeth and shining spectacles. Gone are the flesh and heart and eyes and skull and all that made this man, till only this remains of a little swaggering soldier who fought for his Emperor, and died – this residue of calcium and clay.

"Is that really a Jap soldier?" George squats over the open grave and pokes the ashes. "Do you think it hurt him to die? How did he get killed? Was he bad? Did they burn him, and then spoon him into that bowl?" He sifts the dust through his fingers, stirs the ashes again and smells his fingers as if looking for some odor that he can recognize as man.

"Was he bad?" asks Harry slowly. "No, he wasn't bad – he wasn't good. He just was – and then he died, that's all. He had to die because he was a soldier, and he had to be a soldier because he was a man and there was a war. And he had to be a man because he was born of the race of men – not gods, or apes, or dogs or elephants, who know better – but the race of men who wage war on each other and their own kind. Well – that's all. . . ." Who can explain or make reasonable the great unwisdom of man?

"Did he kill many people, do you think, Dad?"

"Maybe. He had to kill, or be killed."

"Are you glad he got killed, Dad?"

"I feel no emotion about it—except—better he than me. Come on now."

Harry covers the urn, tamps down the dust and we move, George and the dogs leading, past the twenty-foot Japanese cenotaph which stands mass monument to all the graves on this wind-blown hill. We stop to read again the characters which note that here lie buried thus many Nipponese soldiers of His Imperial Nipponese Emperor, who died fighting in Borneo, 1944 and 1945. The dogs use the post for their own purposes as we pass.

"*Sic semper tyrannis!*"—Harry.

The path through the burial hills is a red clay gash cut through light green bracken, dark scrub, gray-bearded vines, and shiny, large-leafed bushes. Lime-green rattan hauls itself up out of the verdant mass by swaying flagella which cling like scaling ladders to the trees, and allamanda flowers shoot up from the rank growth with the garish yellow perfection of crepe paper blooms pinned to painted foliage. Underfoot, rooted tenaciously in the layers of clay and rock, bloom scrawny-necked, mauve, ground orchids which add little to the beauty of the scene, but permit me to say that orchids grow wild in Borneo.

Along this familiar path we continue to the Chinese cemetery—not for the purpose of mourning, nor in search of bodies, nor out of affection for the dead, but because the dead in Asia always have the best view. During the war years, Japanese dead joined the Chinese dead in their journey up this hill to share this view, and now in peacetime deceased paupers from town, the hospital, the poorhouse and madhouse, are joining them to rest. The fresh graves are red mud puddles tonight, washed out by recent rains, and in the shallow, overcrowded bone pits, each filled with several skeletons, the odd tibia and fibia stick out at the surface.

But graves are not depressing when they don't belong to you. What difference do such sights make to me now, I remind myself, in these days when happiness comes frequently? Tonight I feel the awareness of living more strongly, amongst these dead. Perhaps this is only the newly found security of people who have long been insecure, or perhaps it is the triumph of being alive at all, here where all others are lifeless.

Or perhaps it is because today I go for a walk with a well-filled stomach and a well-nourished body, stepping along in the company of my husband and son, wearing white shorts and a Jaeger shirt, with my hair well kept and my face made up, and secure in the expectation that with dusk, we shall return to our bungalow, and leave the dead behind us in the hills.

Perhaps it is the knowledge that at home tonight George and I will read *Yebbin*, or *The Elephant's Child*, while Harry reads the *Straits Budget*, until time for the B.B.C., and then to bed – and these nights we have a bed. Yes, I can afford to say that graves are not depressing when they don't belong to you.

Ahead by the path one wild gardenia bush grows up out of the tangle, with one waxy, star-petaled flower shining against the green. Harry reaches out to cut the flower for me, and as he does so, George sniffs the air, then suddenly shouts in excitement, "It smells like the Jap soap in camp! It smells like Colonel Suga! It smells like Jap soldiers!"

I reach out for the white, strong-scented flower and take it in my hand, and the lemon-sweet smell of the wild gardenia, the smell of Jap soap and perfume, brings it all back. Here again is reality – Borneo under the Japs.

Now these Japs are in graves, the dead ones are all buried, their bones crumble, their urns fall, their cenotaphs rot. The war is over, we are the victors, we win. Our graves, except that of my child who had none, will be kept green.

In the heart of the burying hills there is a red-roofed temple where white-petaled frangipani trees spread scented droppings like heaven-sent dung, and plaster images squat silently on the altar and listen to prayers. Here the abode of Confucian gods is shared by puppet likenesses of departed Chinese ancestors, dressed now in silk gowns with human hair glued to their faces for beards, while the fragrance of incense pervades their plaster nostrils, and paper money is placed for their hands to hoard, and gods and ancestors live on sweet manna, while only the living are poor.

The old man who guards the cemetery – sometimes it is one old man and sometimes another – brews tea at the foot of the altar and boils his rice there, while basins of food stand about for his dogs.

All about the temple are groves of earthenware jars filled with Chinese bones awaiting return to China, or burial here. The jars have earthenware lids weighted down with stones to prevent dogs, rats, and children from poking inside and sniffing the human remains. When omens are propitious or money available the bones will be cleaned and buried in a favorable site, or sent back to China. Meanwhile, chickens, dogs, snakes, and wild cats roam amongst them, while mangoes drop from the mango tree and the temple flowers spread their petals over them. And this is the old man's job – to sweep flowers, mangoes, and chicken dirt off the temple floor and the dead.

It is lonely, isolated work and frequently sought by those who wish to hide. Caretakers come and go, usually lasting only long enough for the police to search for and find – hidden amongst ancestors, gods and incense – stolen goods. Then the old man goes to jail and a new one comes. Perhaps he doesn't mind, Sandakan jail provides a place to sleep and as good diet as a gravekeeper gets.

Harry and I frequently walk through the cemetery grounds, for the graves extend along the crests and valleys of the hills near us, and look down on the lonely outline of the bay. The Chinese in the town below exist huddled closely together, staring each other in the face throughout their lives, but in death they seek a view. It is known to be the habit of spirits to return and sit on spirit seats at the head of their graves to enjoy the view which in their lifetime they have been too busy to see. For a Chinese spirit to return and find himself in a jungle with nothing to look at but trees would be bad luck indeed, being bred to the bare hills of China. The spirits turn naturally to wind and water, and consider these good omens, and the popular burial place is on upper hill slopes from which the spirit may look to the Sulu Sea.

Today there is a new old man in the temple, by name, we learn, Ah Ju. To our surprise we see that he is a very clean old man, his expression is affable, and he doesn't kick his dogs. With less surprise, we see that he has an ulcer which completely surrounds his ankle in a four-inch wide, deeply etched band of rotting flesh. The wound is partially plastered with tree leaves which are glued onto it by the oozing serum. From the foot to above the knee the leg is swollen to shapelessness.

While Harry is forcefully separating our dog from the Chinese cemetery dogs, I am studying the old man's leg, and longing to be responsible for the treatment of that ulcer, to undertake its cleansing, medication, and dosage, external and oral, assisted by the new wonder drug from America.

"Look at the old man's leg!" I say.

Harry looks. "How long have you had that bad leg?" he asks in Malay.

"Only three years, Tuan. I was a rubber tapper, and when those Jap-devils were here I got a little cut. I had no medicine and not enough food to eat, and those Below Level People made me work very hard all the time and they beat me often. So my leg did not get well, it got like this."

Harry examines it closely. "Is it very painful?"

"I am accustomed to it, Tuan. And I do not work very hard here with the dead. I just sweep."

"What have you placed on it?"

"That is grass – pig's dung grass, Tuan. It is very good."

"That will never cure your leg. The most it will do is keep the flies off."

"Well, Tuan, that is something!"

"You must go to hospital for treatment, old man. I will give you a letter to the doctor and you must go tomorrow."

"Thank you, no, Tuan. I have this bad leg three years, I am an old man anyway, so never mind. If I go to hospital I lose my job here."

"If you do not go, perhaps you lose your leg."

"The hospital costs money."

"Very little money, if you go into Number Three."

"Yes, Tuan, in Number Three the money is little, but also the medicine and doctor and food is little."

"For poor men, the food is always little, either in the hospital, or here in the cemetery. But if you get your leg cured you can get a job as rubber tapper again, and make more money and eat better food."

"Many men go in to hospital, Tuan, but they do not come out of it, Tuan."

"That is because they go there too late. If you go in like a dead man, is it a wonder if you come out a dead man?"

"I live here with the dead, Tuan, but I am not yet dead. So thank you, Tuan. I will stay here."

"Harry, let me treat it!" I say aside in English. "Tell him to come to our house and I'll take care of it. I know that new penicillin ointment will help."

Harry ponders, then says, "Old man, we live on the nearest hill just outside this burying ground. My house is the first one you pass on the road to Sandakan. If you will come to my house tomorrow, I will put medicine upon your leg, and in time it will be better."

"Thank you—thank you, no, Tuan. If I leave this temple someone may steal something here, perhaps the ancestors, perhaps the gods, perhaps the bones. . . ."

That anyone would steal the ancestors or gods is most unlikely, as this would be unforgivable, and very bad luck for the thief; the old man does not intend to leave his temple merely to cure his ulcer. He is at home in this sphere and will not leave it for an untested world of questionable foreign benevolence.

But that leg has caught my fancy.

"Harry, would it be possible for us to bring the medicine out here, and treat him? We come every few days anyway for a walk."

"Oh, damn!" Harry sees protracted cemetery walks ahead of him, whether or no. "It would be quite useless to try to treat it until he has soaked it in hot water and thoroughly cleaned it first! We couldn't do that here. You know we couldn't. . . . Oh, well! I suppose you've made up your mind!"

To the old man, "Old man, my wife has made up her mind to have that leg of yours. You might as well agree, and let her treat it. We will be back tomorrow evening at this time and fix it for you."

The next afternoon we returned. We bathed the leg in the old man's tea, because we knew this water had been boiled, we soaked it, and removed what we could of dead tissue and skin, and then cleaned all about it with alcohol. The smell was that of bad meat roasting on a fire. Then we plastered the entire ankle thickly with penicillin ointment from a new supply flown out to me the week before, and wrapped it about with layers of sterile gauze. We told the old man to keep his leg up as much as he could, and not to touch the bandage until we returned in two days' time. He was amiable but unimpressed, obviously humoring us. All the way home I smelled the leg, it seemed as if the odor was in the hairs of my nostrils.

In two days we returned to Ah Ju. As we unwrapped the bandage the smell was worse than before. More dead tissue came away, and the leg was a little less swollen, but otherwise there was no change. Ah Ju said he felt little pain in the leg, but this meant nothing as the sore itself had been without feeling for months. We bathed the leg, disinfected it, covered it with ointment and rebandaged. This time we left internal dosage of sulfa drug, and said we would be back in two days.

For two weeks we went every other day and repeated this treatment, and by the end of that time there was a noticeable change. Under the dead slough of skin a clean red band of raw flesh was beginning to show, and the leg had lost much of its swelling. Even the old man began to take an interest, and followed our instructions with more respect. Now we told him to unwrap the bandage every day and expose the leg to the sun for a few minutes.

Soon we went every third or fourth day and at the end of two months the dogs no longer barked at us but curled up and yawned, the penicillin was gone, and the surface of the sore was covered with a thin new layer of skin. We bandaged the leg with a clean gauze bandage, and felt triumphant.

"We don't need to come again, old man," Harry said. "Our medicine is finished and your leg is well. But you must keep your ankle protected by a bandage for a long time, as any blow or injury will break down that flesh again. We will leave you these rolls of bandage and tape and you can attend to it yourself."

"Yes, Tuan. I see that the leg is well now. Perhaps I shall go to Lahad Datu and get work as a rubber tapper again."

We said good-by, and started down the hill, the dogs following us as friends.

"He didn't fall on our necks with gratitude, did he?" I said.

"No. I reckon he thinks there's something behind it all."

"But what could there be? Except that we wanted to make his leg better?"

"Well, there's a long history of past cases in which we have always wanted something for whatever we gave in the East—either riches, trade, labor or converts for our God. I reckon the old man knows."

"Well, what did *I* want?"

"Oh, to be benevolent, the distributor of largesse—And to prove your new medicine."

"But surely that's good!"

"Yes, the result is. But what I mean is that one's motives are seldom pure, good is mixed up with something else."

A week later when we climbed the path to the temple, no dogs welcomed us and no old man brewed tea on the temple floor, the frangipani petals strewed the ground unswept and untrodden, and the ancestors slept on the altar alone. There was nothing left of the old man but the smell of his leg in my nostrils.

III. Honest Men

EVEN as a long-haired pagan boy with snaky black hair rolled in a rancid bun and brown loins draped in a scarlet rag, Arusap showed independent judgment. When in 1933 Harry, a very young forest officer, had visited Arusap's native Murut village in the interior to distribute wise words about rice planting and cautious ones about unauthorized tree cutting, he was called on at the same time to drink fiery native rice wine distilled with cockroaches for his stomach's sake, and to discuss the problems of hunting pig, buffalo, and deer with the village lads, of which Arusap was one. And when Harry left Kampong Pau with its twisting ribbons of smoke, its redolence of burning wood mixed with decaying meat and fermenting rice, its bright-eyed, laughing children, and languid, wheedling girls – and Arusap – he had, unknown to himself, been chosen.

Arusap packed his few belongings, rice bowl, hair oil, pipe and tobacco, in a square of twisted native cloth, tightened the loop in his long red loincloth, and followed Harry barefoot many miles down to the coast. Catching up with Harry at the nearest seaport town, Arusap appeared before him very politely and said in his soft Murut voice that he had come to work for him and be his boy – for this is the way the native has, he chooses you, you do not choose him.

Harry looked at the adolescent pagan, with straight back, strong arms, hard-gripping hands, feet bare, splayed, tougher than leather, and decided he was just the companion he needed for his travels. From then on Harry was, in Arusap's words, "like father, like mother" – except at periodic intervals when they disagreed about Arusap's self-granted leaves. But then – when a native feels like a holiday he takes it, and why not!

All this happened six years before I came, and by the time I arrived in Borneo, Arusap had been back to his village several times for holidays, and once to wed, and brought his wife Kuta back to the coast with him. Kuta was lazy, ox-eyed, coaxing, vitriolic and dumb, and Harry accepted her tolerantly but without enthusiasm. And when I came I was accepted by Arusap in exactly the same way as Harry accepted Kuta. Wives were a necessity to be put up with, not a luxury like fresh-killed deer or pig, to be rejoiced at.

In time I proved myself with Arusap by producing a son, as in time Kuta proved herself by producing repeated sons – but hers died in early infancy, while our son lived and prospered. The deaths of Kuta's babies were always attributed by Arusap to (1) Kuta's disregard of Murut taboos, and (2) inauspicious witchcraft. The health of our son was attributed by him to good omens.

For two years George grew and prospered, while Arusap mourned his own childless state and gave George his full approval. We became a congenial, happy family, and all existed on the best of terms, and it would suit my story to say Arusap was completely devoted to us all – but rather he was devoted to the relationship which existed between himself and us, that of equal return for equal goods. We were devoted to having a good boy, and he was devoted to getting what he wished from us, and the relationship was never allowed to interfere with his own personal, private, independent life.

And that is the thing the native has above all else. He helps you, he serves you, he loves you, but always remains himself, a very fine fellow who, no matter how many years you pay his wages, is still his own master under your roof to the end. Perhaps that is why we like him; we can't trample on him, and he never loses himself in us.

So it was with Arusap. And in 1941 when there was gossip among the local boys of the probability of war with Japan, and what we then termed the "inconveniences" of war, Arusap began to show symptoms which we had recognized in times before as the pre-vacation itch. His specific goal this time was a vacation far inland with plenty of space between himself and any enemy arrivals. Time had taught us that Arusap's vacation urges were never abortable.

Then fate put in a word. A message was relayed to us from Kampong Pau saying that Arusap's brother, the Headman of the village, had died of tuberculosis, and Arusap was next in line to become Headman. There was no choice to make now between being houseboy in Sandakan, and Headman in his own home town, far from the threat of guns. Arusap went home, and one could not blame him – but one did.

War came. Our Chinese servants stayed with us without wages through three months of Japanese occupation until we were placed behind barbed wire in internment camps for the duration. Occasionally thereafter we heard rumors of the Japanese treatment of other Asiatics in the Asiatic co-prosperity sphere, and we learned that Kampong Pau was not so far inland as Arusap had thought, and that the Japanese invaders were visiting it.

I could envision these visits. I could see the debonair people of Kampong Pau, by nature sociable, hospitable, and amiable – politely smiling, bowing, chewing, smoking, and passing the rice wine to the visiting Japanese as they often had to us – saying "Yes, Tuan, yes! Yes, it is indeed as you say!" – as long as the Japanese were still in their midst. And then, with the turning of straight military Japanese backs and the last sound of Japanese boots, they would pursue their own ends and go their own unlicensed way.

Twice, word came to me through Japanese guards that they had met our old boy, Arusap, and that he had told them "all about us," which phrase always made me nervous. Colonel Suga, the Commander of the Japanese Prison Camp, also told me that he had met Arusap, who had asked after our health and put in a good word for us. I was glad to hear this, as when master turns servant and you look at your own conduct from the servant's point of view, you see your own shortcomings.

When I returned to Sandakan in 1947, one of the first things Harry showed me was a neatly written letter in Romanized Malay, from Arusap, at Kampong Pau:

> Greetings Tuan! My heart is happy because people tell me that you return to Borneo. When there was war people tell me that you and the Mem and Mister Groge are in Japanese camp.
>
> After that people tell me that you are sick. Many times I tell the Japanese that you are a man of good heart. I tell them to take good care of you. Now I hope that you and the Mem and Mister Groge are not sick and have light hearts.
>
> Kuta did not have more sons. Now I have a new wife and a son who is three years old. He is strong and not sick, and very beautiful like Mister Groge.
>
> When I look at him I think of Mister Groge. My son does not have clothes such as it is good for the son of a Headman to wear. This is because we people cannot get cloth since the war.
>
> My heart will be happy if the Tuan sends some cloth for my son such as a Headman's son would wear. Certainly Tuan you will send the cloth I know, because your heart is good. I hope that you and the Mem and Mister Groge will soon come to Kampong Pau to visit me.
>
> ARUSAP

Harry received this letter at a time when cloth was still almost unobtainable in Sandakan, and Harry's memory of Arusap's hasty prewar departure from our household did not lead him to attempt to obtain the unobtainable. Harry wrote him that he was glad to hear he had a son, that his own son and wife were not yet well enough to return to Borneo, and that we were very short of clothes ourselves, having lost them all to the Japs.

The next news of Arusap was after George and I had returned. A friend was traveling from Jesselton, now the capital city, up the Padas River gorge by jeep coach on the lone strip of railroad track, and from thence to Keningau, and across the plains to Kampong Pau. Upon his return from this trip he wrote to say that he had seen our former boy, Arusap, who had asked after us and sent his good wishes; that Arusap was now teaching his own people, the hill Muruts, to plant rice in the modern method which he said Harry had taught him, and was attempting to introduce other modern methods of agriculture among the hill Muruts.

Shortly after this the Officer Administering Government traveled the same route and met Arusap at a meeting held to discuss planting of crops. Arusap, who is a Rotarian by nature and adores thinking in public, had led the meeting. The O.A.G. wrote Harry saying he was very pleased with what the local Muruts had accomplished in growing crops under Arusap's advice.

Arusap sent his version of the meeting as follows:

> Greetings, Tuan, and Mem and Groge.
>
> I have talked with Tuan Governor about the growing of rice and crops. I have told him how is best to do it, and he agrees. I told him that you told me how to do it. We agree you are very smart.
>
> Tuan Governor tells me that you are well and that the Mem writes two books, with a picture and story of me in one. I should like to have this book. Please ask the Mem to send one. I remember you and the Mem as my father and mother, and my child is like your son.
>
> Tuan Governor says you are going on leave, and then you will come back. I have put in a good word for you with Tuan Governor. I send my greetings to you and the Mem and Groge. Tabi Tuan.
>
> My son could fit Mister Groge's clothes very well.
>
> Good-by, Tuan and Mem.
>
> ARUSAP

With this exchange the matter temporarily rests, but I have no doubt that Arusap Junior will someday be wearing flannel shorts and George's old school tie.

2

"I'm firing that old poop Norudin! He's no damn good!"

At first I used to think that Harry meant this threat when he made it, and I would plead earnestly for his withered, opaque-eyed little native assistant in the North Borneo Museum of which Harry was the curator, collector, duster off, and everything else but janitor. Norudin being janitor, I knew that if Harry fired him there would be no one upon whom he could safely take out his annoyance when things went wrong in the museum, and he would bring it home to me. For Norudin had an indestructible capacity to exist untouched by extraneous matters, and in a situation in which other people became hurt or indignant, Norudin just stood politely and listened with his mind on other matters, and an apologetic expression on his face which had nothing to do with his feelings.

When I first saw him, I thought he was very old, but ten years later he wasn't any older, and his ancient face continued to be ancient, rather than aged, or senile. His expression was always benevolent, come good or evil, and his pale blue, far-focused eyes still looked beyond you, concerning themselves with what he was thinking of you, rather than what he saw of you or what you might think of him.

Norudin had worked all through the war with the Forest Department, disappearing with the Department into the jungle to escape both Japanese massacres and Allied bombs, and reappearing in the end to welcome the Allies, and when Harry returned he was there to greet him. With him was a small girl perhaps ten years old, dressed in a faded, ragged cotton dress, with straight, tangled black hair falling over wild eyes out of which she peered belligerently at a hostile world. This was Kamsia, Norudin said, a war orphan whom he had adopted.

As dwelling places were nonexistent in the town, Harry appointed Norudin nightwatchman of the Forest Department premises, which position gave him the right to doze about the place during the night as well as through the day; it gave Kamsia a roof for her head, and the two lived in the office godown, and cooked over a bucket of charcoal. Since essential foodstuffs had quadrupled in cost since the war, and salaries had not, it was soon obvious that Norudin's war starvation was continuing into peace-time, and Kamsia looked ready to snatch at a bone.

As it was difficult to get enough young men in the Department for orderly service, Harry decided he would solve two problems at once by hiring Kamsia as orderly. He replaced her ragged dress with a female version of the khaki orderly's uniform, with a skirt instead of shorts, and told her to comb her hair, wash her face, keep her uniform clean, and deliver letters.

Kamsia hated getting washed, but she didn't mind delivering letters, although at first she caused some comment as the only female orderly in town. She would push a letter onto an office desk, and the orderly book under an officer's nose for signature, and then bend hotly over the recipient like a small wild animal scenting his smell, while deciding whether to scratch or purr — and in those days you felt sure she would scratch.

But in time, aided by the curious, teasing, half-admiring glances of her clientele, Kamsia learned to purr, to look at people without glaring, to smell without sniffing, to wash her face and comb her hair and like it, and to be what we call civilized. Soon she began to dress up the uniform skirt with a fancy native blouse above when going to visit her favorite offices, or set off the uniform top by a tightly wrapped sarong below, and when she looked at people she smiled challengingly now, and did not hurry away. And one day after a pay check, she appeared with her hair tightly crimped in a permanent wave, and the same day old Norudin complained to Harry that she was spending her wages on hair oil, bangles, silk blouses and perfume — would Harry please stop it? But this was the sort of thing no man could stop; men had occasioned it.

Then, by Harry's orders, Kamsia financed a bicycle for orderly use on her orderly's pay, but she refused to learn to ride it. She would push her bike along the road, park it outside the office to which she was delivering, leave the letter, and push the bike back again. Harry said he would take the bicycle away from her if she did not learn to ride it by the following night. She learned, and from then on wherever I went I met Kamsia on her bicycle, pedaling swiftly along with a tightly wrapped sarong wriggled

KAMSIA

well above her knees, her wind-resistant curls battling the elements like wire springs, her sleazy silk blouse sticking like skin to breasts that no longer needed rounding.

Now, the coincidence of Kamsia and trouble became one hundred per cent, whether in her own office or other offices, until one day Harry told her that he was prepared to send her to school in the evenings so she could learn to read and write, and then give her a desk job in the herbarium, but he could not keep her any longer as orderly. Kamsia looked at him with bold black eyes, softened now with blandishment, ran her slightly grimy thumb back and forth for a minute on the edge of his desk, picked at the turquoise blue blouse which banged up and down with her heart, pushed back a black-shaving curl, and said, "But I do not like to learn to read and write, Tuan! I like to be orderly and ride my bicycle!" It sounded so much like George that Harry wanted to laugh, but the eyes looking brightly at him from the speaker's face were the wheedling eyes of a woman.

So as Kamsia grew into her skin she grew out of her job, was fired, and "that old Poop Norudin" took over the bicycle, and the official position of orderly. Now instead of Kamsia's hot, panting body bending above the recipient of official forestry letters, Norudin bends there, with all the sex appeal of a withered tree shaking its last leaf from a trembling bough, and the bicycle is his during office hours. But from five o'clock on any afternoon Kamsia rides again. Six days out of the week, with the wind plastering the rayon of her latest blouse, she pedals the road to town, wheels through the afternoon strollers, rolls slowly back and forth several times past the coffee shops with their idling lads, and then back out the road again to the Forest Office.

But every seventh day she parks her bicycle in front of the Educational bookstore where local school books, and Chinese and English magazines, are on sale. Here she joins the crowd of small boys of every size and color who bend breathless over the newsstand snatching anxiously for the latest edition of *Nyoka, Jungle Girl*, *Gigi the Gorilla*, *Manuka the Monkey*, and *Panuka the Punk*, printed in Malay, for this is the day the comics come from Singapore.

3

From the day that I first saw old Hatib squatting on his rattan mat and chewing sireh surrounded by his fawning wives and leering relatives of wives, while he condoled gently with me over my ruptured wooden fish, I knew he was an artist.

"It is beautiful, Mem, but not made after the fashion of the Suluk people."

"It was given to the Tuan and me by the *Imam* who made us man and wife," I explained, "and we would like you to make one like it."

"My people use different patterns for making beautiful things," he said firmly. "I will not make you a food container with the same pattern as this one, but I will make you one with the patterns of my people on it."

The item under discussion was a wooden platter carved with fish which had been given us by the minister who married us; it had, for us, considerable sentimental value, and was said to symbolize fertility. When the damp heat of Borneo began to splinter the fins and split the fish and the platter became unusable Harry suggested that we take it to a Suluk friend at Bokhara village not far from Sandakan who could copy it for us.

But old Hatib would not do this, for no native likes to follow the design of any other. But he did in time carve us a whole series of platters with a variety of native ghosts, phallic symbols, and Suluk emblems which outdid the original in hopeful suggestions of what to do with spare time.

Hatib was always hard up, thanks to his wives, offspring, and buttonhole relations, for the whole village was connected by blood or marriage, and he was almost the only breadwinner among them. At regular intervals he would arrive at Harry's office and ask for a loan, on which occasions Harry gave him cash, and an order for sufficient carvings to cover the credit. In this way the carvings cost us nothing, as we figured we had to help Hatib anyway, and the carvings were handy to use for wedding presents.

In spite of his expert workmanship, he complained of bad eyesight, which oddly enough did not seem to affect the delicacy and beauty of his work. As there is neither oculist nor optometrist in Sandakan, we started Hatib on a series of spectacles as supplied for local consumption by the Sandakan equivalent of a drugstore, which stocks a wide variety of goods unsalable elsewhere. Throughout the years of our friendship Hatib went regularly to this shop to try spectacles on his unbridged, almost invisible nose, each time searching until he found a stronger pair to suit him, and then charging them to us.

Before the war we went frequently to visit Hatib at Bokhara, a picturesque coast village which makes native life resemble a South Sea movie. The houses are built over the bay near a grove of tall, swaying bamboo, where in deep, cool shadow chattering children play noisily, young men loll, young girls flirt as they comb out their long black hair, old ladies gossip, cough and spit, and an occasional old man bends low over his work. We always enjoyed going because we were greeted like royalty and made to feel, as we distributed biscuits and cigarettes, that we were fine people, amongst fine friends.

Old Hatib was always busy. Squatting on his little veranda where the waves lapped softly under him, surrounded by the carving tools Harry had bought him, with his bit of wood in his hand, Hatib would talk. He always held the object on which he was working close to his myopic eyes as if outlining it with the end of his nose, while the clean, delicately cut, precisely executed design gradually and very perfectly emerged, and Hatib talked of his troubles.

His wife Lana was much younger than he and, although the pleasures of the marriage bed were enhanced, the responsibility of her extravagant nature offset this. Lana, it seemed, was perpetually smoking, chewing sireh, adorning herself, buying new earrings, a new sarong, having a new bit of cloth, and now in addition she had just produced a new set of in-laws from a distant Simunol village who claimed the right to Hatib's support. Meanwhile Lana stood at old Hatib's shoulder giggling, chewing, smiling and agreeing to it all very pleasantly, which is probably the best thing a woman can do towards getting her own way. And in the end Hatib's stipend always included the little bit extra needed for her new anklet, new in-law, new sarong, or new friend.

When we returned after the war, we found a sad change in Hatib. I cannot say honestly that this was due to the cruelties of the Japanese, for Hatib's village was not noted for overloyal resistance, but rather for a certain spirit of opportunism which reckoned that if there was anything good to be had out of occupation, it better be had. I can easily imagine the village receiving the visiting Japanese as they had us, as new lords in the old manor, new friends among friends. The Bokhara people were accus-

LANA

tomed to living on crumbs from other men's tables, and for them the backbone of existence was not who sat at the table, but whether or not there were crumbs.

But for Hatib the occupation had meant four years' passage of time, no new spectacles, and no drugs to fight the development of an undiagnosed disease which we now suspected was diabetes, and which was changing him rapidly from merely an old man to a very sick old man.

The first time he came to Harry's office he was brought in by Lana, who said she had to support him all the way from the village to the beginning of the bus route, about a mile. The old man had dwindled to nothing, but he was respectably dressed and combed, and gave Harry the Muslim greeting, then fell into a chair shaking violently, and it was some minutes before he could pull himself together and formulate the same old request – glasses and money.

We bought him a new pair of spectacles, advanced some cash, and suggested that we take him to see the doctor. This he refused to agree to, saying he was sure he could get on very well indeed, now he had his new spectacles. He agreed to carve a model of a native boat for us.

A month later we walked out to the village; the boat was scarcely begun, and Hatib, looking more ill and shaky, and peering blindly, said the spectacles were not strong enough, and Lana produced a new set of relatives to bargain for. We inquired whether the villagers had any old, native brass rice containers to sell, and Lana undulated about from house to house, finally producing several lightweight modern ones which had no value. When we told her so, she answered that the Japanese plus the Allied military occupation had removed all worth-while native possessions from the country. We left, telling Hatib that if he would come to Harry's office the next morning, Harry would arrange for some more spectacles.

Early next day Hatib came, escorted by Lana, and again he selected a pair that he said he liked, again Harry asked him to go to the hospital for examination, again the old man refused, saying that he could not be bothered, and Lana took him home.

Next week, a message came from Hatib that the spectacles were not strong enough, and he would be in the following day for better ones. He arrived with Lana and a terrible toothache, and said he must have his teeth out before he changed his spectacles. Harry made an appointment for him to go to a Chinese dentist the next day, promising to send him in the motorcar.

The next day Hatib arrived and sank into the chair by Harry's desk in obvious pain.

"Tuan, don't be angry with me – I just came to tell you – I can't be bothered to go to that tooth man."

"Of course you are going!" Harry said. "I will send you now."

"Oh, Tuan, no. Don't be angry – but I cannot be bothered."

"Certainly you must go; this man will fix your teeth, and then I will get you another pair of spectacles, and the doctor will give you medicine and you will be better again. You know you must finish that boat for us. Where is there another man who can carve as you can carve? That talent must not die."

Hatib's voice and hands shook, tears spilled from his eyes down his folded cheeks, as he slowly shook his head. "No, Tuan, I cannot be bothered. I will not need spectacles or teeth any more."

Harry could not change the old man's decision. Hatib rested some time, coughing, belching and weeping quietly. When at last he got up to go he peered sadly and intently in Harry's direction with faded, filmed eyes, the eyes of old people all over the world no matter what color their skins, eyes that have seen too much and joyed too little, eyes that no longer see visions and see now only bare facts, eyes of those who have ceased to care.

"I am too old, Tuan. I am going back now to die," he said.

Two days later Lana came in, smoking, chewing, crying, keening, with real grief in her face; Hatib had died that morning, he would be buried in his boat. Could she please have some money for his funeral, and for the feast for relatives who would be attending?

4

"Do you remember Osman *bin* Saleh who lived up the Kinabatangan at Temegang? The lad who made us stay in his house that night in the storm, when the Chinese shops refused to let us in?"

"Of course I remember him. He was wonderful. I'll never forget the shock of finding a spring bed to sleep on a hundred miles upriver in the jungle. I reckon it's the only one in the whole of Borneo, since the war. I always wondered how Osman got it. Probably some governor went tootling up the river determined on comfort, taking his bed and collapsible bathtub with him, and he left his bed behind."

"Sounds more like the Martin Johnsons to me! Well, whoever the bed belongs to, Osman is in trouble now. Nick tells me he is accused of stealing Government funds. They think he's been forging receipts for Government money, instead of paying it out on behalf of Government, and he's been brought to Sandakan for trial. Nick is going to take the case in a day or so."

"Oh, Harry! And he was so nice—and Mrs. Osman too! I don't think he's guilty at all. Do you?"

"Well—all the proof seems to be against him. Osman swears that he's innocent, but there's only his word against the fact that the money's gone, and the men haven't received it. In actual fact, his salary as native clerk was so small that he should never have been permitted to handle large sums. He wasn't a safe risk—there's too much temptation."

"In a position like that at home, wouldn't he have to be bonded?"

"Yes, and I doubt that such a low-salaried person in a job of so much responsibility would be able to get a bond."

"Have you any idea what his sentence will be, if they decide he is guilty?"

"A heavy fine, I should think, with probably the alternative of a jail term if he is unable to pay."

"He'll never be able to raise a big fine. Those people never keep money, even if they make it. Oh I wish we could help him. He helped us when we needed it."

"Don't worry, we'll have plenty of opportunity to help him, I'm sure. They'll probably be up to see us. Nick said they were asking about us."

We were sitting drinking tea on the veranda the next afternoon, looking down the steep path which leads to our house, when we saw two people mounting slowly towards us. The girl wore a turquoise-flowered *baju* and a henna-colored sarong, and the man was wrapped in a checked green and yellow sarong with a white silk tunic, but the attempted finery could not deny the dejection of Mr. and Mrs. Osman. It is a terrible thing, I thought as I watched them approaching, to be able to tell by the way people place their feet, move timidly forward, turn their heads anxiously, look hesitantly about, that the world has succeeded against them, that they are defeated and they know it. And if they know the fault is their own, it is even more sad.

As I went to the door to meet them I remembered the pride I

had seen in those two faces nine years ago, when they had given us their best hospitality, the pride of people with something to give. Now they had only the shells of being, and their utter emptiness was worse than tears or moans.

Meticulously we observed the decencies, touching forehead, eyes and mouth, extending the right hand held by the left hand to prove we concealed no weapons, before we sat down. We asked the proper things about each other's health, and recalled the dark night on the river and the storm, and then I told them of the birth of George. For a moment I thought I saw warmth in Osman's dark eyes, before they again lost life. Mrs. Osman continuously twisted a small, bright handkerchief in her delicate, child's hands, with her lips relaxed in patient resignation, while her great, liquid eyes touched the face of each speaker in turn with a child's questioning gaze.

For almost an hour we sat talking of nothings, while I wondered how long Harry would stand such evasion, and who would break it first. Then Osman forced himself to begin.

"Tuan, you know that I am in trouble? Very great trouble?"

"I know."

"They say I am a thief, they say that I keep the money belonging to other men, and then sign the names of other men on those receipts."

"Men have told me this thing."

"But it is not true, Tuan! I swear to you! Now I will tell you. . . ."

And Osman gives his version. He was entrusted with Government funds to deliver, and he delivered them, taking signed receipts from the recipients. Now the recipients claim they did not receive the money, and did not sign the receipts. When shown the receipts, they say that Osman has forged the signatures. This, Osman says, is not true.

"My case was tried this afternoon, Tuan, and because all these other men tell lies about me, the Magistrate has judged me guilty. But I am innocent! Tuan, I am innocent! Tomorrow the Magistrate will sentence me, and I have heard from friends that he will sentence me to pay $500, or to stay six months in jail."

"What friends can tell you what the Magistrate's sentence will be, before the Magistrate himself speaks the sentence?" Harry's voice is indignant and his eyes are cold at this violation of magisterial secrecy.

"What friends, Tuan? Why people say, Tuan, people say . . ."

Always there must be a clerk to copy a magistrate's report, and the clerk has a friend and the friend has a friend, and after that the leaves of the jungle, the drops of rain, the whispers of wind tell the story.

Harry is forbiddingly silent. Osman presses anxiously, "Tuan, a jail sentence disgraces me before all men. If I go to jail, then truly I am a thief. But I am not a thief. Yet I do not have money to pay the fine. I am honest, Tuan. I am honest! I swear! I swear!"

Harry remains silent.

There is no comment I can make. The facts of Osman's story as he tells it convince me neither of his innocence, nor of his guilt. But when a man looks at me and swears that he tells me the truth, it is difficult to believe that he doesn't.

Osman moves anxiously.

"You do not say anything, Tuan? Do you not believe me?"

Finally Harry answers slowly, "If the evidence before the Magistrate did not prove your guilt, the Magistrate would not judge you to be guilty."

"But the Magistrate is wrong! He says that I signed those receipts! But I say that I did not do so. I know what I sign better than he knows what I sign!"

Osman's brown, honest eyes – and I would swear they were honest eyes, even if I caught him thieving – go from Harry's face to mine, while Mrs. Osman twists her handkerchief. Watching Osman now, I see clearly that the important thing is not to determine whether or not he has been dishonest in this instance, but to take care that something does not happen to him which will confirm him in dishonesty. I am even willing to argue it his way – he may not have resisted that temptation to steal. Ah, but that was in the past. The important facts in this act of "stealing" have all been altered for him since the act. For now he sees that theft, that is, the juggling of other men's money, is accompanied by something disgraceful, by the greatest of all disgraces in the Asiatic mind, discovery! That changes the face of it all! Surely, a man may not steal if he is to become thereby a thief in the eyes of all!

I feel convinced that if we keep Osman out of jail this time, there will never be another time. But if Osman serves a jail sentence now, then he feels that he is a thief and he becomes a thief, and it is useless for a thief to try to be honest. This reasoning is not ethical, but I am sure it is Osman's.

I look at Harry to try to discover the workings of his mind, hoping to transfer by thought wave my sudden clear conviction as to what he must do.

Harry is speaking to Osman. "You know that after this trial, whether or not you go to jail, you can never work for Government again? And they cannot recommend you to anyone for a job of official trust?"

"I know that, Tuan," Osman answers sadly. "But I will get other work."

"When is the Magistrate going to pronounce sentence, and when must you have the fine?"

"Tomorrow in the court at ten."

"Be at my office at eight tomorrow morning before the court convenes. Now good night."

"But you know that I am innocent, Tuan? You believe I am innocent?" Osman is like a child promising to be good next time, without quite admitting that he has been bad.

Mrs. Osman and I listen anxiously for Harry's answer. She, childish, irresponsible despite four children, hangs with pathetic necessity on Harry's decision; as he judges Osman, so is he.

"You believe me, Tuan?" presses Osman.

Harry hesitates still, while I am praying that he will sacrifice a little of his natural forthrightness. Then Harry speaks.

"I do not believe that Allah placed you on earth to become a thief."

The answer is not entirely satisfactory to any of us. Yet, what answer could be? And perhaps it is the most that Osman can expect – accompanied by the $500 fine (from Harry) at eight tomorrow morning. Osman bows his head. It is the will of Allah – Allah's will be done – with a little assistance from good friends.

IV. Angela

THE people of Sandakan need almost everything, but the least of these things is probably tatting. Infants are vestless, babies are pantless, boys without drawers, adults without shirts, bachelors need mending, beds need bedding, houses need curtains, but my friend Angela tats colored tatting for handkerchiefs.

Angela is a prewar survivor, and she makes the pilgrimage up the hill to me once a week, when the day is hottest and she looks limpest and I feel sorriest, and my yards of brilliant tatting grow. With this vivid edging, innocent little pieces of cotton goods may be made expensive through art, for the wiping of European noses. Harry accuses me of buying tatting from an inability to say no. But I don't. I buy it deliberately, in the name of democracy, and in the memory of bananas.

Angela herself, whose ancestry is Indian and Filipino, is nice to look at and titillating to the senses; with eyes like chocolate drops on white frosted cake, and skin like a bisque meringue, she was created by nature to sweeten rather than to sustain. To her natural confiture of being, Angela adds lipstick lips and fuchsia cheeks, a peroxide bleach and permanent wave, a peasant blouse, dirndl skirt, and purple barefoot sandals on spindle legs. She weighs little more than a toothpick, is shaped like a child, but her ardent eyes hold amorous lure.

Angela's life is pursued by a dark-browed fate. Her husband is always out of work, her relatives break their bones, her babies have colds, her childbirth is complicated, her miscarriages are never convenient, and her dwelling places are regularly robbed, burned, and blown away, but Angela retains her adolescent figure, baby face, and ingenuous mind.

Her reactions to the cruel Nemesis which pursues her is to embrace it with the resignation of a girl for a too brutal lover who hurts her, but leaves her with something to talk about. And as if to compensate for her domestic ill luck, Angela buys raffle tickets and wins prizes of face creams and powder compacts, she bets on horses and wins silver trophies, she enters dancing competitions in the Club and brings to her devastated and adversity-stricken home silver-plated mugs, electroplated percolators, flower-embroidered tray tidies, and cut-glass cocktail shakers.

Angela comes to our house either at 10 A.M. when I am writing, or 3 P.M. when I am bathing, and any hour is the wrong one. Today is the third anniversary of the decapitation of her father by the Japanese, in the Sandakan May Day massacre, and Angela comes this morning to review the scene again to a guaranteed listener.

"It was after the American motor torpedo boats came to Sandakan on May 26th, 1945," Angela recalls. "They shelled and torpedoed the harbor and town and the Japanese ran away into the jungle. The Americans landed and came into town and people rejoiced and were very glad to see them and gave them food and anything they wanted. My father was one to help them, and we were all happy because the Americans had come at last.

"But they went away again that night, and the Japs came back into town the next day. Then they asked all people in town to tell them who had helped those Americans. Some people who were afraid told on the others. A few had warning, and ran to the jungle and escaped, but the Japs arrested sixty-seven who did not run away that night. They were the best people in the town, Indians, Chinese, natives – and one was a white woman, Mrs. Linkhe, the Jewish lady who came from Germany before the war, and was always sick.

"The Japs took them to Military Police headquarters, and for many days the police were asking them questions, and we did not know what was going to happen to them. Then one day we saw them taken away from the police offices in army trucks, and two of our men followed secretly to see. The trucks went up Ernestina Lane and stopped at the rubber trees and the guards made everybody get out.

"Then they started to kill them. They tried to cut their heads off, but the soldier whose job this was, was not clever, and his sword not sharp enough. He killed some O.K. but others he could not get the heads off, until finally even this soldier himself got sick with the mess. So then they had to shoot them. But the Japs were so confused by not killing these prisoners neatly, that one Chinese escaped.

"Mrs. Linkhe was very brave. She did not weep, she only prayed – until they killed her. And my father was the last. My father was a very handsome man; they never found all of him. He was buried with all the others, sixty-seven in one grave under the rubber trees on Ernestina Lane. So that was the end of my father."

Angela stopped, and drank her ginger beer.

I remembered her father well, a swarthy, gallant-mannered Indian whom I had often talked with at Government House garden parties. We always talked of birds and flowers, because one must at such parties, but in spite of synthetic horticulture he had registered in my memory as a man.

I also remembered Mrs. Linkhe, a little, nerve-worn, under-nourished refugee German Jewess who had come to Borneo with her husband to escape from the Nazis, who had buried her husband here as the victim of past brutalities, who had then herself survived alone amongst Asiatics for two years after the other

Europeans had been interned, only in the end to meet the bungled sword blow and ill-aimed gun of a fuddled executioner. In life her outstanding quality had been that she evoked pity; now in the valor of her death she commanded respect and admiration.

We ourselves live on Ernestina Lane and pass the site of this mass grave frequently. It has several times been exhumed by bereaved relatives in the effort to sort out bones; they always give it up and toss the residue back in the clay pit again.

"What happened to your mother then, Angela?"

"Very soon then my mother goes crazy; all females in her family go crazy quite easily. So she must live at the mad house at Buli Sim Sim. Then my sister Mabel gets tuberculosis, and all she does is cry and cry. Then my sister Mary gets rheumatic fever and she cries and cries.

"When the Japs came in 1942 I got married; it was not good for a girl to be alone then. So I married a Filipino boy, and I have a baby, and the baby is always weak because we all have malaria and not enough food. Then I have another baby who is also weak because of malaria and no food. Then the Japs kill my father, and my husband runs away from Sandakan to hide in the jungle.

"Then peace comes, those Australians come, and everybody thinks everything will be happy again. My husband comes in from the jungle and we get another baby, and this baby is sick also because I still have malaria and no medicine and no food and no cloth for clothes. The oilfield opens in Brunei again and my husband gets a job there and makes some money. But soon he gets sick and loses his job and we come back to Sandakan, and my mother comes to live with me.

"Now my third sister, Elsie, who used to work for the timber company has lost her job because she can type, but not good enough. So will you ask Mr. Keith if he would like her to do his typing?"

"Mr. Keith already has too many people who can type not good enough. However, I'll ask him. Tell me, Angela, there is a teacher at the school called Maria Cardenas; isn't that your mother's family name? Is she related to you?"

"She is my mother's youngest sister, Aunt Maria. She has a very sad tragedy in her life. Her boy friend was Richard Brown from Labuan. He is a Eurasian with light skin, lighter than yours, and a very nice clever fellow, only careless, very careless. And because he was careless he got leprosy; it was his own fault, you understand, through carelessness."

A significant pause here implies a form of carelessness which Angela's delicacy restrains her from naming.

"So now he cannot marry. But he is not sent to Berhala leper station with the other lepers, because he is Eurasian, and he is kept in isolation upcountry. Now even Aunt Maria cannot see him because his face is going, disappearing, rotting – and he is a very tragic sight, his mother says. So he is just a tragedy now, and my Aunt Maria who is already old, she is twenty-five years old, will never marry."

"Is she going to teach school all her life?"

"Well, yes – she must just give herself up to the education of the young now. That is her life. She herself has reached the Sixth Standard and so much knowledge must not be wasted. Besides, if she marries and has babies she will assuredly go crazy because all her family goes crazy after having babies."

Leaving Aunt Maria caught between leprosy, insanity, and pedagogy we turn our attention to the Club, the rendezvous in town of Asiatics, Eurasians and bachelors, with European Lady and Gent Patrons. The Club is noted for its large oil-burning refrigerator which supplies cold drinks, and its large radio-gramophone which supplies hot music.

"Are you coming to the Saturday night dance at the Club, Mrs. Keith? I never see you there."

"No, Angela, my husband does not go out much. I expect that you are going?"

"Yes, I shall be there and dance an exhibition tango with Mr. Minchen of the Singapore boat, if he is in port. We are clever dancers together. I am always popular with boat gentlemen; also with the H.M.S. boats after the war when many came in to Sandakan. All petty officers call me Angela like old friends, and some still write to me. That is really my hobby now, writing letters to my pen friends. The stamps cost much money, but it is educational for me to have pen friends."

Pen friendships of English-learning Asiatics are vivid still in my memory from wartime censorship, and I would not use the word "educational" to describe them. I let the conversation drop in the hope that Angela may leave soon, but she still has matters to impart.

"Have you seen Serena Mathews since she came back from Singapore?" she asks.

Serena is the most industrious and efficient Filipino Eurasian in town, and the accepted styles-dictator of night club life. She is an expert typist who receives just less than European wages and lives on Asiatic standards, and probably has more spending money than any other woman here. Serena suffers the Eurasian frustration of being too good for what she can get, and unable to get what her ancestry breeds a desire for. She stood off the bachelors before the war, and the Japanese through the war, and has resisted the forces of triumph and peace since, and now at the age of twenty-five, the virginity which was an asset at fifteen becomes a liability.

Angela: "Serena comes back from holiday in Singapore now with one thousand new dresses, all New Look, and beautiful upswept-hair permanent wave."

"What will Serena do with a thousand new dresses in Sandakan?"

"She will wear them to the Club dances one after the other, a new one for each dance through the year."

"Still, even at the rate of one dance a week," I ruminate, "that's only fifty-two a year, leaving Serena with a surplus of nine hundred and forty-eight unworn dresses still at the end of the year!"

Angela dismisses my mathematics with, "Well, never mind—I shall have a new dress myself for the dance. It will be white with sequins purchased per yard by order from Singapore, and I shall wear my twenty-four-dollar shoes. They also are from Singapore with very high heels, and I cannot walk in them."

"Then how can you dance the tango in them?"

"That is different, and only for a short time. After my tango

I remove them. Those shoes will make me taller like my friend of the Singapore boat, Mr. Minchen."

"Is he a good dancer?"

"Not as good as Mr. John Grant was. When he used to tango with me before the war everybody admired us greatly. But now he is married. Do you know his wife? She is a beautiful Eurasian girl with skin much, much whiter than yours, and yellow hair all very curling."

"Yes, Angela, I do remember Mr. John Grant."

He was one of many prewar gallants with lusty ways who did his best to go to bed with every pretty girl in town, and the only pretty girls were Asiatics. Living someplace else he might just have had fun, but here there is no fun, the choice is between intercourse or silence, bed or boredom. The pretty girls liked Mr. Grant, and didn't like boredom. Soon distracted parents were dispatching seductive daughters to the sticks, or marrying them off to boys of their own race. Perhaps only the arrival of the Japanese with priority contracts prevented interracial sin in the grand fashion.

"How are your children now, Angela?"

"They have a little influenza now, and maybe a little tuberculosis. My family all has the t.b."

"Who takes care of the children when you are away selling tatting?"

"My mother takes them – she is not so crazy she cannot take care of a few babies."

"Here is the money for the tatting and a few dollars for your mother, and two tins of milk for the children. Now I must go back to my work."

"Thank you. I will tat you some more tatting soon."

"Couldn't you make some children's dresses instead? There are a number of babies that I would like to get some plain dresses for. I will supply you with the material, if you will sew the dresses."

"No, thank you Madam, I am not educated in plain sewing, only in the fancy stitches for making things beautiful."

With the milk tins in her hand, with the extra yards of tatting wrapped in an American comic section, with her red rayon umbrella held over her bleached permanent wave and her expensive imported complexion, with her blue dirndl doodling about her spindle legs, Angela trips down the hill, a fragile figure of elegant incompetence, an epigram on Asiatic independence.

And to me she is the memorial of her kind, of a class of persons here who by ill-birth and limited opportunity, in their incompetence, childishness, shortsightedness, and improvidence, were unable either to settle with the Japs for profit, or to win with us. But they are people who, when we were starving behind Japanese barbed wire, were improvident and shortsighted enough to risk their lives to smuggle food to us; who were childish enough to help our prisoners of war escape; and many of whom were incompetent enough to face a firing squad and give up their lives in our name.

During the war Angela smuggled food to me in prison camp. Today she tats tatting; that tatting means something more to me. This yard of azure blue is the tin of milk that came through the Jap guards and barbed wire on Berhala Island, our first prison, "For George, from Angela." This coil of brilliant green is the bunch of bananas which was hidden for us behind the latrine, this livid mauve is the dried prawns which arrived for us in the dark and the rain, and this bilious lavender signifies the first letter smuggled to me from outside the wire, signed by a brown hand with the words, "We do not forget you, we are your friends."

With the proceeds of her tatting Angela will buy a new dress with which to dance the tango on some hot night in this hot town. The neon lights of the Club will shine whitely on the gaudy best dresses of the Asiatic ladies, on the genteel best dresses of the European Lady Patrons, on the starched white cotton of the young Chinese, on the ultramarine shirts of Youth Filipino, on the loose checkered blouses of *Muda Malayu* – but not on the natives of Borneo who will not be there. Conversation is forced, fraternizing is awkward, Lady Patrons smile resolutely, Gents push to the bar for something stronger to ease their pain, and the gramophone plays.

Sitting barefoot in our house above the town we hear the music to which Angela dances the tango, glittering in her sequins, her twenty-four-dollar shoes pinching her feet but adding inches to her stature, the powder on her dark face unbecoming but adding whiteness to her skin. Beyond the glare of the neon lights, up the dark, scented alleys of the town, her crazy mother dandles her sniffling children, her husband loafs, her neighbors gossip, and her house is burgled or burns.

V. To Have a Little Land

I FIRST met Kam Chu Hak in 1940: I was standing in front of the Forest Office in a clean white dress looking with disgust at the dirty old Chinese taxi Harry had just driven up in. He always would get that taxi because he was sorry for the driver, Sing Fook San, who used to be a procurer but had reformed now and kept taxis instead. His taxi was always filthy, I always protested, and the taxi continued to arrive dirty. Now I was too busy with annoyance at the taxi to notice that it held an extra occupant.

Harry jumped out to open the door, while old Sing, seeing me, reached swiftly into the back area with the long, rainbow-colored feather duster, and fluffed languidly at the dust. This duster was used for everything except jacking up the car, and now its molting feathers joined clumps of mud in the bottom of the car, and ineffectually smeared the dust, cigarette ash and grease on the seat.

"Not dirty now, Mem," said Sing, with a polite smile.

It was so typical, I thought, to try to clean off mud with

feathers, not with any idea of ridding the taxi of dirt, but merely as an amiable concession to my foibles.

"Why don't you wash your car sometime?" I said crossly. "Water is cheaper than feather dusters."

"Not dirty now, Mem," said Sing happily, pretending not to understand.

"Come on, get in, dear, we're late already!" Harry urged.

"Not dirty, Mem!" Sing urged.

"I'm sick of polishing his dirty seats with my white dresses," I muttered. "But I suppose I should have known better than to dress like a human being when I go driving in a Sandakan taxi!" I bent my long back double, and entered the old-fashioned back seat in a jackknife pose which landed me almost in the lap of a young Asiatic who was a stranger to me.

"Well, yes, you really should," Harry agreed. "Dear, this is Mr. Kam, the new assistant in the Agricultural Department. He will be driving with us every week when we go to the Experiment Station. He has charge out there now."

"How do you do, Mr. Kam," I said glumly, without in the least wanting to know how he did – or to take him with us on our pleasant weekly inspection trips to the station.

Little did I know as I said those words that someday how Mr. Kam did would be a matter of life and death to the Japanese secret police, and later to the Australian occupation officers, for at this moment Mr. Kam seemed of utterly no importance. And yet, thinking about it later, I see that this first trip of his to the Agricultural Experiment Station to mark his promotion in the department probably decided his destiny.

"I do very well thank you, Madam."

Mr. Kam was answering my question which I had already forgotten, in a literal way which I was to learn was characteristic of him. He was looking at me with a confusingly straight stare, and I saw for the first time that his face was handsome in what I styled to myself a Tartar way, combining pleasant Asiatic features and characteristic Asiatic hairlessness with fierce eyes and a challenging boldness of glance which belonged to a warrior more than a farmer.

During the afternoon we thoroughly inspected his new domain, about five square miles of semi-planted land and secondary jungle, now in partial use for agricultural experimentation and being rapidly expanded for emergency. Mr. Kam raced ahead of us at blue ribbon pace. He was built like a Mongolian pony, or my idea of one, all muscle and spring and hard flanks and smooth, shining hide, and I quickly imagined him married to a gypsy-like creature with shining, blue-black mane streaming behind her in long straight wild ribbons of hair as she ran tirelessly beside him.

"Are you married, Mr. Kam?"

"Yes, Madam, I have a wife and five children."

"Five! How long have you been married?"

"Five years."

This time I saw her running beside him with slightly less speed.

"Does your family live in Sandakan, or China?"

"In Sandakan, Madam. I am not from China. My wife used to teach school here."

The blue-black ribbons of hair changed quickly into a permanent wave.

"My wife is born in Sandakan. Her father Chinese – mother Japanese."

I gave up the gypsy strain completely for Mrs. Kam, and focused on Mr. Kam instead.

"But you were not born in China, Mr. Kam?"

"No, Madam. I am born in Korea."

"Do you like Korea? Or do you prefer Borneo?"

"Borneo is better," he said decidedly.

After this, we drove regularly every week to the Experiment Station, and I came to know Mr. Kam as a quiet, self-contained man, who neither asked nor gave confidences or favors, but was prepared to succeed on his own efforts alone. Harry told me he was unusually competent, and had studied for several years at a university in Korea. When I met his wife one day in the town, I thought her colorless compared to him, and years older in appearance, a look no doubt contributed to by the birth of five in as many years. However, the two of them lived together in peace, industry and hard work, without time perhaps for sentiment, but not, I learned, without dreams.

One day I asked Kam why he had left Korea, and he answered bitterly, "No Korean is free in Korea."

"Perhaps Korea will some day become independent again?"

"When I am very young in university there I join fight to make Korea independent from Japanese. But no good! Only, I get into very much trouble. Then my father say, go away! He is frightened for me so I come here, get married, now have many children. No good for me now to fight."

"I should say not! Your business is to raise your family."

"My wife – he do that. My wife – he has ideas."

"What do you plan for your children?"

"My wife, he say, all children must go to school!"

"Well, that's a very good idea. And you – don't you have ideas, too?"

"No ideas! I just take care of wife and children – and some day, maybe, have a little land."

He was the last man whom I would have said would get excited about a war, when earning a living was the important thing. In Asia, men fight all their lives for mere existence, and adding a national war to the daily one does not transport them from a state of peace into strife, but merely adds one more hazard to the fight. Kam should have taken the war with Japan in his stride. But then – Kam was born in Korea.

I had been working in the censorship of Asiatic mail from the outbreak of the European war, and with the advent of Pearl Harbor, Japanese mail became our greatest problem. Mr. Kam, because of his knowledge of the Japanese language, was called on to help. Working with him in the censor's office I soon felt in him the same sense of painfully controlled hysteria and tightly drawn tension that we Europeans found in ourselves during these weeks of waiting for the enemy to invade our shores.

One afternoon we had completed a speedy and exhausting tour of the Agricultural Station where emergency acres of tapioca were frantically being planted for use when the rice supply should

be cut off, and sweet potatoes were literally springing from the ground. Even Kam had sweated slightly on our rounds, and on the drive home we suggested that he stop at our bungalow and join us in a cold drink. Now with the iced glasses in our hands, I was thinking that to be without ice would distress us Europeans almost as much as to be without rice would the Asiatics; I was thinking that the Chinese had the advantage of us because they had less to lose in comforts in any war than we who lived on luxuries, when suddenly some words of Kam to Harry caught my ear –

". . . and so – he very frightened now!"

"Who is very frightened, Mr. Kam?"

"My wife, he very frightened!"

"Why should your wife be frightened? What do you mean?"

"My wife, he ask me, When the Japs come – what shall *I* do?"

"But she will be no worse off than the other Chinese here, will she? They aren't worrying much!"

"Yes, my wife more trouble because he half Japanese!"

"How will the Japs know she is half Japanese? Anyway, if they do, isn't that in her favor, in their eyes?"

"Japanese always know everything. It is on their papers in Tokyo about every Japanese," Kam answered doggedly. "And it is worse for my wife also because he is married to me – to a Korean."

"But that's foolish," I said, still happy in those days of ignorance, and strong in the belief that when the Japs came they would act "reasonably." "That's foolish! If she is married to a Korean they will expect her to be prejudiced in favor of Japan."

"No Korean ever have prejudice *for* Japan! He know too much," Kam said bleakly. "No Korean ever forget he is Korean, and no Japanese ever forget a Korean not Japanese."

"I'm afraid you are right, Kam," Harry said slowly. "And I have been thinking for some time that you ought to get out of here before the Japs occupy, especially as you have been doing censorship of Japanese mail. I think you should take your family and go up to China, and get lost. Sandakan is too small a place for marked men. I can get you passage on a Hong Kong steamer, I'm sure. I don't like to lose you, but I think you should go."

"No good, I think. In China – I am Korean!" Kam answered heavily. "Also – here I make my food – have place to live. If I go to China, what do we live on? My children must eat."

To this we had no answer. No man is free while his children are hungry, nor safe when his heritage is divided.

Shortly after this, all the local Japanese nationals on the east coast in North Borneo were interned by our government in undeniably bad living quarters at Berhala Island Quarantine Station, but with a good diet and facilities to purchase extras from the shops including an alcohol ration. The Quarantine Station was a temporary measure until better quarters now being built in the grounds of the Agricultural Station could be completed and the internees moved out to them, where they would have access to their own food crops. Meanwhile, the Japanese nationals thus interned were fishermen and fishing industry coolies who lived normally on a very low standard, with a few shopkeepers and rubber estate managers. The majority of these internees were living on a higher standard in internment than they were accustomed to as free Oriental laborers.

But we, the Government, were conscience-stricken about the bad conditions in the old broken-down ex-Quarantine houses—especially so as we could foresee our own turn coming very soon. There was much talk amongst us about "those poor fellows out there!" and much sympathy expended on their problems, and those of us who had friends amongst them saw to it that the poor captives got extra cigarettes and as many soft drinks and whiskies as noncaptives were entitled to.

Meanwhile Harry, Kam and I continued our weekly visits to the station in an effort to speed up crop production there. Our visits left us with increasing depression at the sight of the uninhabited and very drab huts which were being built, row on drab row, to hold the Japanese—and which would all too soon probably hold ourselves. The Japanese had already occupied the west coast of Borneo, and it was obviously only a matter of weeks, or days, before they would be here.

This day Harry turned to me and said, laughing with the laughter we were learning to cultivate to hide our fears and tears, "Come along, dear! Let's choose our own hut, and tidy it up a bit! You and I had better keep on Mr. Kam's good side, as he'll probably be out here guarding us. Will you speak a good word for us, Kam, when you're outside the barbed wire, looking in, and we're inside?"

Kam looked sober.

"What else can I do?"

"Nothing," Harry answered. "Nothing. The only thing you can do, as long as you didn't get out of the country, is to try to continue to work with the Japs when they come in. Just go ahead and continue to produce food crops for the locals. That's your job. But don't mix politics in it. Remember, if you remain loyal to us, this war will be over sometime, and Korea will become independent again. Then when you return to your country and take your children with you, they will not be as you were, the children of conquered men born to suppression, but free people."

Kam said slowly, "Yes – I hope it is like that. But before that time comes – there will be much trouble. Even now the Chinese do not trust me. Neither will the Japanese trust me when they come. Yet I wish evil to no man, if he does no evil to me. I wish only to care for my wife and children, and to have a little land."

The conquerors came, and we were imprisoned. Throughout three and three quarter years of internment we heard and knew nothing of Kam Chu Hak.

Before his return to Borneo in 1946 Harry received a letter from José Agama, his senior Filipino assistant in the Forest Department, telling him of the terrors of the past and discomforts of the present, and urging him to hasten back. Mr. Agama had himself sent help to Harry, George and me, and other internees, all through the war, risking his life repeatedly to do so. This and many other acts of loyalty and bravery during the occupation were later to gain him the highest award which the King bestows on a non-British subject.

The men of the Forest Department, Filipinos, Chinese, Malays, Eurasians, and natives had worked steadily through the war years under peril of imminent death and reigns of Japanese terror, while the department offices shifted in and out of jungle, according to Japanese, or Allied threats or edicts. But in 1945, with the burning of the town of Sandakan, department headquarters were destroyed, and only a few of the valuable books were saved by being secreted in homes of the men, or hidden in jungle huts. The men of the department, all Asiatics by then, had remained almost a hundred per cent loyal to the Allies, the best tribute which could be paid to the decency of the white man's rule in Borneo.

In his letter Mr. Agama said Mr. Kam had had a bad time, as at first he had been under suspicion by the Japs because of his Korean birth, and because of this fact and his wife's Japanese blood, he had been forced into apparent connection with the Japanese Military Police, although Agama believed Kam had remained loyal. Now since the Armistice these facts had brought him under suspicion by the Allied occupation authorities, and especially by local Chinese in reference to the execution of a Chinese in the May Day massacre of Sandakan.

Meanwhile Harry started the long trip back to Borneo. On the last lap of the journey, crowded into the cabin of an old ex-army M.F.V. traveling from Jesselton to Sandakan, a letter was handed to him by an Australian occupation officer, who said he had the letter from an officer who had it from an officer who had it from a man. The letter was addressed to "H. G. Keith, Esq., through the kindness of Capt. Blank. Or, if the letter is not delivered to the addressee, it may be delivered to one of the following: 1. H.E. the Governor. 2. The Director of Works. 3. Hon. the Resident East Coast." None of these other men had returned to Borneo.

The officer told Harry that Kam was at present wanted by the Allies to give testimony against the Japanese Military Police, but two days before, Kam had disappeared, and no trace could now be found of him. In searching for Kam, someone had remembered having seen a letter from Kam addressed to H. G. Keith, and here was the letter. Did it have any bearing on Kam's disappearance?

Harry opened the letter, which was dated in October, almost six months before, and was addressed to Harry in the Army Relief Camp in Labuan to which we had been taken immediately upon our release from prison camp, and where Kam had evidently hoped to reach Harry quickly. The letter said:

DEAR MR. KEITH:

This afternoon, I met Mr. Johns of the B.B.T. Coy., and an Officer by the name of Capt. Blank, who informed me of whereabouts of you and your family. I am so glad to hear that you are all safe. The God has blessed you.

The war is over and people all over the World must be happy. Thanks to the Allied Nations, my mother country Korea, has an opportunity to become an independent nation. How we Koreans feel glorious! It has exactly come to truth what you told me once at your bungalow, that I might have a chance to return to Korea after the War. I hope so.

Now I wish to tell you how I was getting along since you left us, carrying out agricultural work for the increased production of foodstuffs, as you advocated while you were here with us. I was mostly spending my time in Sandakan district.

As you are not aware of, when you were imprisoned in Sandakan I narrowly escaped my life from the sword of Japanese troops when they landed in Sandakan, because of my Korean blood. But it was not all. When they heard of attack from the sea by the American force on 27th May they round up many of leading people in Sandakan. The Japanese Military Police was making search of me, but luckily I was not at home and was excluded from being round up. After consulting with Chinese friends, I decided to obey Japanese Government order and followed to place of destination for Civilian Japs, just to save my six members of my family who were remaining in Sandakan. After spending a jungle life for more than four months, I return to Sandakan on 5th October after peace. Now I was happy when I heard of the Victory gained by the Allies.

In the jungle I have been suffering from chronic malaria and insufficient food. When I returned to Sandakan, my friends could hardly recognize me I was so thin.

Now I wish to tell you that I am again swinging between life and death. And you, and only you, understand that I gave my service to the British Government, even at the cost of danger to my life since the war, when you were so kind to tell me that I and my family should be sent away from Sandakan to safeguard our lives. You were right. But it was too late!

Even now since the British force landed in Sandakan I am in trouble. The story is that I am said to be responsible for the killing by Japanese of Mr. B— of Sibuga Road in the May Massacre. I have never dreamed of killing a man! And I still believe the God of Justice is protecting me. How can I, in the world, be responsible for the death of Mr. B—, when I was away from Sandakan for more than four months, and when I was in jungle 80 miles away from Sandakan?

The enemy of my father as well as myself, has been and is, the *Japs.* I have not lived for opportunism although I served with Japanese while they were ruling here, in order to save my life, as well as for bread for my family, and to help the local community. But I could not please all 30 thousand Sandakan people!

There is now no European here who understand me, as you do, or believes me a true man. In this critical moment when my life is in danger, nobody can save me, unless you. I would not ask for any forgiveness, if really I killed or caused to kill any human life in the world. But I did not.

I am writing this letter in a hurry, hoping you can see some way to clarify my standing, and to save me from danger, although I doubt if this letter will reach you in time. I have to leave everything to the God, and I must obey to the order of the British Authority to save my personality from being destroyed.

Lastly I wish to mention that our valuable herbarium specimens and your valuable books were all lost, although I as well as Forest and Agricultural staff tried our best to save them.

Best regards to you and your family from self, my family and the Agri. and Forest staff in Sandakan.

Sincerely yours,

KAM CHU HAK

Harry closed the letter, turned to the officer, and asked, "Do you know any of the details of Kam's disappearance? This letter was written six months ago, just after peace came, but Kam knew even then that he was in for trouble. I am certain that he was not disloyal – at least, no more so than any man who survives an enemy occupation must be to survive."

"We first ran into this Kam type," the officer answered, "when orders came to collect Jap Military Police in Sandakan, and anyone connected with them. Kam was in and out of the Military Police all the time through the war – or so the Chinese said. Anyway, his wife was half Jap, and the Chinese didn't trust them. Nobody had anything they could prove against him, but the chap just didn't sound too good. He was born in Korea, too, and that's about the same as being a Jap.

"But when we couldn't get anything definite on him, we figured we'd give him a break – we told him he'd have to help us by testifying against the Jap Military Police himself. He knew plenty about them, we figured.

"Well, Kam said that suited him all right. He had no sympathy for them, and he'd just as soon help to hang them, as not.

"The trial was to be in Jesselton this week, so we loaded all the Military Police on the LCT that runs along the coast now, about fifty of them, and some Jap officers, and sent them to Jesselton for trial. Now this Kam type has disappeared."

"Where was Kam last seen?"

"Well, we know he got on the boat, all right. My bloody oath he did! But he never got off it – he just wasn't there when the LCT reached Jesselton."

"Kam was under separate European guard, I suppose?"

"God, no. We just bunged them all in together!"

"You mean you loaded Kam onto the same boat with a gang of fifty Jap Military Police he was to testify against, without any protection?"

"My bloody oath, we did! We haven't time to bugger about with details at a time like this!"

"A time like what?"

"Oh, you know – a war, and all that! Anyhow, the guy's a Chink."

"I thought it was peace now, and it's your job to see justice done to everyone here. It strikes me that this is pretty poor propaganda, to say the least, for return to white rule."

"Well, my bloody oath, you can't treat these Chinks square! They don't understand it."

Kam Chu Hak has never been heard of since. His insignificant insurance and tiny pension for Government service have been delivered to his wife, and on this penurious sum she and five children exist in a crowded cubicle in a stranger's house on ten square feet of other men's land.

PART THREE

Boy in Borneo

I. Boy in Borneo

The sky is vivid azure now and cool from last night's storm, the pale Damascus roses tremble with dew, the lemon-yellow allamanda bends under the weight of sodden leaves, the pink oleanders quiver with the last puffs of wind, and the great albizzia tree shakes rain-laden tears onto the garden, temperate and beautiful now, soon to be breathless with heat.

At the less exotic approach to our household, matters are also being attended to. The Labatrine Lady has successfully snatched the latrine can out of the privy without maiming or wounding its occupant and whisked it away to the vegetable garden, the gardener has watered the plants already soaked from last night's storm and collected cigarette butts for himself from the drain, Ah Min has whisked the dust from shelves to floors and swept it up to shelves again, Ah Kau has washed clothes, dogs, and babies in the painless early sun, and Ah San returns from market, laden. Even Harry and I, assisted by caffein and nicotine, are energetic to solve the day's problems. George alone sleeps.

"George, get up! It's time for school!"

George in his little bed has wound himself about his sheet, eaten or otherwise absorbed his pyjama top, thrown away his trousers, and buried his head under the pillow. Sleep is a thing he does seriously, and being awake is the same. George at seven is either full-speed or full-stop, an incredible likeness of Granny at plus ninety-five.

"George! Get up!" I remove the pillow, and the end of his nose twitches slightly.

"George!" My mouth is close to his ear. "George!"

Like a young nocturnal animal unjustly aroused by day, he stretches gently, yawns, and goes to sleep again.

"George, get up! It's almost time for school."

I extract the sheet, which involves almost amputating a leg, and his somnolent breathing is only simulated now as he feels the end impending. I tickle, and the end comes.

"Oh, Ma! . . . Stop!" A stretch and a yawn. "Oh, Ma, I don't want to go to school today! Please, Ma, let me stay home. I don't learn anything there, Ma. And besides, I feel sick. Honest I do."

"George, get up."

"Why do I have to go to school, Mum? Teacher just jabbers Chinese louder than the rest."

"Now, George, you know you have to go to school. How are you going to learn enough to earn a living if you stay home and sleep all day?"

"I'm going to keep a big fish trap like the natives do. They don't have to learn their multiplication tables. All they have to do is go out in their boats and sit at the *kilong* and wait for the fish to come."

"But they have to count the fish and weigh them, in order to sell them in market, and to estimate the price. That requires arithmetic."

"I'll hire someone to do that for me. I'll just catch fish."

"It's no use arguing, George. And don't forget to clean your teeth."

"Oh, Mum, look! I told you I was sick! See, I think I got worms again. See?"

"Nonsense! That's a red elastic band, and take it out of there!"

Pleased by his own ingenuity, he is at last out of bed, and stands before me like a caricature of a boy, a caricature of youth and all it means. With legs too long and thin and bones too slender, with shoulder blades too sharp, and belly sucked against his backbone in a concave curve, with silky flesh tattooed by cuts and scratches, with youthful face still sweet with dreams while his tongue makes dirty answers, my son stares back at me.

"Hi, Mum, what you thinking about?"

"What am I thinking about? George, you'll never know – until you look at your own son the way I am looking at you."

"Why? Is it nice?"

"It's frightening . . . And wonderful."

"Oh!" George gapes. This thing has gone far enough! Still, the mood may have some use.

"Mum, if you go downtown today will you please get the new *Nyoka, Jungle Girl* comic at the bookstore?"

"Dad says no more comics."

"The kids all have them at school, Ma. And I want a new one to trade with. You ask Dad, will you, Mum?"

"Well – I'll see. Hurry up, now. Breakfast is ready."

But he doesn't hurry, he dawdles, and a world of thought transpires between placing a canvas shoe on one naked foot, and then on the other. Fortunately he wears few clothes, and in time the Airtex shirt and cotton shorts are on, and he arrives at the table.

Breakfast consists of tinned Australian orange juice, Lilliputian eggs from local pygmies, a strip of bacon when the boat is in, and milk from a tin. For fifteen minutes George dawdles at the table, and then in one minute actual eating time, he swallows his food, and starts for the garden.

"George, don't forget your books!"

"I'm going out to see the bear. Dad's not ready yet."

There's always a bear in the family, and this one, a young black honey bear, was given to George several months ago by natives from the Kinabatangan. Its predecessor, a baby female called Sheba, was killed by wild dogs; this one, a male, called Heba, kills dogs. Heba is three feet long and weighs sixty pounds, has a magnificent silky coat and is, Harry says, the most beautiful bear in all Borneo. On his black chest he wears a heart-shaped, cream-colored, fur shirt front which tucks like a bib under his soot-black chin, his face is like a Disney dream, and long, cruel, frightening claws more than an inch long project on his padded feet.

His disposition is less than idyllic, and sometimes he goes crazy with impatience. The cause of this may be the rain, the sun, the wind, the storm, the ants, ourselves, or waiting for his food, his bath, his sleep, and when the feeling sweeps him he boxes his own ears with exasperation and beats his chest with anger for that poor black bear! He acts exactly then as I feel like acting sometimes, and as George still does.

Because of his disposition he lives in a large wire cage which once held neighbor Chuck's chickens, and the wire is chicken strength; by the cage ruse Heba is assumed to be safe in captivity, whereas he really spends his time making holes in the cage and then chasing people across the lawn.

"Ma, the bear is out!" George calls.

Always at the most inconvenient time!

"Harry, the bear is out!"

"Well, *I* can't do anything about it now. I've got to go to the office. Just leave him loose for the day, he won't hurt anybody."

"That's what you think! When he's loose I spend my whole time decoying him away from people by exposing my own body to him. And his claws are terrible."

"Oh . . . Well . . . Call Ah San then. Ah San! The bear is out!"

It is Ah San's duty to feed the bear twice daily, and the bear loves Ah San and Ah San only, and Ah San, I believe, loves the bear. Sometimes when called Heba will follow Ah San like a pup, and snootle along docilely with his wet muzzle against Ah San's thin shanks and his sharp claws retracted—sometimes. Other times, although he never offers to hurt him, he will not follow, and then his sixty-pound bulk, reinforced by long claws, taut nerves and intense feelings on every subject, is not to be played with. Such times, Ah San and I sit patiently behind trees to intercept him from the road and warn passers-by, while we wait for Heba's appetite to develop so we can tempt him back to the cage.

"Ah San, the bear is loose!"

Ah San comes. He carries the battered bear food pan with rice and fish in it, and goes towards the front garden. He is making noises that bears are assumed to understand.

"Hurry up, George," shouts Harry. "We've got to get off for school."

"Wait a minute until we see if Ah San is going to have trouble!" I beg. "George is helping him catch Heba."

George is playing my part of the human decoy, and he gambols in front of Heba with his bare brown legs a tempting target for outstretched claws. As he entices Heba towards Ah San, the food, and the cage, Heba ambles clumsily after him in frolicsome mood. From the road below us two barelegged small Chinese boys scrubbed to early morning perfection, with schoolbooks, indigo shorts, and green hair pomade, scream with joy, hoping against hope that the bear will eat the boy.

"Amiable today, thank God! He's getting him in, Harry—call George now if you like. We can cope."

George comes, and he and Harry climb into the battered jeep and leave for school and office. Ah San appears with a diffident, persistent smile which means he has a mission.

"Can talk, Missee?"

"Yes, Ah San. I see you're still alive!"

"Missee, that bear too much money! I show you." Ah San presents me with the crumpled but legible itemized account of Heba's upkeep for the past month, and I see that Heba has consumed thirty pounds of rice and thirty tins of condensed milk in this period. "The most beautiful bear in Borneo," I ruminate. God knows, he should be!

"Ah San, I give you the bear. It is you that he loves, anyway, not us. The bear is yours. Now you buy rice and milk."

Ah San yells like a wounded bull, for this is carrying love too far – "Too much money!"

"Too much money for Mister, too!"

Ah San laughs at this; by his standards we rival Rockefeller. Then he adds, "You busy, Missee? Can talk?"

"Yes, Ah San, what do you want?"

"Missee, every night baby wake up and cry. I no can sleep! Ah Min say, baby cry, let baby suck milk in night! I say, Missee tell me no – baby too big! Missee, what can do?"

"Suppose baby cry, I think baby hungry, Ah San. Suppose give more food every night before baby sleep. Suppose give soft-boiled egg every night for supper, very good. Egg very good."

Ah San looks skeptical. He is uncertain of the virtue of an egg diet for a baby, I can see – or perhaps of Gung Ho's liking it. I try to reassure him.

"Gung Ho will like egg, you will see. All babies like egg."

Ah San looks at me sadly, and wails, "Egg eleven cents one piece! Too much he like egg!"

Between the bear and the baby there seems little future.

George attends a Roman Catholic mission school built of palm-leaf thatch at which he is the one European student amongst two hundred Asiatics who range in age from six years to twenty. Most of these boys are at school for the purpose of combining a religiously advantageous course of Catholicism with the economically advantageous one of English and sums, but George, whose one scholastic accomplishment is to speak the English language, is now rapidly losing this gift. The boys about him speak pidgin English, Malay, or Chinese, and George, who likes to blend with the herd, says reasonably, when I protest, "Aw, Ma, dey all spik like dat!"

"Why don't you talk Malay with them? Your Malay is excellent."

"But, Ma, they want to learn English."

"But that's not English you are talking. You must stop."

"O.K., Mum. I no talk like dat any more, eh?"

When George came back to Borneo with us, we reckoned it was not a matter of ourselves showing Borneo to him, but of Borneo seen anew by us, through George. Through him we would learn what tropical food was like to a small boy's taste, what it was like to speak other languages more frequently and more colloquially than your own, we would observe if Oriental pastimes were more fun than British games, and if the lack of Anglo-Saxon small-boy companions would be made up for by companionship with Asian children.

We would learn whether life here broke down race barriers for a child, or built them up, what effect the tropical climate had on a small white boy several years older than the acceptedly desirable age for the East, and what clothes, if any, he would use. We would learn if the lack of artificial amusements in Sandakan made George self-sufficient, or left him suffering from unremedied boredom, and whether the kind of schooling available in Borneo had any educational value for an English boy who must in time return to the Western world.

Most important of all, we would discover whether a father, mother and home influence during the next three years could contribute as much that was necessary for George's development as would a school at home with European teachers, and the unequaled discipline of those of his own age and kind, without father, mother and home.

Here in Sandakan George's schoolmates were predominately Chinese, Filipino boys, Malays, Indians, and Eurasians, and almost no natives of Borneo. The absence of native boys in school had two explanations – one, that natives did not by choice live in coast towns, but up the rivers, on plains, or in the hills, where each small group was both isolated and self-supporting. And two, that native parents too often reasoned that they were "too kind" to their children to make them go to school and study, if the children did not "wish" to do so!

The primitive native sees no sequence between book learning and increased pleasure in living. His reasoning is that to plant and hunt equals to drink and eat. The Chinese run his shops, the British run his country, and this brings him no alarm if it doesn't interfere with the native's running himself, which so far he has always succeeded in doing. This attitude to education is changing slightly under the tuition of a small group of better-educated young Malays and natives outside of North Borneo who are urging the advantage of native self-government, but as yet the natives of North Borneo regard education as an unkind, unnecessary chore.

George's attitude is that of the native, and he also sees no sequence between learning and living. His life in Sandakan leads him to believe that he is a rich man's son, although any place else in the world we are people of slender means. But here he is Small Master, a documentation he accepts, not because he draws a color line or makes the choice, but as the line of least resistance. He prefers fishing, swimming, boating, hunting with Dyaks, Muruts, Malays, Filipinos, men of the jungle and sea, to soccer, cricket, and movies with other Small Masters.

The young Chinese and Filipinos at school are a different quantity; they are earnest workers and will learn everything offered, as far as their own cultural and intellectual capacity allows. They are mostly the children of shopkeepers, small merchants, clerks, laborers and coolies, and their lives and their parents' lives have taught them that they must learn in order to earn in order to eat, to live.

"There's a secret society at school, Dad, and the boys wear red and white badges and the password is Lavatory. Why would the password be Lavatory, do you think, Dad?"

"Lavatory? You don't mean Liberty, by any chance?"

"Oh, yes—maybe that's it—Liberty?—Lavatory? Yes, that's it. But when the Chinese kids say it, it sounds like Lavatory."

"That's just their trouble," grumbles Harry, "they don't know Liberty from Lavatory!"

"Who do you say won the war, Dad?"

"Who! Hell! . . . Still, maybe that's not a bad question. Who do the Chinese boys at school say won the war?"

"They say it this way—The Chinese won the war, so the

Chinese are Number One nation now, the English are Number Two, the Japs are about Number Nine, and the Germans and other people about Number Twenty. But that's not right, is it, Dad? Did the Chinese win the war?"

"Guess they've been reading Allied propaganda about themselves! They didn't win the war, but they survived it, which I suppose is the crucial thing in war. What do the boys at school call you? I thought I heard them calling *tai lalat* when I picked you up."

"Oh, Fly Specks! Yes, that's for my freckles."

"Do they bully you?"

"Oh yeah – well, sometimes they slap me and pinch me. But I throw stones at them."

"Hunh. That's like 'em. Couple of hundred gang up against one foreigner."

"That's like all small boys," I suggest.

"Y-yes. But it hurts more when they're Chinese. I saw old Lobos today, Agnes, the first time since the war."

"Has he started his barbershop again?"

"No, he's managing a timber camp at Batu Tiga. I asked him if he knew what Mamie Jimenez, his cousin, was doing now, and he gave me a suspicious look and said 'My dear! Have nothing to do with her! She's just a woman of private parts.' "

George is about to ask for an anatomical diagram when I interrupt, "George, do you remember the little Murut with the baby face and bright black eyes who works for the telephone department? He was up here to fix our wire today, and he asked me how 'the baby' was! He always remembers you at your prewar age, and still expects to see you in my arms."

"Hunh!"

"I saw young Lo this morning, dear."

"Which Lo? With or without?"

"Without." Brothers Lo are always distinguished from each other by the absence or presence of their own widely discussed affliction of piles. "He wants to come up to talk with you about America. He speaks American, as a matter of fact, more than English. He studied at Lingnam University in Canton with American teachers, and during the war he acted as Chinese interpreter for the American Army in China."

"What does he want to talk to me about?"

"He wants to go to the United States to take a graduate course in engineering. During the war the American Forces more or less promised to arrange for some of their young Chinese interpreters to return to the U.S. for schooling after the war. But when matters changed in China, the whole scheme was forgotten. I think Lo wants you to help him."

"How would he get into the U.S.? On a temporary permit?"

"I suppose. Although he says that U.S. passports for American-born Chinese are on sale in Hong Kong for $500 each!"

"He couldn't get by on one of those for very long. Perhaps he can get in for study purposes. But how will he get dollar exchange?"

"I expect he has plenty of 'cousins' there who can manage it for him. Meanwhile the older Lo brother has been back to China to have his piles operated on, before young brother goes away."

"What will he talk about if his piles are cured?"

"His wife's pregnancies, I guess. He gave me a graphic description of the present one. Or his mother's falling womb."

"After twelve children, something had to fall."

"There are a hundred Los in three generations in Sandakan, and an entire village of several thousand, all Los, where the old man comes from in China. Too bad there aren't more. They're good people, straight, and smart and honest. And the old man's not far from a saint — the only Buddhist I ever knew who lived up to it!"

"What's a Buddhist, Dad?"

"One who follows the teachings of Gautama Buddha, the Indian Prince. He was the first teacher to expound the religion of love and virtue to the Eastern World, just as Christ in another age brought love and virtue to the West."

A very good Christian, I think to myself. That's what Harry is — only preferably always in the name of Buddha, Allah, or Mohammed.

II. Curry with Brotherly Love

"MA, could Ronald and I go to play at Surjit Singh's house this afternoon?"

"Why don't you bring the boys here to play? There's more room here."

"There's more fun there. Isn't there, Ronald?" A jab in the ribs reminds friend Ronald of where there is more fun.

"Yes, please, Auntie, there's more fun there," dutifully says Ronald, a guest in our house this afternoon.

"Because I'm not around to stop you sling-shotting birds, I suppose?"

"Yes, Ma – I mean no, Ma. It's more fun at Surjit Singh's house because there are more kids there to play with."

Seven Gill Singhs live in a two-room house nearby, surrounded by other two-room houses of Asiatic clerks, all filled with families of seven or more, and fun.

"All right, you may go if you will promise to come home at five o'clock. That's the Gill suppertime anyway, and I promised Ronald's mother to bring him home early."

"O.K., Ma!"

As I expected, at five o'clock nobody has come home. I get in the car and drive out North Road to old Government House grounds where, since the war, half a dozen small *atap* houses act as temporary quarters for Government Staff. I pass the old sign-in-the-book sentry house at the entrance, the only remnant of gubernatorial glory, and follow the drive past the charred

ruins of Government House. Beyond the foundations, in the overgrown but far from abandoned garden under the trees, is the settlement of small houses. I stop at the furthest one, the home of Mr. A. Gill and family, the Hospital Bacteriologist.

As my car comes to a noisy stop, every aperture of the house is suddenly filled with handsome, small dark faces, which peek out with smiles from under white turbans, and a slender woman in a dark sari with a bright, worn face, ardent Indian eyes, and a glowing smile, appears at the door. She waves me to come in, using the Indian gesture for welcome which is one of pushing away.

I shake my head, and call out that I have come for George and Ronald, and cannot stay. But she continues smiling and shaking her head and urgently beckoning me in until she is joined by Mr. Gill, a handsome figure in a green and blue checked sarong, with chalk-white turban bound neatly above classic Indian features and brilliant eyes. I again indicate that I have come for the boys, but Mr. Gill steps down from the veranda to the car and says earnestly:

"We are honored to see you. You will enter our house please."

"Oh, no, thank you, I cannot stay. I must take the boys home."

"But the boys are about to take curry with us. You must not take them away before they eat, please. My wife prepares the food now. You must come in and share with us."

"But I have promised Ronald's mother to bring him home early. The boys really must come, or she will be worried. They will stay with you another day."

"Oh, please do not take them away before the meal. My wife fixes the curry now. Please enter our house and observe our children eat together in brotherly love. It will make us all very happy to see them thus."

It is obvious now that to take the boys away is to refuse the brotherly love, even more than curry. But to stay is to strain the sisterly love of Ronald's mother by arriving later with her child, I well know – yet at this moment relations with her seem less important than with the Gills and curry.

"Perhaps we can telephone to Ronald's mother," Mr. Gill suggests. "I will go down the road to the hospital telephone."

"She has no telephone," I say.

"Please stay," he urges.

Our sons have chosen, I am thinking, and these children are their friends. To take them away from a meal which is to mark that friendship is impossible. Children go through life gathering to them the events of living which in the end serve to make them the adults they become. Today can be an event to help enroll these Indian children and our English ones in a common world, or to separate them further; it can be a day marked by the thought, We are friends! or long remembered in the phrase, "They wouldn't eat with us."

"The food is almost ready, now," says Mr. Gill. "It will not be long. My wife prepares it. Stay."

This day, I tell myself, can go with George and Ronald all their lives, reminding them if they hear a disparaging phrase, "All Indians are – " that all Indians are not; reminding them that the Indians they know are hospitable, friendly, intelligent, kind.

"You will stay?"

"I will stay."

Inside the small neat house are a small neat table, two chairs, several small stools, and a long rattan chair which the smallest Gill now uses as a bed, tucking himself up in folds of cloth to peer safely out at me from security. For decoration, a bright calendar advertising beer is pinned on the thatch wall, and another advertising tinned milk. In a corner the blond heads of George and Ronald and the snowy peaks of Gill turbans bend over a pile of worn comics, while reading is frequently interrupted by scuffling, and trips to the kitchen to inspect the curry.

Mrs. Gill has disappeared, and Mr. Gill and I sit down together, out of sight but not out of scent of preparation of the curry, in whose creation everyone except ourselves takes turns in helping. Our job is to entertain each other.

"I don't remember you in Sandakan before the war, Mr. Gill. Where were you during the occupation?"

"I was in Singapore until the Japs came, then I lost my job, and could not get food for my family. I heard there was work in Seria Hospital in the Sarawak Oilfields in Borneo, so I bring my family and come. There is only my wife and three children then, and I go to work in the hospital as bacteriologist for the Japs. This is when Dr. Burn, a European doctor from Sandakan, is working there."

Sardol Singh, age fifteen, enters and spreads a white cloth on the table and disappears.

"I hear that this doctor has been in jail many months," Mr. Gill continues. "The Japs beat him up and treat him badly, and sometimes they make him walk through the streets in chains with a sign saying 'This is what happens to WHITE MEN.' But he was always very brave, and not afraid of them, and clever too.

"One day Dr. Burn says to a Jap officer who talk with him in jail, 'Many people sick here with dysentery, malaria and typhoid. By and by Japanese soldiers get sickness too. You need a good doctor here. I am a very clever doctor, but you make me stay here in jail. I think *you* are not clever.'

"So the Japanese take him out of cells and tell him to go ahead and be doctor, but not to talk. So when I work in the hospital, I look under microscope for germs but do not talk with him. He tells me, 'Don't have anything to do with me, or else it make trouble for you!' To know any European then, even to speak English, is bad and makes the Japs suspicious."

Here Surjit Singh, age thirteen, enters carrying a large steaming bowl filled with shredded white fish, eggs, and a coconut in curry. This he places reverently on the white-covered table.

Mr. Gill continues, "I wish only to work and try to get enough food for my wife and children. But the food costs a great deal and money is worth very little. Soon we cannot get cloth for our clothes, or even to make our turbans. We bind our heads in anything we can find, and the children do not have turbans.

"Now my wife is about to give birth again. When her time comes, she is very sick, more so than with babies before, and I am very frightened. I go secretly at night to where Dr. Burn lives and ask him to come to my wife. He comes to the house and delivers the baby, and that one is little Afta Singh. When Dr. Burn leaves he says better not to speak of this, or it will make trouble for me that he comes."

Just here little Afta Singh, now age six, enters proudly bearing with great concentration a large savory plate which contains potatoes, beans and eggplant, colored yellow with turmeric.

"But a few days later a Military Police officer comes. He says to me, 'That English doctor is your friend. He comes to the house for your baby. You speak English. You sympathize with white people. All that is bad.'

"I answer, 'I wish only to care for my family. I do not sympathize with anyone but my family. Other men's business is not mine, but my baby is my business. It is only for that the doctor comes.'

"So the officer goes away. But he comes again two days later with guards and they take me to jail. They ask me many questions. They say, 'What do you know about English people? What do you know about prisoners who escape to Australia? Where are money and jewels hidden here by white people before the war? Where is ammunition hidden here before the war?'

"I answer that I do not know any of these things, I only know my family and children, and they must eat, and this alone keeps me very busy."

Now a third large plate appears holding braised prawns and curry, carried deftly by Bebe, age eleven, the only girl, as straight and slim as her brothers, and with the same soft dark eyes.

"So then the Japs are very angry. They beat me, and jump on my stomach, and hit my head, and always grow more angry because I am not guilty of the things they say. For many days they keep me in the cells and treat me badly and there is very little food. But I do not say yes to the things they say that I do, because I do not do them.

"So then one day the police captain comes in and says to me '*Sodeska!* We see now that you are not guilty!'

" 'I was never guilty,' I say.

" '*Sodeska!* That is what I say – you are not guilty!'

"I say nothing because I do not know if he is about to kick me again, or reward me.

" '*Sodeska!* You know that you are a very lucky man not to be guilty? We are very kind to all Asiatics, but if you are guilty, even kind Japanese become very angry and treat you very severe!'

"I say nothing, because I think now he wants something from me.

" 'There are plenty people sick now with a disease of the stomach and bowel,' he says. 'I think maybe it is typhoid. Japanese Commander decide to release you. You go back to your microscope and look for typhoid germ. You very lucky man not to be guilty. Be careful! Do not be so bad again!'

"At that time, although I am six feet tall, I am very thin and weigh only about five and a half stone from starvation. My chest is weak where they hit me, my stomach is sick, my face is bruised – with kind treatment of the Japanese – because I am not guilty! I leave the cell very weak and go back to my wife and children, and they feel sad to see me this way. I tell them this is war! Just be thankful I am still alive!"

And here comes Bobo, age four, and rounder and plumper than the others as though with his advent in the family came peace and more food. He carries a saucer of chopped mangoes with peanuts, most of which reach the table safely.

"Then finally people begin to whisper that peace is coming. Some say that already the Emperor signs a surrender. The Japanese soldiers do not admit it, but they act different, and they release people from cells. Then the Allied soldiers come in, and free all the prisoners of war. When the Sikh prisoners see my boys growing up without turbans they say it is very bad, they must have proper turbans, and I must teach them to grow up to be proper Sikhs. I say never mind, we are very lucky to be alive at all, with or without turbans, after four years with Japanese."

The cooking team has been working behind the scenes in semi-privacy and much hilarity, and as each item comes out of the cooking pot onto a plate, one of the cooks has brought it in, never bringing more than one dish at a time. This system prolongs the appetizing process and the air now reeks with spices and aromas. My appetite is well aroused, but my anxiety keeps pace with it as I watch the minutes pass on my wrist watch, and visualize the annoyance of Ronald's mother.

Now in rapid succession small dishes appear on the table holding chopped ginger, pickled onions, green and red chutneys, and four small saucers each holding a lightly fried egg with concentric circles of yellow perfectly preserved from white, and two other saucers which hold two fried eggs each. I imagine that these latter are to be for George and Ronald. There is a plate with a large pile of fresh cut bakery bread, but no *chapatis* — perhaps because it is difficult to get good fresh flour here.

Now, one by one, the cooks come out of the kitchen, each bearing before him his own plate heaped high with a generous amount of rice, George and Ronald leading the way. They look untidy, with shirts discarded, feet bare, and hair standing on end, but all the Gills have somehow managed to stay smart and clean. And Mrs. Gill glows both with the heat of the stove and with excusable pride for the beautiful repast she offers us.

She passes a basin of water to each one to wash his hands, and a towel for each to dry on, and then the moment comes. Mr. Gill places a chair for me at the table, and the four Gill boys, George and Ronald, draw up a variety of stools to perch on. Mr. and Mrs. Gill and Bebe stand back smiling hospitably upon us.

"Are you not going to eat with us?" I ask, although it is obvious there is no space at the table, no chairs, and probably no plates.

"My wife and I are not hungry," says Mr. Gill discreetly. I myself have sometimes experienced a lack of hunger with the arrival of sudden guests.

There are knife, fork and spoon at my place and at the places of Ronald and George, although there is nothing on the table which cannot be eaten with the fingers, or sucked up, licked up, smacked up, if you are clever. Mrs. Gill stands by the table ready to assist George and Ronald if they are bashful, which they are not. They join immediately with the Gill boys in molding rice balls with the tips of their fingers, dipping these into the curries and chutneys, and popping them into their mouths without the aid of spoons.

George sucks, smacks, and licks as if he had not touched food for a week, and had little hope of eating anything so good again. Perhaps some of his enthusiasm for Eastern dishes comes from his first memories in prison camp, when the only tasty food he ever had was smuggled in from Asiatic friends. Now he prefers rice to potatoes or bread, and tonight he and Ronald eat twice what they would eat of European food. The Gill boys eat along in businesslike manner, with matter-of-fact satisfaction which seems to say — Of course it's good! So what! This is not to be treated as a feast by them. After all, its secret is not alone in the curry and spices but in the friendly hands which bring it, and the priceless ingredient of brotherly love.

Now it is well after seven o'clock. Everything is eaten, hands are again washed, discarded shoes and shirts accumulated, and we say good night, and thank you. The Gills stand on the veranda, father and the five children waving good-by in the Western manner, while slender, worn, gay little Mrs. Gill says good-by in her own way, waving us in by shoving us off.

Now is the time to think of our guilt. I have kept Ronald two hours after home time. As we race through the town headed for his house a figure dashes out of the police station and waves at us, a figure which even in the distance in semidark carries a quality of hysterical anxiety which marks it as a distraught mother.

"Oh dear! . . . Where was he? Where were you? What happened? I went to the next house and telephoned — you weren't there! I called the neighbors, you weren't there — I went up to the house, you weren't there! Nobody knew anything — I went to the hospital — I searched every road — I called the police. Oh dear! Where were you? Why didn't you . . . Oh dear! I thought he had fallen out of a tree — fallen into a hole — fallen into the sea — been bitten by a snake! Oh dear, oh Ronald, oh dear!"

Ronald and George cuddle snugly together in the back seat, smugly innocent this time, confident that it is not their fault, for I was along. I was to blame.

Now Ronald's father arrives from the direction of the hospital where he has been seeking the corpse. We begin again with all the misfortunes which could have befallen these two — but didn't, all the things which happen regularly to them, but this time didn't — because instead they were eating an Indian curry with their best friends, served with the priceless ingredient of brotherly love.

III. Tommy

Harry has just returned from the capital city of Jesselton with astonishing stories, to us who know the old Borneo, of two hundred and forty strange white faces, new to the East, unlined and carefree, of palm-leaf houses built with modern enamel plumbing in contrast to prewar timber houses without plumbing, of caviar served with drinks, and gin with everything, and of white tie and white gloves worn at Government House.

Along with this wide-eyed tale of prosperous postwar living, Harry brings something that is of more interest to George, a long, covered wooden box with wired slits at both ends, and strong with the smell of animal, at which George anxiously peers.

"Oh, Dad, what is it? What did you bring me?"

"Peek in the end through the breathing slot, but don't open the box until we get up to the house. It's something you'll recognize."

George peeks.

"Oh, it's Tommy! The Bryants' Tommy from Menggatal Estate! Oh, I love Tommy. He won't bite, he's perfectly tame. Did they give him to you, Dad? Is he to keep? Oh, Mum, isn't that wonderful?"

I withhold comment. I have no heart for animals in captivity now, I have been behind the bars too long myself. But in spite of this we have a macaque monkey, four guinea pigs, four white mice, six telescopic-eyed calico-goldfish that bump their eyes on the goldfish bowl, a semi-Siamese cat, a wonk dog, a tree shrew, four white doves, two parrots, a honey bear, and two recently come by mud tortoises said to be engaged in the process of reproduction. The owner of these is George who dotes on them, but hates cleaning their sleeping quarters and feeds them only when he remembers. We have them in spite of my principles, because native friends bring them to George, and I haven't the heart to say no.

But when we arrive at the house, and Harry carries Tommy's box to the veranda and opens the end and reaches gently inside and brings out clinging to his arm a magnificent, tame, silky-furred palm civet cat, I catch my breath with joy and pain. Here is a ghost of our early days in Borneo, and my first loving jungle friend, beautiful, dangerous, Georgie the Musang, whom Harry and I had loved long before.

Soon I saw that Tommy was incredibly more handsome than Georgie had ever been, and where Georgie had been wild, wild, animal to the tip of his long bushy tail, this creature was gentle and playful, a mixture of beauty and beast. Where a true musang has boldly streaked markings, Tommy was delicately blended and shaded, a mixture of gray, brown, yellow and black; where a musang has strong odors both fishy and musky (to be complimentary in description!), Tommy was comparatively scentless. In place of the usual bushy tail, Tommy had a two-foot drape shaped like a bottle cleaner and blending from soft gray into a glossy, sooty blackness. From nose to tail tip he measured twice his tail's length, a total of four feet.

Most important of all for beguiling my affections, Tommy was as soft and silky to the touch as the underside of a kitten. To hold him in your hands and fondle him, to feel his heart pound wildly yet trustfully while his short, strong little back legs gripped your arm in friendship, to see his wedge-shaped jaws open wide in a gentle yawn while his pointed bright face gazed confidingly at you, was to feel the unity of life in all things beast and man, and a love and respect for life in every living thing.

His little face was pointed like a baby fox's, keen but not grotesque, with large, shining, nocturnal eyes, and a wedge-shaped mouth with small pointed teeth and a red-purple tongue. His characteristic action was yawning, and he would yawn and yawn and yawn, if awakened at any time before the dark hours of cool night brought him his natural rising hour. Yawning thus with head well back, his rosy tongue curled against the roof of his mouth like the inside of a shell, he was an elegant and comely guest in any home.

Although by nature he was a wild creature, Tommy had been born in captivity on a rubber estate near Jesselton. At the time of his birth the two small sons of the estate manager, who was a friend of ours, were staying with him for the holidays and Tommy became the children's pet and pride. When the boys returned to school in Australia and their father gave Tommy to George, Tommy already knew that his place was in the heart of a family, well-beloved and trusting.

Tommy moved into our household without a hitch. He occupied the bottom shelf of George's wardrobe for his diurnal slumbering, where it was quickly recognized that he needed the yellow silk pillows more than we did. Soon Harry and I were padding our own wardrobe shelves with silken tidies and soft shirts to curry Tommy's patronage, for we valued him as much as George. George took for granted Tommy's warm love and attentions, his kindness and splendor; even Tommy's exciting and sensuous enthusiasm for life seemed unremarkable to George, for life was like that for him, too.

But we knew that Tommy was nothing common, his trust not cheap, his beauty and joy were not to be taken for granted; Tommy was rare, he was life as it should be, but isn't. We cherished him for his perfection, with the knowledge of its value.

Tommy was always uneasy on the ground, and it was obvious that he understood that his safety was in his quick scenting of danger, and his self-defense was in his power to climb. His legs were short compared to his body, and for speed he galloped, producing an odd thumping noise described by Harry as gallumping. His back legs had a strong grip and he could climb up or down any perpendicular object as long as he could get his legs partially about it. He would descend drainpipes head downwards for any distance, as no domestic cat would do. He would ascend to the top gutter of our two-story house and lurk there in the drain with nothing visible except that long, round black tail hanging straight down from the roof in the air, and his progress along the gutter was noted only by the trailing of that long back handle in the air, which was the equivalent of a sign, "Tommy at work here!"

If teased or frightened Tommy would open and close his mouth as if mouthing a silent scream, but only after the greatest effort imaginable would an infinitesimal, pathetic, scarcely audible little squeak emerge, and it was obvious that if he ever needed help, he couldn't call a friend.

From early dark till 9 or 10 P.M. was a time of concentrated gaiety for Tommy, associated with our bathing time. Our bathrooms and bedrooms open off opposite ends of a rear service veranda which runs the length of our second story. On this veranda Tommy's food was always placed, a bowl of condensed milk with a raw egg, and a couple of bananas which were always trailing along the floor half eaten.

With the coming of night, Tommy would awaken, yawn and stretch as a child does with the coming of day, then abandon his silken pillows and cozy wardrobe and start to prowl. George would take him to the garden for a play, Tommy riding on George's shoulder with his tail about his neck. These two would dash up the hilly lawn to the garage which perches on the highest elevation, and here George with Tommy on his shoulder would crouch on the grass while the two held a moment's conversation. Then shouting "Race!" George tosses Tommy into the air ahead of him for a start, and the two tear like mad ones down the slope to the veranda. George arrives first and Tommy leaps on him, mouthing him all over very gently with sharp pointed jaws, gripping him lovingly with his strong little back legs and rubbing his soft little belly all over him up and down, until the race ends with the two rolling on the grass in the dusk, with Pooch, the dog, coming in to join by nuzzling and prodding at boy and beast.

Pooch accepted Tommy into the family as soon as he saw that we did, and Tommy, although wary at first, quickly took Pooch as his friend and soon learned to climb on his back for a ride. Although we have had many animals in our Borneo history, orangutans, apes, monkeys, honey bears, mouse deer, goats, guinea fowl, musangs, civet cats, moon rats, white mice, binturong, squirrels, tree shrews, cats, tame and wild, and several tarsier, we have had only one creature that our dogs would not accept as a friend as soon as they saw that we did. This was a crocodile, and no friend of mine either, which perhaps the dog knew.

At night when we went to bed we fastened the hooks of our bedroom screen doors to keep Tommy out during his active hours, as otherwise we had no sleep. First we had tried leaving the doors unlatched; Tommy would nudge them open, jump on the bed and chew ears, noses and edible parts, then race off and claw the doors open, mount the drainpipe to the roof to slide under the eaves and enter the air space between inside ceiling and outside shingles. Up here he would thump and gallump up and down, back and forth for a time. Then just as we had adjusted our ears to this rhythm and were about to fall asleep, he would slide down the drainpipe, push the door open, leap on the bed and nibble again at any human parts which protruded, then back to the roof again, and so forth.

Now we latched our doors with Tommy outside and through the night I would hear him on the ceiling overhead. With dawn he scratched on the screen and waited till I opened it, then bounded on the bed and rubbed himself over us, nibbling ears and embracing us with his back legs. As the sky grew brighter and the sun came he finished with fun, going leisurely and with luxurious yawns to the wardrobe to curl up and sleep.

When George went to bed at eight after an exhaustive play with Tommy which left them both swinging from the light fixtures with excitement, we would turn Tommy out onto the back veranda. Here he would lurk on the top shelf of an abandoned bookcase waiting for Ah Min to bring our baths. She was nervous of animals and terrified of Tommy, which he knew. He would lie on his belly, with his nose pointing down over the edge of the shelf, watching for her. It was Ah Min's belief that when she went by with the bath water, he would hurl himself on her and eat her alive. Consequently she never brought the baths until she had screamed for Harry or me to drag Tommy from the shelf.

But on one night when she carried the baths upstairs she did not call for us, and when we went up later there was no sign of Tommy. Even when we returned to the bedrooms after dinner and put the lights on again there was no sign of him. I thought he might have jumped from the roof into a nearby tree, which he had done once before, and although I was a little worried, I was confident that Tommy could take care of himself if he stayed up high, as he usually did.

All through the night I was disturbed by the fact that there were no noises overhead. I lay awake to listen for the thumps and bounds that ordinarily assured me that Tommy was about, but never a sound. I anxiously waited for dawn, in the hope that I would hear him scratching at the door. But the sun arose and shone brightly and hotly, and no Tommy came. I knew that if he was in trouble he had no voice to call us, only a frightened squeak.

From dawn until nine we searched the house and grounds, looking in wardrobes, standing under trees and calling, and sending George into the roof space with a torch, but finding nothing of Tommy. By nine o'clock we knew it was no use continuing — wherever Tommy was now, he would stay until dark came.

Just before noon, the Chief Police Officer, a friend and neighbor, telephoned me:

"I hear you lost Tommy last night. Have you found him yet?"

"No."

"Bill Carlton telephoned me just now. He says that his dogs killed a civet cat last night — a cat with a magnificent pelt, that I am to have if I want. I'm afraid that sounds like Tommy."

The grief that I felt then does not sound reasonable. I know war, starvation, and death, I have read of Hiroshima and Buchenwald, I share on the radio with the grief of Europe — surely I should know better than to weep for a skunk!

The very trust we had taught Tommy to have for man and dog had betrayed him. Now I could envision it all – Tommy, thumping along our roof that night, had been called down by some new scent, then thumping along the ground in the dark thinking that the world was his playground, he had been put up by the dogs. Then, standing for a moment instead of running – that was his mistake! – he would have glared with nocturnal eyes into the dogs' red ones until suddenly he saw blood in them. In that second his body must have stiffened, his heart pounded more fiercely, his mouth opened in the terribly effortful but soundless infinitesimal call for help – before he ran! But too late! We, his friends, had taken from him by kindness his only defense of fear.

Soon the dogs would mouth ferociously the bedraggled, lifeless body of fur, while the owner came out of his safe house at the sound of barking. Good dog! Good dog! A nice pelt this! One more of those damn things dead!

I could not bear it. And I could not bear it for George.

When Harry came home at noon he took me aside to say, "Bob called me this morning. Carlton's dogs got a musang last night."

"I know. Tommy. But don't say anything to George. If Tommy just never turns up he'll soon lose the feel of him and forget, and never know how terribly he died."

"I wouldn't have minded," Harry mourned, "if he had just disappeared and gone back to the jungle the way Georgie the Musang did. Then we could know he was happy and free. But to think of the dogs getting him! Pooch was so good with him that he trusted them all."

"Those horrible black beasts of Carlton's!" I cried. "If I ever shoot anything again in this country, it won't be wild animals – it'll be these damn, damn, damn horrible dogs of his!"

On this same day one of our guinea hens had taken umbrage at her husband, and flown from our place to the other side of the road, and then whirred and scuttled through the ruins of an old house to fly up into a tall tree and make her nest. The speckled mate, her husband, refusing either to pursue her and bring her back, or to give her up, stood on the crest of our lawn from

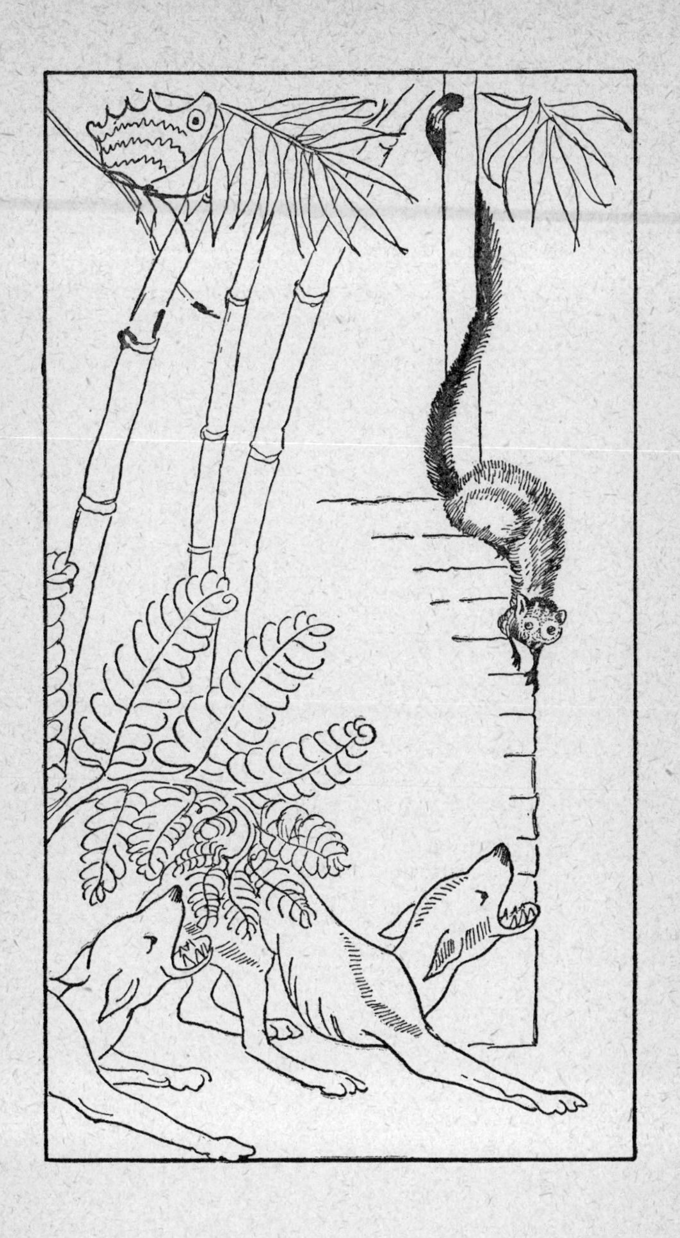

9 A.M. until 4 P.M. calling her with his inimitable voice which is like the scraping of tin being torn into pieces to the accompaniment of chalk scratching on blackboards – the voice of the guinea fowl calling for its loved one!

By four o'clock I could stand it no longer to hear the guinea fowl alive and squawking, and to know that Tommy was dead. I asked George, who had Michael and Carol with him for the day, to go down to the tree and throw pebbles at the guinea hen, with the idea that if she was driven from the tree her hubby might persuade her to return home, and then himself shut up. George dashed off, trailed by Michael and Carol. In a couple of minutes they were back, George gasping out excited words.

"Tommy's dead! They've got him! Their dogs got him! I went through the Carltons' garden on the way to the tree and they called me to come, then they held up Tommy's body by the tail and said 'Is this your musang?' "

George stops now, and looks at me in horror, while he waits for a cue for action, knowing that he cannot cry before the other children.

Then Michael, "Yes! They got your musang! The dogs got him! Yes, they did! They did! We saw him!" Michael's voice holds the tone of pleased excitement with which children always spread bad news.

And Carol, "Oh yes, they held his body up for us to see!"

I look at George, and I see that he is trying to shrug it off, and act as if he didn't care. To me, this is the worst, to have him be tough about Tommy, even to save his face. It is only decent that he should mourn for a friend.

Michael is twitching to be away. "Come, George. Let's go and play!"

George looks at me miserably for a moment. I can make no suggestions. I only know what I must do myself; I start to cry. George sees my tears with considerable embarrassment, then he turns and runs off with Michael.

Carol lingers as if wondering what to say – then sits down to read *Winnie the Pooh*, with a swish of her short skirts, and a gentle feminine adjusting of silky brown tendrils of soft childish hair which cling to her translucent, white-tropical skin. *Winnie the Pooh* will give comfort.

That night, when I kiss George good night in bed, he says, "Don't feel bad any more about Tommy, Mum. Dad'll get us another musang."

"Oh, George – !" Then I stop. There is no way to say it. Only life itself can tell him. Tommy was his pet. His pet is dead. One gets another pet.

Tommy was not my pet. Tommy belonged to life, his death was the death of life, which does not belong to any man, and part of whose strange, terrible, and beautiful essence is in its evanescence.

IV. Sailor Hat

The idea of a thousand American gobs in Sandakan haunted all responsible authorities. A dozen gobs here would make news, a thousand would make history.

"How shall we entertain them? What will they want to eat and drink?" I asked Harry. "I do hope they don't break things!"

As the only American in Sandakan, I had been consulted as authority on the habits and ways of American sailors, pending the arrival of the U.S.S. *St. Paul*, Flagship of the Seventh Task Fleet, with a complement of a thousand men, in Sandakan.

"The U.S. Navy has the best food in the world, and the sailors are probably better fed than we are," said Harry.

"How discouraging! But we must find something to give them. What is typically American? Do you think they'd like ice cream sodas?"

"No! You can't bring American sailors to the South Pacific and feed them ice cream sodas!"

"Which do you think they'd rather have, coffee or tea?"

"Don't try English coffee. They get plenty of good Java on

board ship, and I never heard of asking a sailor to tea. The Navy is dry – better give them beer."

We settled for beer, Coca-Cola, tinned biscuits and cheese, to be distributed by a volunteer canteen force in the hope of localizing damages, and then we waited anxiously for the day. The prestige of a nation rises or falls on the behavior of its visiting navy.

There is a place in the garden from which you look down on the pastel blue bay framed by the silvery trunks and shimmering foliage of the albizzia trees, and on this exact halcyon blue spot the *St. Paul* finally anchored. In perspective she seemed to bridge the bay, lying from shore to shore, and as I looked down at one of the greatest ships afloat in all her majesty, I could not help but be proud.

"Isn't she wonderful, Harry! Sometimes I don't seem to have any patriotic feelings at all, but then something like that ship happens, and I feel frightfully American!"

"Too bad she couldn't have happened in 1941!"

Sailing with the *St. Paul* was the Vice-Admiral of the Pacific Fleet, Russell Berkey, a friend of a friend of ours, a relationship which in the East makes you closer than kin. By midafternoon we had met the Admiral, discovered the friendship, and he and his party came up to the house. The Admiral was known as the Count, and he did things with a flourish, no matter whose bottle he was opening. He possessed a display of ribbons which he never wore, and medals which he didn't remember, and had friends whom he never forgot, and because he was a man to begin with, being an Admiral came easy to him.

It was three o'clock and very hot and for lack of other occupation we served tea. Harry and I had tea, Steve and John had Coca-Cola, Frank and Roy had rye, and the Admiral had Scotch on the rocks and pretzels. It was six-thirty and still hot, and we went to a cocktail party. The Count had Scotch on the rocks and cocktails, kissed the hands of the eldest ladies, and left them asking him when he would return. We went on board for dinner, and while the Count opened his air mail from Guam, rattled off orders for his ship, organized his party, and whipped out some new motion picture films, we had dinner with, of course, ice cream, and partook in the strange practice of the American Navy, of being dry when afloat.

We returned to the shore to the Club, and here the ship's band played such music as Sandakan doesn't know, and the best party I have ever seen in our town progressed from good to hilarious — such a party as could never have taken place in the segregated club for Europeans, only in prewar Sandakan. Filipina, Chinese, Indian, native and European women danced alike with all who came, the Count danced a rumba, and a samba, and a conga with as many different nationalities, I danced a rumba without knowing how, even Harry danced something, and for once in its custom-bound social life Sandakan had carefree, color-blind fun.

For two days following, in the steaming town at the foot of the hills where the faces in shops are foreign and voices speak strange tongues, where the essence of day is heat and odors of rancid oils, and the fragrance of night is frankincense, Sandakan became Little America. The brilliant colors of native groups, the harsh blue and dead black and white of Chinese costumes, were washed off the streets with the flood of sailor white; the shops were filled with gum-chewing, grinning, freckled souvenir seekers, the football field inundated with players and spectators, and only the movies were deserted, for Sandakan pictures had been seen long before by the Navy.

Every Chinese taxi bulged with leggy forms and cocky faces, every bicycle was pedaled madly by fast-moving white legs, the fourteen miles of road from the bay to the jungle's edge were a long white naval parade, and a steady stream of coasting bicycles whizzed down the steep hill into Sandakan, driving private motorcars from the road.

The sailors' ideas of money values were fantastic, and the fact that they were not cheated was charity on the part of the locals. One U.S. dollar was worth three Borneo ones, and with every purchase the sailors would pour out an uncounted palmful of Borneo currency, and let the shopkeeper make change. When the salesman counted out his due, and handed the surplus back, the sailors suffered from shock; they had never been in a town like this before, they said! What was wrong with it? They were used to being cheated! But American sailors were so rare a sight in Sandakan that nobody knew enough yet to cheat them.

The canteen was perpetually crowded and a great success. The American boys might have been accustomed to better food than we could give them, but they were overcome by the fact that we gave them anything. They helped wash the dishes in the canteen, talking steadily with everyone, especially those who knew the States.

They said, Gosh! We didn't know English folks were like this! My mother cooks like that, too! My sister looks like you! My dad says that himself! They said, Thank you, for everything, and when refreshments ran short they just sat and talked, while gratitude shone in their faces. The beer went down like water, cheese and biscuits were eaten at the tables, folded into sandwiches and chewed on the streets, and carried back to the ship in tins. We'll never forget Sandakan! they said. We sure want to come again! And Sandakan wanted them, too.

On the last morning of the ship's stay the school children were invited out to the ship and they lined up all morning waiting for launches. George felt that he had a private interest in the ship, being half American himself, and when he and the dozen British children went out with special friends they had made from the boat, he was looking forward to a wonderful time. He was away several hours, and when he arrived home just before the ship's sailing hour, I looked for a display of admiration, wonder and pride. Instead his expression was sultry.

"Well, dear, what did you think of the ship?"

"Oh, she was all right, I guess."

"Did you see all the big guns? Aren't they wonderful?"

"Oh, good enough!"

"Did you see the ice cream machine?"

"Oh, who wants to see an ice cream machine!"

"Didn't you like the ship's crew?"

"They're all right, I guess."

"George, what *is* the matter?"

"Oh, nothing, nothing! Only I don't see why that little Basil should have an American sailor hat! He's only an English boy — he's not half American like me!"

"Tell me about it, George."

"After they took us all over the boat, Basil asked the sailor if he could have one of his sailor hats, and he gave him one. And I wanted one too, only you always tell me I mustn't ask people for things. So I didn't ask, and nobody gave me one. Now Basil's got a sailor hat and I haven't, and I'm half American!"

The fault was mine, I saw that plainly, and no way to remedy it. I saw a long future ahead of me in which Basil wore his sailor hat, while George, cut to the heart, wore none, and I, the stupid moral force which said "don't ask for things," had occasioned this hatless state.

"Well, never mind, dear, in a few weeks you'll forget it all. But I am sorry you didn't get one."

"It was all your fault, Mum, and now I will *never* have an American sailor hat!" He was trying hard not to cry.

"Basil will probably lose his sailor hat," I said hopefully. "Come along, dear, let's walk up to the hilltop and wave good-by to the ship. She's under way now."

The *St. Paul* sailed out of Sandakan Bay with never a fuss or a fight, with honor to all sides, and good feeling from all, and with everybody happy with one exception — George, with a broken heart.

Basil did not lose his sailor hat. Instead he looked indescribably cute in it, and attracted everybody's attention, and for weeks all the home folks said "How very cunning!" and all the visitors said "Who is the darling youngster who wears the American sailor hat?" Every place George went, to meet the boat, to meet the plane, to say good-by to the boat, the plane, Basil went in his sailor hat. Basil got the spotlight and took the bow — and George hung back like a crippled child, feeling that not to have an American sailor hat was the equivalent of a clubfoot, or a glass eye, or wire braces on your teeth.

I hoped he would forget it after a few days, and I began to think by his actions he had. But I was wrong, he was only biding his time. Several weeks later when I was having a bath in a very great hurry, George came and stood outside my bathroom door, and shouted at me with glee.

"Hey, Ma! Ma! Basil doesn't want his sailor hat any more! So I've traded him for it!"

"What did you trade him?" suspiciously.

"Oh – I just traded him that old mechanical clown that jumps over the horse, and the toy telephone, and a few things he liked!"

But I knew that this was not nearly, nearly, nearly enough! I knew that to equal that sailor hat George would have to give all he had in the toy line. There must have been coercion someplace. I shouted back through the bathroom door:

"Well, you will have to trade it back to him tomorrow morning, because I know he won't want to lose that hat when he thinks it over. Anyway, his mother will want him to trade it back. And besides, I have told you not to trade with him because he's too young. He's three years younger than you, and it isn't fair."

"Oh, Ma! He *wanted* to trade! Honest he did. Anyway I've got the hat, and I'm going to keep it! Please say I can, Ma!"

"Well, if he still wants the trade to stand tomorrow morning, then it's O.K. But if he wants to trade back, you will have to. And I'm sure that he will want his hat back!"

Then I opened the bathroom door and there was George with the hat cocked over his eye, looking instead of the frightfully cute, awfully sweet little cinema laddie playing sailor with a big gob hat the way Basil looked – looking instead like a very young, very tough, very adolescent but genuine youngest gob in the U.S. Navy – and drunk with triumph and glee. I looked at him, and my heart hurt me for some future day when he would wear a uniform in all seriousness.

I sighed. "Well – I do hope you can keep it, dear. But don't set your heart on it, because I'm certain Basil will want it back."

The telephone rang. I answered, I listened. My telephone voice spoke.

"Yes, yes, I know he did . . . Well, I'm sorry Basil is crying and feels upset . . . I have already told George that he must trade it back tomorrow . . . No, I don't know what happened,

I was taking a bath . . . Yes, I agree that Basil is too young to trade with George . . . Yes, Basil *did* look cute in it – oh, much cuter than George! George just looks tough in it . . . Yes, I knew you wouldn't want him to trade it, dear . . . Yes, all right, they can change back in the morning."

I turned from the telephone. There was George with the hat on his head, and streaming down his cheeks were tears. To have made the trade, to have won, to have had the hat on his head – and then to lose! I could remember moments like this one all the way back through my own life, and nothing has ever made me forget their pain.

"I'm sorry, George," was all I could say.

"I won't! I won't give it back to him! The silly little . . . He traded it! I have a right to this hat, and he hasn't. He's only an English boy!" And then he broke, "Oh, Mum, I want – I want a sailor hat, Mum – and I'll *never* have one now!"

It wasn't the first time that blood had flashed in my eye and inspiration suffused my brain to comfort my son's hurt.

"Write to the Admiral!" I said.

It took two days for George to write that letter, with all the things he, and we, felt he ought to say.

Harry: "If you're asking for hats, better ask for one with gold braid on it!"

George: "Aw, I don't want one of those! I like the gob hats better!"

I: "Don't forget to tell him that you hope he comes here again."

The letter was mailed, and the waiting ensued. Every night now the Admiral was included in George's prayers, and the hat was covered by the open clause, "Please God, get me a gob hat – *somehow!*" Every mail day George questioned anxiously, "Did my sailor hat come?"

Only once did his steadfast vision falter. One night he said to me, with a hint of future maturity, "You know, Ma, I'm so anxious to get that hat! Only maybe after I get it – maybe it won't make so much difference!"

The American Navy has never been put to a severer test than

it passed through during those weeks of waiting. Finally, at 4 P.M. on a Friday, three weeks after George had mailed his letter, an air-mail folder arrived, and in it was a sailor hat from the Admiral.

That was a very important day for George; on that day the American principles of democracy and valor were vindicated forever in his heart. And the fact that the sailor hat now lies upside down on the shelf as a catchall for round, polished stones, sea shells, old clock springs, shiny nails and glass marbles, makes the memory of that day none the less valiant.

60

V. Rat Race

In Sandakan we offer three recognized ailments, malaria, dysentery, and pregnancy, the simplest of which is pregnancy. When you have a baby in Sandakan you lie down on the bed, if you have a bed, and push if you can push, and after that somebody pulls, and everything is just fine, or else just too bad. No nonsense is encouraged about this process; anesthesia, thought control, sterile delivery rooms are beyond us; I recall that a stray dog dozed under my hospital bed during the moments of George's birth, and a cat tried to get in with me. Sandakan delivery routine calls for clean hands, a private corner (not too private, as the other side of the thin partition usually has the bed of a young bachelor against it), and a big push, after which the baby cries and the womb falls.

From serious illnesses, there is little appeal. This is not the fault of the doctors we have, but of the fact that we are always short of doctors, and those we have are overworked and underpaid. There is also an insufficient number of nurses, and a shortage of drugs, medical equipment, and hospital space in which to handle serious cases, and no X-ray to assist in diagnosis.

The answer to a bad epidemic here is the graveyard, or get out. This formula applies to both Europeans and Asiatics, only more Europeans can pay for transport out, if transport is available. The first year after the war there was almost no emergency escape from Sandakan; a year later the way out was a weekly RAF plane to Singapore; now it is two planes. But the majority of local Asiatics cannot afford either air passage or a seven-day boat passage to Singapore, to discover whether they have constipation or peritonitis.

A number of infantile paralysis cases have recently developed in nearby Borneo towns. There is no iron lung in Borneo and none available from Singapore, and two children have died. The first Borneo cases appeared among a group of laborers recently imported by steamer from Sarawak, and now the disease is following the steamer's route.

Today George is ill with a virulent cold, cough and flu; infantile paralysis begins with a cold, cough or flu. Harry is away, and there is no one to tell me not to be ridiculous.

I spent the day nursing George, making him inhale steam vapors from Friar's Balsam, rubbing his chest, wiping his nose, feeding him penicillin throat lozenges, and reading aloud to keep him quiet in bed. At six o'clock I left him to drive to Sandakan and buy ice cream for his supper. When I returned ten minutes later he was outdoors riding his bicycle dressed only in pyjama pants, madly circling the flat space behind the garage, in a race with Ah Kin, on his larger bike. George was coughing, sniffling, and shouting in a hoarse croak:

"Hey! Hey! Ah Kin, I win, I win!

"Tee hee! Ah Kin! I win!"

while Ah Kin good-naturedly braked his own bike to allow George to hold the lead. I was annoyed, but reassured; George couldn't feel as badly as I thought he did.

An electrical storm in the night got me out of bed three times to close, open, close again twelve pairs of long French windows in our proud white mansion on the hill, and by that time I was wet, cold, and wide-awake. The damp air made George cough incessantly, and when I went to his room I found that although he was sleeping, his respiration was bad. For the rest of the night I alternately (1) placed him in an iron lung with his respiratory muscles paralyzed, or (2) saw him suffocating because he was not in an iron lung because there isn't one here. I also mentally prepared a cable to Malcolm MacDonald, Commissioner General in South East Asia, asking that an RAF plane be sent to Sandakan to take George to Singapore where there is an iron lung. Mentally.

By the next morning George was better, and so cantankerous that I transferred him from the iron lung to the Reformatory — and by afternoon, to the Penitentiary.

I went to the bank in the morning to cash a check and found the doors closed with a notice — Closed until further notice because of the devaluation of the pound. I turned away with the feeling of alarm and helplessness which closed bank doors give.

Ah Lin, Harry's Chief Clerk, was passing on his bicycle, and seeing me at the bank he stopped and asked if I wanted money, and how much. I said apologetically that I guessed fifteen dollars would help. Ah Lin said, "Fifteen? That's no good. I'll get you a hundred."

So we started down the road, Ah Lin wheeling his bicycle beside me, towards a Chinese shop where he said he could borrow the money. But before we were out of sight of the bank, the Assistant Manager saw me from the private office, and ran after us to say that he would cash my check. He told me the pound was now pegged at U.S. $2.80, instead of its previous U.S. $4.04 — bad news for us as we changed sterling into Canadian dollars.

Before I went back to the house, I cabled to Harry in Jesselton. I couldn't think of any appropriate words of consolation, so I just wired, "Don't worry, I don't," to show him the blow had already been broken, and that I knew that as usual our dollar had less than a hundred cents.

Time passes and now George has hurt himself — the only wonder is that he didn't kill himself. *How* do boys live to grow up? I stroke his hair gently and allow myself an instant's softness, thinking — My baby with the poor sore leg!

"Mum, you smell bad!"

"Oh — sorry! It's that antiseptic stuff I'm using for your leg, I guess. It's on my hands."

"Well, it smells worse on your hands than on my leg. That leg looks bad, eh, Mum?" George looks proudly at his leg which is propped up on a pillow on his bed. The skin is off in a long graze from ankle to groin.

"Perhaps that'll teach you to enter the bathroom through the door, instead of climbing up the outside drainpipe! You might have broken your back when you fell. Only wonder is you didn't! If you hadn't caught on the outside stairs you probably would have."

"All right, all right, all right, Ma!" George's tone is exactly like his father's, when a point has been made against him, and it's time to drop it. "All right, Ma, let's forget it. Any new comics?"

"I'll see when I'm down shopping. Now listen, George, don't you dare to get off that bed. I want you to keep your leg up. If it gets any worse the doctor will have to take you into hospital. I can't take the responsibility if you don't do what I tell you."

"Oh, Ma! I'm not going to hospital and have those nurses around me when I'm undressed!"

"Then do what I tell you and stay quiet. The doctor is afraid of infection. You rubbed a lot of dirt into your leg when you fell, and the soil around here is full of infection."

"O.K. Ma, O.K.! Who's that? Listen – somebody's calling!"

Below us from the sloping main road comes a staccato, carefully controlled call, repeated with metronomic regularity, "Jargch! . . . Jargch! . . . Jargch! . . . Jargch!"

"Pacifico! Oh, Ma," George is half out of bed, "call him up!"

"All right, all right!" – I push him back – "but don't forget to keep that foot up! And *no* roughhouse!"

Pacifico proves to be also Reynaldo, Ferdinando, and Pepito. Finding George in bed with his sores uncovered and making the most of invalidism, they stand about him with admiring gazes, while George describes the accident.

"My fadda he tell me not to go up dat drainpipe, eh, Pacifico? But always I am smart with climbing. You know dat, Pacifico, yes?"

Pacifico nods, proud to know this intimate detail. George's narrative continues well embellished, and I leave him the happy center of misfortune and excitement. In half an hour I return with the latest assortment of comics from Singapore which I have with difficulty inveigled away from the newsstand hordes of small, glowing-eyed Malay boys with their Muslim hats knocked crooked in the push, from Indian lads whose eyes flash and whose white teeth gleam with joy at the antics of newspaper apes, and from chattering, tenacious Chinese urchins, whose little blue-trousered backsides press eagerly forward as they snatch for their modicum of romance and allure, brought to Sandakan this day in the Singapore mail.

At home, I am greeted with cries of welcome from all, and everything is pushed aside, toys shoved hastily off the bed, ginger beer glasses upset in the rush, and the sore leg almost sat upon, while four heads of black patent-leather hair and one of tousled fawn bump against each other in amicable excitement in the breathless pursuit of the adventures of Lightning-throwing, Death-defying, Atom-blasting Superman, who brings terror to the jungles of Malaya, and joy to the lives of striplings.

Silence, practically breathless, ensues for an hour. When with the coming of early tropical dusk I suggest to the visitors that it is time to start home, they courteously agree and each one calls graciously back as he leaves, "Tank you, Jargch! Goot-by. Tank you, Jargch! Goot-by!"

And George answers happily, "Goot-by, Pacifico! Goot-by, Reynaldo! Ferdinando! Pepito!" Then hastily, "Oh, Pacifico! *Mari-la!* Come back! I tella you someting!"

Little indigo-shirted Pacifico, quick as lightning in his movements both mental and physical, zips upstairs again to the side of his bedridden friend, and a long, whispered conversation follows, while the other three wait on the lawn, gazing bright-eyed into space, their pants pockets bulging with broken mechanical toys which will be reconstructed when they get home to comfort their juniors of whom there are bound to be many, and their little brains still whizzing at supersonic speed with Superman. When Pacifico rejoins the group a burst of chattered Malay tells me that George's sore leg and its treatment are the subject of the conversation again, and I am touched to think that his leg can rival Superman.

"Goot-by, Pacifico! Reynaldo! Ferdinando! Pepito! Goot-by!" George's clear voice from the upstairs tells me that he has hopped to the window and is calling out of it, despite my instructions.

"Get back to bed, George!" I shout.

The next day the leg is neither better nor worse, the flesh is still open and oozing, but there are no signs of infection. In the afternoon I am glad to welcome a visit from Pacifico as a means of keeping George both happy and quiet, especially so as Harry and I are going out for the evening. The two boys are playing contentedly together, George's leg propped up on the pillow, and having thought of everything I can to tell them not to do, we leave. We return at ten o'clock to find Pacifico away, George sound asleep, and everything in order.

Next morning early I hurry in to inspect the leg, the third day being the crucial one with infections. A terrifying sight confronts me. My child's naked leg lies on the white pillow, black from ankle to groin, and covered with a black, thick scab. George himself is awake, and looking surprised, but not pained.

"George! Your leg! What have you done to it?"

"Nothing, Mum."

"You've put something on it! You must have. It's awful!"

"No, Mum, I didn't put anything on it. It's O.K."

"Do you feel sick, dear? Do you think you have a temperature? That leg! I can't bear to look at it. Are you sick?"

"No, Mum, I'm fine. Don't make a fuss, Mum. It's nothing." He tries to cover his leg.

I grab his hand.

"Don't! Don't touch it. I'll get the doctor."

"Aw, Mum, don't fuss. Can Pacifico come up this afternoon? Will you telephone his dad for him to come?"

"I don't know, I must find out about your leg first. I never saw anything like it. Are you sure it isn't hurting you worse today?"

"No, Mum."

"I'll have to call the doctor. I wouldn't dare let it go."

"Oh, no, Mum!"

"Yes, I must."

The doctor comes.

"Very alarming! I never saw anything quite like it. There's always tetanus to be feared around these parts, you know. You haven't been using any medicine besides the ointment I gave you?"

"Oh, no, Doctor, just the antiseptic ointment."

"Well, I'll have to take him to the hospital and give him anti-tetanus treatment."

Shouts from George, "No, Doctor, no! Not the hospital, please! My leg's *not* worse."

"Now, George, your leg may be in a very dangerous condition," the doctor urges.

"Yes, dear, it may be very dangerous! You don't want to lose your leg, do you? Something alarming has happened to make it turn black. You must go right into hospital and let the doctor give you antitetanus shots. It's no use arguing."

"Oh, no, Mum, please! I don't want to go to hospital! That black is snake bite medicine that Pacifico bought in market yesterday from the Indian fakir. It's guaranteed to cure snake bite, and Pacifico and I thought it would cure my leg. Honest, Mum, that's all it is. Pacifico just did it to make me better. Honest!"

Relief fights with indignation. "But I asked you! . . . But you told me! . . . But you *said* you hadn't put anything on your leg!"

"I didn't, Mum, honest! Pacifico rubbed it on. You should see the snake bites the man in the market cured with it! Pacifico said he reckoned it would cure most anything! See, Mum, here it is – here's the bottle."

George leans over and fishes under the bed, the ordinary hide-out of empty ginger beer bottles. He brings up a dirty, quarter-filled beer bottle with a thick, dark liquid inside. "And you know, Mum, Pacifico had to pay a lot of money to get it for me! Wasn't that kind of him?"

The doctor leaves soon after, with little to say. Pacifico arrives for the afternoon. George gets up, and they play cowboys in his room, both boys armed with water pistols. I guess if that leg isn't infected now, germs aren't as strong as legs are.

Ah Sing the gardener appeared with his year-old son, Ah Ping, in his arms.

"Baby sick two days, Missee. Very hot now."

I felt the baby's forehead and neck, and he was very hot; I took his temperature and it was 104°.

"You must take baby to hospital. I give you chit for doctor."

"More better you give medicine, Missee. This doctor always angry."

"Nonsense! Don't be so silly, Ah Sing. He isn't angry, he just sounds that way. Today, I give you medicine for baby. If baby better tonight, O.K. If not better, tomorrow you take baby to doctor."

Ah Sing agreed with relief. He and his Hylam wife, Ah Li, had both been in Sandakan throughout the war, and I knew they were suffering from a chronic state of malaria and undernourishment, which they had not been rid of for years. The baby no doubt had malaria, and was obviously teething, so I gave it a dose of milk of magnesia and a small dose of eau-quinine, the form of quinine best adapted to children and one which I always kept on hand for George. As Ah Sing's wife lived three miles away at her brother's truck garden, and was employed all day burning garbage, I told Ah Sing that the baby must remain at our house with him, if I was to be responsible for the child.

Evening came and Ah Ping's temperature was 105°. I gave him sponge baths throughout the night, and determined that when morning came he must be taken to the doctor. The child obviously had malaria, but I was not certain how much quinine I dared to give, and did not like to fool with a high temperature when there might be complications.

Before drinking my coffee in the morning I wrote a note to the doctor asking for medical care for the sick babe, and sent Ah Sing to fetch Ah Li from her garbage burning, then sent the three of them to the hospital. An hour later as I was sitting at my desk writing, and hoping that I had succeeded in passing on the responsibility of a sick infant to the proper quarters, I heard the blood-chilling, unrestrained, all-out wailing with which the inscrutable Chinese loudly meets emotional upsets. I looked out of the window and saw Ah Sing and Ah Li with their shiny black heads bowed over the cloth-swaddled bundle in their arms. I hurried down to the door to meet them with fear gripping my heart.

"What's the matter?" I called. "The baby? Ah Ping?"

Wailing increased as they approached, but no explanation. As they entered the house I grabbed at the swaddling cloth that covered the infant's face and pulled it down, and to my great and happy relief the child started to bellow, and although his little face was rust-red through his yellow skin with fever, he obviously had energy still to yell.

"For God's sake stop your noise, Ah Sing, and tell me what's the matter! The baby's not dead, anyway."

"Doctor poison baby!" Ah Sing sobbed. "Doctor put poison down Ah Ping! I very frightened. Baby die soon!"

"Don't be silly! What do you mean, the doctor poisoned the baby? Now tell me just what happened."

"Doctor take Ah Ping's blood and look. He say have got fever. Ah Ping must stay hospital. He say baby's momma stay too. But she not like to stay because she have work to do burning garbage, and she say no can stay. Doctor angry, so I tell doctor, Never mind, Missee will give medicine, I take baby to Missee! Then doctor more angry. He say No! You leave baby hospital, you Chinese . . . ! I frightened because doctor very angry. But I say No – doctor please give me medicine for baby. I take baby home to Missee. She take care. Doctor more angry. He shout, No. Hospital good for sick baby. You take baby away, baby die! Doctor swear plenty."

"But why didn't you leave baby in hospital, Ah Sing? That's what I told you to do. The doctor was right."

"I no leave baby in hospital because too many sick people there. I no like baby with sick people. So I tell doctor never mind! More better I take baby to Missee. She got plenty medicine, all kinds medicine."

I could imagine the doctor's expression at the substitution of the Keith nursing home and my doctoring, for his. "Well, go on, Ah Sing. What then?"

"Doctor more angry and shout more. He tell dresser bring medicine. Medicine come. He take Ah Ping and hold nose and make medicine go down. He tell me take medicine away, take baby away, go away!"

"Well, isn't that what you wanted, Ah Sing?" But my heart sinks at the thought that I am still responsible for the administration of the medicines. "What are you crying about?"

"Because doctor very angry now, he like to kill baby. He put poison in medicine, and now baby die."

I look at Ah Sing marveling; he believes it! To him it is perfectly reasonable that this strange, indignant white man must take revenge in some way – and the helpless Ah Ping is the perfect victim!

"Ah Sing, give me that medicine the doctor gave you."

Ah Sing hands me a bottle of clear liquid, and a small package. I open the latter and it contains a dozen tiny packets filled with shining white powder. I taste one and decide it is aspirin.

"Which medicine did doctor give Ah Ping in hospital?" I demand.

"He put bottle medicine down throat."

"And you think it is poison?"

Ah Sing nods his head. "Yes, Missee, for sure poison!"

I pull out the cork, put my mouth to the bottle's mouth and take a good, big swallow. It is terrible tasting stuff, but not poison; it is liquid quinine. My expression at the bitter taste is not reassuring, but it is obvious that if death is to be dealt out of that bottle, I as well as the baby will soon be dead. Ah Sing looks at me with goggled eyes, and even the baby ceases howling and waits for me to die.

"All right, Ah Sing," I say. "If I die, never mind give baby any more medicine tomorrow. But if I no die, tomorrow you give baby two medicines like doctor say. Now put baby to bed. And bring me a glass of water!"

Ah Li giggles hysterically. But Ah Sing does not give up his point easily.

"If you get sick, Missee, I call Misiter quick. He kill doctor!"

The mouse house is a small, perfect, mouse-size establishment built in miniature on the principles of government housing, being approximately a square box, six inches by six by eight, freshly painted outside with a hole in the floor for plumbing, and fully equipped for the needs of modern mice in substantial but unpretentious positions. The edifice has a glass front through which you may follow the activities of the occupants on two levels, and the upper and lower stories are connected by a slide. The upper floor is semi-secluded by half-partitions for purposes of mouse repose, but the lower floor is in open view of the onlookers, and here is installed the perfect machinery for government offices, a mouse wheel.

As soon as the slumbering mice awaken and move about upstairs, they automatically trip through the opening in the floor, are precipitated down the slide and onto the wheel, where they tread conscientiously and tirelessly until hunger or exhaustion diverts them. The minimum food for maximum mouse needs is placed in the receptacle just behind the wheel, and when the mouse lags, he notices it and stops for a nibble. Then with vigor renewed, his first revived step will take him onto the mouse wheel again. Harry calls the whole setup "the Secretariat."

This typically Chinese joke on mice and men was brought by Ah Kin from Hong Kong for George some months ago, with four white mice occupants. George was crazy about them at first; to see these helpless little living forces compelled by the urge to survive, to go through the motions of existence under glass before him, fascinated him. But soon the sameness of their daily routine began to bore him, their blind following of instinct palled, their lack of free will and originality made him call them stupid, and the perpetual clicking of the mouse wheel through the night annoyed him. The daily acts of a mouse's existence, which had once been so fascinating, ceased to be so. Soon the mouse house stood at the end of the sideboard, and everybody wished that the Secretariat would close down, but nobody had the heart to make it. We could not let the mice loose in the house for fear of destruction by our domestic animals, nor in the jungle for fear of wild ones.

Then mortality struck. The all-white mouse died suddenly from eating buttered toast crumbs (no butter on mice-toast, Ah San told me later), and another one died of shock when George transferred the mice momentarily to the goldfish bowl, while he was washing the mouse house. Today, the third one ate his way out of the house, got lost in the luggage in the upper hall, and met death under my wardrobe trunk when it was hastily moved in the search.

Tonight, when I came in the house at midnight after dinner with friends, the first thing I heard was the click-click of the mouse wheel. I shone my flashlight and saw the little, lone white-and-tan riding his mouse wheel madly, earnestly, ambitiously, as if it would get him someplace – much as man rides the wheel of progress. And all night long I could hear the sound of the little mouse going forward.

It seemed to me a forecast of the state of the human world, after we drop enough super bombs on all who interrupt our progress, or tempt us to cuddle lovingly in corners. There will be nothing left for us then but to ride the wheel night and day.

In George's mind, the two mice who died first will always be remembered as the best – they died before boredom set in. My favorite is the one who ate his way out through the wooden roof; that took great courage, to break through instinct and tradition, and risk security. Now the final fellow still treads out his mouse destiny in the little house while the cat stares at him savagely, the dog paces alarmingly nearby, Ah Min bumps into his house as she passes causing a major quake, and I mention wearily that the house, the once busy Secretariat, smells bad, and George complains that he can't be bothered to wash it.

George loves birds. Yet George shoots birds with slingshot and gun. George finds a wounded bird on the road with shot in it, and he brings it home to me to nurse and revive; he breaks a bird's wing with a sling, and he picks it up and asks me to splint it and make it well.

George loves doves. The other day I arrived home to find him on the grass nursing a wounded white dove from our dovecote, one more victim of the hungry, five-foot monitor lizard in the garden. Eight months ago we stocked the dovecote with twelve doves, now there are only four, the rest all having been pounced on, dragged away and consumed by the scaly monster who inhabits the valley below the wilder slopes of the garden.

At hungry intervals the lizard visits the domesticated upper stretches of turf, and lies like a rotten log half hidden in long grass at the edge of the sunny slope where the doves feed. There with slathering jaws twitching and saliva drooling through reptilian teeth, he waits; the doves peck, and hop, peck and flutter, their wings chalky white, their eyes glowing ruby red; the lizard slithers out, snatches, and slithers away, and the doves whiz upward, one dove less.

We have seen this ugly, crawling visitor vanishing in the distance, we have run out after him with a gun, we have chased him to find his hidden lurking place, but always by the time we get there he has again become successfully a part of the jungle background. Although my sympathy is with the doves, being always on the side of beauty against the beast, their stupidity annoys me. It seems to me that when eight have been taken in the same fashion, the survivors might learn to keep watch while feeding on the ground.

We tried throwing their feed in other places, but the doves returned hungrily to the lawn; then we moved the dovecote, but the doves refused to follow. Instead they fluttered confusedly about and finally came to roost in the big albizzia tree nearby, which situation left them open to the attacks of kites and snakes as well as the lizard. So we returned the dovecote to its place, and left survival to solve itself, with odds on the lizard.

Today, from his bedroom, George saw the doves whiz suddenly up from the lawn, and knew danger threatened. He ran to the garden to see the lizard disappearing with a dove in his mouth. He threw a stone, hit the lizard in the head, the lizard dropped the dove and disappeared into the underbrush.

When I arrived George was examining the wounded bird. She had a bloody wound on her back where the lizard had buried his teeth, a gaping hole under one wing, a broken foot, and a bitten tail, and she could neither stand nor fly. I thought she must surely die and I wanted to put her out of pain, but George was so certain I could doctor her successfully and he begged so earnestly for her life that I gave him a little lecture on the sanctity of life and brought her into the house, and bathed her in a warm solution of mild disinfectant. She was shivering with terror and chill, and I wrapped her in a soft, warm towel and placed her in a small cage with water and corn, and hung the cage in George's bedroom high enough to escape the fierce, threatening gaze of the jealous cat.

The dove lay quietly for several days, with her ruby eyes unblinking and the ruby holes gaping through her soft white feathers, while each day we bathed the wounds in disinfectant. The fourth day as I was working with her she hopped up on her good foot, balancing with difficulty as she couldn't lift one wing, and from then on she stayed on one foot. Apparently she didn't eat at all, as the quantity of her corn remained the same.

Ten days later I had her out of the cage and was bathing her healing wounds when she fluttered both wings in a trial of strength, then with an excess of flapping flew out of the French window, across the lawn, and up to the albizzia, where she took up her stand on one foot again, soon to be joined by the other three doves, all very solicitous. George was disappointed, as he had hoped she would become tame.

Some days later we noticed that she was always perched on the mass of elkhorn fern in the first branch of the albizzia. George climbed the nearby papaya tree for investigation, and came down saying that she had built a nest in the heart of the fern. In time he reported there were eggs in the nest, and now she spent little time on the ground.

Then one day I heard a call from the garden, "Mum! The eggs are gone!"

I hurried out to find George in the top of the bending papaya tree, imperiling the season's papaya crop which was just turning faintly golden, as each oval, emerald fruit clung, delicately attached, in the crotch of a smooth, green branch. The tree was bending under George's excited weight as he strove to make certain that the dove's nest was really empty. The mother dove was feeding nonchalantly on the grass.

"They're gone, Mum, and there are no baby birds, either! Oh, damn that lizard! Oh, I wish Dad would find his hole and kill him!"

"That big lizard couldn't get so high up the tree. A python has taken the eggs, I'm sure. If the mother had had sense enough to make her nest in the dovecote, the snake might not have gotten them."

"Gee, Mum, I was going to catch those baby birds and bring them up to be tame!"

"Oh, weren't you going to shoot them?"

George looks both abashed and wounded. The battle about shooting birds is an old one.

"Not doves, Mum!"

"Well, anyway the snake took the eggs for food. But when you shoot birds you do it for what you call fun. If a lizard gets a dove, you ask me to nurse it back to life, if a snake takes the eggs you feel sorry. And when you shoot birds I feel sorry. Now what's the difference between the lizard, the snake, and you—except your skins?"

"I'm sorry, Mum!"

I had taken unfair advantage, but I don't give up this battle easily. Boys kill to test their own skill, and to show prowess in competition: if they can once come to believe in the value of life to every living being, they may grow further from the stupidity of human destroying human.

PART FOUR

Golden Rain

Golden rain in other lands,
Icy rain in mine –
Better mine for me.

– From a Malay Proverb

I. Bird's Nest Caves

THERE is a long slow, brown, warm stretch of river in North Borneo which is known as the Kinabatangan, and is the greatest volume of mud and crocodiles in the country. Watching the turbid water of the river's mouth where it muddies the clear bay, it seems impossible that this same liquid once raced down steep stream beds, threw itself recklessly over glistening white stones and polished moon-white boulders in the violence of its first fine, free, turbulent descent towards the Sulu Sea and Sandakan.

This river takes its way unsung through a country that is little known to those who won't take time for native boat and carrier travel. It is along these upper stretches of the Kinabatangan that Borneo myths and legends flourish and flower, rooted deep in native mud and native minds. Up this river, Borneo ceases to be British or Chinese, and reverts to its own tribesmen, becoming a country of primitive customs with primitive virtues and vices. It is up this river that civilization should spread, as it has done up the waterways of many countries, and could do in North Borneo – but hasn't.

Occasionally oil company geologists or Government officers stagger up the river on foot, or journey up by Government launch, touching for a couple of hours at Government stations, and making entries in notebooks about metamorphic rocks or sedimentary governments. After five or ten days' travel up the river, according to the depth or shallowness, the ebb or flood, of its water, they return to Sandakan, the geologists to write Yes or No, to the one question that interests them; the officers to write a Government report saying that the need is great to have European Government personnel stationed far up the Kinabatangan, that it is imperative to have regular medical attention and drugs carried up this waterway to spread from its distributing centers into all primitive living, that primary education in hygiene and child welfare must go with these things hand in hand, and that scholastic education and agricultural guidance must follow before there will be prosperity. This report is then sent to and engulfed by The Authority with one or two possible results – no money, or no answer.

Still further above this region which is exposed to the visitations of Government officers, the tributaries of the slow-moving Kinabatangan rise in tall mountain ranges where the air is clean and cool, where white water dashes down through handsomely forested hills and country which has little in common with the mangrove and nipa covered stretches below. Least romantic of rivers as it opens its muddy mouth, yet its course from headwaters to the sea is actually the unwritten saga of primitive peoples evolving into twentieth-century ones.

In the year 1880, a fiery little man named Pengiran Digadong Samah ruled the Kinabatangan. Shriveled and brown, with legs like mangrove roots, fists like elephant hide, sad, bright, liquid eyes of a Pekinese, and a conscience that was not his guide, he was a man who with wider opportunity, modern weapons and ways, and a geopolitical outlook, might have challenged national boundaries and liquidated world states. As it was he ruled his river in Borneo with native poisons, knives, and daggers, blackmail, and a fierce cruel cunning.

It was a day when human sacrifices were made to pagan gods, when head hunting was a happy pastime and human heads hung from native roofs as coconuts hang from trees, and the bird's nest caves were to early Borneo what gold was to pioneer California. The Gomantong Caves alone on the Kinabatangan produced $25,000 worth of nests yearly, a huge fortune in those days,

PENGIRAN DIGADONG SAMAH

and this sum represented the greatest native wealth in all North Borneo. Possession of these caves was claimed by a peaceful, timid, native tribe, the Buludupies, whose leadership Pengiran Digadong Samah had forcibly acquired by being the opposite of peaceful and timid. Soon the Pengiran came to consider the caves as his own private property, although he still generously permitted his tribesmen to do the work of collecting the nests, a specialist's job for which their life training fitted them, of climbing to great heights on bamboo poles and rattan ladders.

In addition to bird's nest marketing the Pengiran ran other rackets. He strung rattan across the river and when a boat passed up or down he collected tithes from the occupants, and also collected taxes from neighboring villages. If spies were sent to outwit him he plied them with wine and women, or poison, until they went to bed or the grave.

Being a sturdy individualist and not one to go along with progress, when the states comprising North Borneo were turned over to the Chartered Company and the white man came to rule, the Pengiran did not fall into line. He continued to collect taxes, distribute poison, hack up his enemies, promote his friends and collect wives—and his favorite song became his "death song" which he sang many times, without dying:

> I am a Buludupi man
> I have always ruled the Kinabatangan
> No one—Suluk savage, Bajau pirate, nor white man—
> Shall take the river from me.

Finally a time came when the police of the white men had enough of this rugged individualism, and they went up the river with guns. But this wasn't the old story of the native who had no guns: the Kinabatangan people under the Digadong's tutelage had old muzzle-loaders and tower muskets, and in addition to blowpipes, knives and poison, they met the police with these. When the white men saw the natives with guns, the Digadong's last chance was gone. The guns spoke, the Buludupies' decadent muskets lost aim, exploded, went wild. Not so the white man's—Pengiran Digadong Samah fell, and a legend was done.

With his death we can only guess what rejoicing there was among other tribes, what relief among his own, what sorrow among his wives who adored him, and what tears from his three small children, for that story is not told.

What is told is that the Government confiscated the Gomantong Caves. From then on Government hired contractors to work the caves and collect the birds' nests, Government to keep one half the gross profits, and the contractors and their hired labor the other half. For the people who had once owned the nests there was nothing, except that the work of collecting must be done by them for a share in the contractor's profits.

Today, the most satisfying source of revenue to both natives and Government is the harvesting, sale, and export to China of birds' nests from the fifteen famous cave groups of North Borneo which are a byword wherever bird's nest soup is sipped. The bird's nest industry now brings yearly to this country almost $100,000, plus a goodly sum for export duty, all acquired at the expense of the birds alone.

The vital ingredient of bird's nest soup is not feathers, sticks, twigs, or grass – but, as is known to epicures, it is the inspissated saliva of adult swiftlets. This is a secretion from the salivary glands of certain swiftlets, with which they make their nests. The saliva hardens on exposure to the air into something like isinglass, and this is the edible ingredient of birds' nests.

Nests are attached at great and inaccessible heights inside the inky chambers of the limestone caves when the nest-building urge comes to the small, dark-plumaged, white-bellied swiftlet. When nests are completed and eggs are ready for hatching, both nest and eggs are collected by natives, leaving the frantic swiftlet balked of its mission. Once, twice, and a third time the bird makes its nest every year, and the third time the swiftlet is permitted to hatch her eggs and the nests are not taken until after the birds are fledged. Even then, nests are sometimes taken too hurriedly, and many of the immature fledglings fall to the floor of the cave, to die or be eaten by cockroaches. If nests are taken more than three times in one year, the bird becomes exhausted and frustrated, refuses to build another nest, and its posterity is lost.

The nests are classified as black or white by their color, which is determined by the species of swiftlet which makes them. Nests are collected by expert native climbers from several tribes, among these the original Buludupies, and the Orang Sungei, who with lifetime training mount rattan ladders to daring heights of four to nine hundred feet to steal the nests.

The caves are also inhabited by myriads of bats, and the winging beat of their startled flight floods the caves with eerie sound as the intruder feels his way through darkness, drawing his breath with acrid distress from the ammoniated fumes of bat dirt. Feeling his way over the damp floor of the caves he creeps over a moving, seething mass of cockroaches and cave centipedes, as he looks upwards in vain for a view of the nests. Not until climbers mount and light the cavern roof with torches and candles will he see the drab, nonspectacular, grayish cups clinging far above him to damp cave walls – cups which mean home to the swiftlets, and epicurean soup in China.

Birds' nests are classified in North Borneo as forest produce, and in most cases the caves are in Forest Reserves. For this reason the harvesting, revenue, responsibility for and conservation of the industry, except in the case of a few native-owned caves, is in the hands of the Forest Department, and is of vital interest to Harry. My own first nightmare jungle trip in 1935 was to the most famous of all bird's nest factories the Gomantong Caves, and so is George's to be, years later.

"Now don't worry about him, dear, Gomantong is the obvious place to take a beginner – it's a fairly easy trip," says Harry.

"Easy! I thought I'd never live to get home! That was years ago and I haven't forgotten a minute of it. Or how I hated you when you pranced ahead of me looking so fit and happy. If I didn't murder you that day, I never will."

"But you insisted on coming!"

"I didn't know any better then."

"Well, I always told you the trips were too tough for you."

"They weren't! I'm glad of every trip I ever took – only I'm not going again."

"Don't worry about George," Harry says quietly. "This isn't a hard trip, the way we are making it. When you and I went to the caves we went there and back in a day. That was almost a record."

"*I* thought it was a record!"

"Yes, it was good going. But George and I are taking five days, and going upriver by launch and back by the new trace, the new route for the bird's nest people to bring the nests down to Sandakan. If there is any possibility of making the track into a jeep trail I'm going to do so – that would speed up collecting and marketing of nests. At present it's only a freshly blazed trace, crossing and recrossing streams, and I imagine the log bridges will be out since the rains. But don't worry about George. I'll take care of him."

"All I can say is that you and George will know a lot more about each other by the time you come home!" I answer hopefully.

In the land of Borneo there are two kingdoms for the sojourner to inhabit; one is the small town life of big town Sandakan and Jesselton, with pseudo society, synthetic gaiety, mock amenities, and easy, costly living. Here European adults and a handful of children follow a quasi-civilized curriculum as a substitute for real life, here nothing is genuine and the best is only an imitation good enough for the far east, and life itself is not rooted in reality.

But there is another Borneo which has little to do with the city way, and in this land to have a white skin, pale face, long legs, and leather shoes is a disadvantage. A tough brown hide, a short body with balance near the ground, and lifelong calluses on a pair of bare feet, mark the aristocrat. This is a life of discomfort, uncertainty, and adventure, breeding a flat stomach, strong legs, and an appetite, and the hero of this Borneo is not the aristocrat of the town.

The damp wind whips at your face, the thorned vines tear at your hair in the jungle, crocodiles threaten your bath in muddy rivers, and exhaustion, despair, and leeches stumble into bed with you each night. One night you sleep under a moon like a ripe melon with stars like peelings of tin and praise God for its beauty, the next night under a sky like a broken drain when the storms come down. Mosquitoes and sandflies bite you till morning, you sleep scratching, and awake aching, you are never clean, and never comfortable, you curse it and hate it and swear you'll never go again if you live to get home this time—but you do go again, and you know in your heart it is this for which you were born.

You learn to know those things by which man lives—the knowledge of strength in himself, the joy of struggle, and the making of himself one with the things against which he struggles—one with the earth, sky, water, fire, storm, and every living, breathing, restless thing, and this knowledge leaves you more respecting of nature and less respecting of self. This was a Borneo Harry and I had traveled together; now it was George's turn. For the next seven days I went to the jungle with him, in mind, as intensely as I had ever gone in body.

I spread my raincoat on the long wild grass under the lone tree in the cleared circle of sunlight cut from the jungle darkness, and lie down to wait. It is high noon at Pengkalan Suan Lamba up the River Lanut, and I have come to meet husband and son a week later at the end of the jungle track. George should know now what the jungle is like.

The Dusuns working in the jungle here are still cutting the unfinished track from this end to meet the trace to Gomantong Caves, and they tell me I am foolish to wait; the track is only blazed trees, the bridges are down, and no party with a child can travel nine miles from the caves in a morning.

But Harry has said he'll be here. I decide to wait in comfort lying down in the shade, and no sooner have I touched the ground than my ear catches a new sound. High above the layers of steaming air which hang over the jungle comes a shrill, human note penetrating even the insects' whine.

Quickly I call, "George! Oh, George!"

"Ma! Hi, Ma!" comes the faint answer.

I jump to my feet and stare towards the stretch of metallic green grass and scrub, taller than man in height, which stretches like a glittering thicket between the clearing and the jungle. Soon its shimmering surface undulates as if being parted from below by the passage of bodies, and as the green wave moves towards me I see glimpses of skins through the grass, and then I distinguish Harry and George, followed by others. Of George, I can only see blue bathing trunks, and the fact that he is triumphantly in the lead. What he was like behind the trees is not shown.

His voice comes in snatches as he shrieks the news to me—"Shot a croc . . . a pig . . . red monkeys . . . Dad and I . . . fun!" in the effort to let me know immediately what a trip they had. And there is something about that intentionally high, penetrating child's tone which says to me even across the grass and space, "I have made a man's trip with men, Ma – and now I must be treated as one!" While I still scarcely see him I hear in his tone that the jungle has not left him as it does me, humble and hobbling.

Now he is near, and the first thing he says is, "Ma, I'm going to the jungle with Dad again next time. I want to go, and Dad says I can, too."

I look questioningly at Harry. "Didn't he ever reach the zero hour? The one *I* always hit when I swear that I won't ever, ever, ever, go again?"

Harry smiles discreetly. "I believe he did say something about never believing anything I said, when I told him for the last hour before getting here that the river wasn't much further away. This morning was quite a test – but just the same – he wants to go again!"

"Well, tell me!" I urge. "Tell me more – tell me all about the trip. What happened?"

"Oh . . . nothing. We just made the trip – and here we are home – and on time."

"You mean that in seven days in the jungle nothing happened?"

"Well, nothing unusual. It takes you to sweat the last drop of anguish out of the elements!"

I turn hopefully to George. "You tell me, George. Tell me all about it, dear. What happened?"

But George takes his line from Harry. Laconically, "Oh, nothing much. Mum, is the bear O.K.?"

This is too much! Am I to know nothing about my son's first trip?

At home that night: "Harry, may I see your diary of the trip? The part about the caves?"

"Here you are."

Diary: "Arrived at Caves 7 A.M. on foot. Climbed hill (1200 feet), and entered caves through Semud Puteh. Very spectacular, and George enjoyed it. Kulibabang Besar just being rigged and collected. This cave has not been collected since before the war, and all the rattan climbing gear rotted and fell to pieces and had to be replaced. Men actually now collecting at top of fragile bamboo ladders with recesses of cave dimly lit by flickering torches. Quite spectacular. Agnes would like it. George in fine form all along."

"Oh, Harry, I wish I'd gone!" In spite of myself I remember the lure of those eerie caves. "And were the cockroaches and centipedes still thick on the ground? And did you have to squirm over them on your stomach in the dark to get down into the cave?"

"Well, it was worth it. It was the third collection of this year in the largest chamber of Semud Puteh. Some of the nests had been taken too early, and the floor of the cave had numbers of fledglings too young to fly; they had fallen out when the nests were taken. George and I picked up a number and tossed them into the air or put them on ledges. I told the contractor he must see that it doesn't happen again. Of course, he claimed that the mothers had pushed the fledglings out too soon, and the nests were already empty when collected. But if they do it again the birds won't nest next year."

"Were they collecting the highest parts? That's really exciting to watch."

"I've never seen them collect as high as this time, some of the men in the top gallery were about a hundred feet above the cave floor. It's certainly a specialist's job. I don't think a white man could do it, using such primitive gear. The native build is perfectly suited to climbing, small, compact, tough, hard, and they use their hands and feet in an almost prehensile way. George was crazy to be up there with them. He's the right size, and pretty good at climbing. But I thought about what you'd say if I came home without him."

"Not that *you* care much about him!"

"He gets on well with natives. He has about the same mental capacity, at the age of eight. They are extraordinarily gentle with him – with their own children too. No native ever strikes a child."

"He's having some unusual experiences. Do you suppose he'll remember any of it? Has any of it any use for him in his future life?"

"It's always some use to know that all people are human."

Yes, that was use, I reminded myself – the biggest use that anybody could get out of learning – to know that all men are human.

Later that night as George goes to bed, I say hopefully, "George, dear, you haven't told me anything at all about the trip. What did you like best of all?"

"I liked the little birds that fell out of their nests in the cave, and we picked up. I wanted to bring one home, but Dad said it would die before we got here."

"What did you see that was most exciting?"

"Oh . . . nothing. Except an elephant."

"Where was he?"

"Standing by the Gomantong Caves track. His stomach was rumbling."

"What did he look like?"

"Oh – just like an elephant."

"Wasn't that exciting? Weren't you surprised?"

"No, not much, we were looking for an elephant. I say, Mum, did you know that Galpan, he's the bird's nest cave contractor and a great friend of mine, Galpan's going to bring me a baby tree shrew the next time he comes to Sandakan? And Dad says I can keep it, too."

"Yes, dear, of course. So it was a good trip, eh?"

"Oh, sure, Mum. But nothing much happened."

To meet it all as a child does, I thought, without surprise, or hurt, or excitement, or indignation or apprehension, or preconceived prejudice – just to meet life as it comes – that's wonderful! But that is what makes a child a child.

Unless you know jungle travel you will think it ridiculous that a limestone hill full of sizable caves is lost, when it is within a known radius of seven miles. But if you feel about mileage in the jungle as I do, there is good reason to let the caves remain lost.

However, the Buludupies, Orang Sungei, and Dusuns, to whom jungle miles are nothing, will give you what is to them a more practical explanation for the fact that the lost bird's nest caves, despite their reported fabulous value which is greater even than the Gomantong Caves, remain both lost and unexplored. The natives will not talk of weather, broken bridges, or mud, but of a dark, evil, all-powerful Spirit, a Shaitan, who guards the approach to the caves. They will tell you that upon the tread of any mortal foot in this vicinity the lurking, vigilant Spirit deluges the jungle with torrential rain, thunder and lightning, and makes arrival at the caves impossible. And if the Spirit for a moment sleeps, and a human being successfully invades his privacy, the retribution on him is worse even than the angry elements – it is the loss of the thing the native values most greatly – the loss of posterity.

High up the flooding Kinabatangan where legends take on visible proof as legends always do for those who believe in them, I met a man who met a man who knew a man who once saw the Shaitan. From this first-hand evidence I give my story.

Some years ago a middle-aged, short-bodied, splay-footed little Dusun with a family to feed and support was out in the jungle hunting wild pig when he fell through a tangle of creepers into an acrid-smelling hole in the ground. This proved upon exploration to be the entrance to a series of caves, deeper, darker, larger, more rich in bats and bird's nests than even Gomantong Caves. Exhausted by his day of hunting, the little man of the jungle lay down in the caves to rest, and fell asleep and dreamed exultantly of his rich discoveries. But even while envisioning his future wealth, he was visited by the Shaitan, who warned him that the nests from the caves would never be available for human profit until the payment of *sagit*, or blood money, was made. This *sagit* would consist of human sacrifice in the shape of the son of any discoverer who should seek to exploit the caves. With this threat, the Shaitan vanished, leaving the hard-pressed Dusun parent prostrate on his jungle bed, to awaken in a cold sweat at the thought of his favorite son, Amir, threatened now with a terrible fate.

Hastily the little Dusun gathered up his draggled loincloth, his faded, crimson head square, and his priceless, well-sharpened jungle knife, vowed by all his pagan gods never to visit the caves again, and ran home. That night over his fire, toasting his pig and puffing stinking Dusun tobacco with a feeling of gratitude at having survived, although without the wealth of the caves, he told the story to Amir with gestures and warnings. The fond father cautioned the boy never, never to look for the caves, and Amir, being a dutiful son, or possibly a lazy one and more interested in pig-sticking than commerce, did not protest his orders, but instead spent much time telling the story at neighboring campfires, and every campfire passed it on.

Since this first discoverer, only one other person had ever risked the Shaitan's malevolence by visiting the caves. This was Iman Usub, the holy man, who may have thought his holy connections could outbalance the Shaitan's wrath. In spite of the Shaitan's well-directed warnings of rain, thunder, lightning, and all the obstacles which the Apparition had promised, Iman Usub succeeded one day in crossing the turgid, green-black swampy area which abounded with elephants, snakes, five-foot lizards, and vines, and entered the mouth of the caves. Here he gaped with awe at a cavernous underworld, and marveled at the frantic flight of myriad swiftlets who beat the black air at his entrance with distraught fear for their nests and eggs. Then the excited Usub returned jubilantly to his jungle home to make plans for sale of the nests, and to anticipate happily great benefits to come.

What was this holy man's horror and guilty sorrow to experience then, and be helpless to halt, the tragic deaths in rapid succession of his nine children by accident, illness or fate. These deaths were immediately recognized by Usub and all his neighbors to be the vengeance of the guardian of the caves. With this terrible episode the Shaitan's secret and the treasure of the caves became seemingly invulnerable.

A friend of ours, a Buludupi named Galpan who acts as agent for Government and for the natives who hold contracts for the removal of the birds' nests from Gomantong Caves, has never been quite satisfied with this ending to the story. Although Galpan lives six days up the Kinabatangan, which is wilderness by Borneo travel standards, he also knows the sophistication of the city. In his capacity as agent he has made many visits to Sandakan, occasionally bringing with him his wife, children, and followers, of which last, as a self-respecting Muslim family-head, he never travels with less than ten.

Coming down the river in small native *prahus*, Galpan and entourage reach the bay and cross to Sandakan, there to paddle a short distance up Elopura Creek which acts as river, drain, and sewer to the town. They tie up in the creek's channel by the market place, and wonder and goggle and gaze throughout the day, and sleep soundly in their boats at night. Here in the center of town they quickly become familiar with the habiliments of civilization, and purchase puce-and-red cotton dresses for their naked babies, sweet-water perfumes, blue plastic combs and hair oil for modest Muslim ladies, gilt earrings, brassières, and marriage baubles for the teen-agers at home, and T-shirts, firecrackers and sunglasses to take back for the ancients.

On these visits there takes place a variety of consultations with Government as represented by Harry, and several events in Society, as represented by me, with tea parties which start at 2 P.M. and run the sweetly sick gamut of soft drinks, tea, coffee, lemonade, ginger beer, orange crush, sarsaparilla, soursop and soda. This schedule finished with all decorum and affectionate farewells, Galpan and entourage go back up the Kinabatangan – there to be regarded by the home folks as people who have struck it rich, who have made the Grand Tour, and to whom no form of modern sophistication is unknown. And, indeed, compared to their neighbors, they are now people of two worlds.

By reason of this two-world view, Galpan was skeptical of the Shaitan's powers of vengeance, and decided to challenge it. One day he suggested to Harry that they organize another search for the lost caves, an undertaking which, if successful, would profit the Government a worth-while sum, and double Galpan's own takings as contractor. This proposed expedition was to Harry's exact taste, and he decided to accompany Galpan, taking George with him for his second jungle trip, and also George Brown, his young Scots Assistant Conservator of Forests, a man of real jungle talent and true Scots character.

II. Return to the Jungle

Harry's diaries are always accurate and specific, and they inform the reader exactly what hour and day he arrived and departed from each given destination, and they are filled with correct and precise data, but human emotions have no place in them. This is quite impossible for me to understand, as Harry himself is exactly the opposite.

Any man who puts "Married 4 P.M." as a description of his wedding day, and "Son born 9 A.M." for final comment on the birth of his son and heir, is not one to paint the jungle with anything more colorful than mud. However, Harry promised me that on the forthcoming trip with George he would strike a real literary key – if he remembered, if he had time, and if there was anything to tell! Meanwhile I began to feel myself getting backed unwillingly into another jungle trip.

When the men of my family returned ten days later, it did not surprise me that they both assured me that "nothing had happened," and each hurried off to his own preoccupation, George to a comic, and Harry to the office. I could wait for evening; then I knew I would be permitted to see the small black leather book.

Evening came, the black book lay open before me, and I turned hopefully, then less hopefully through its pages. I closed it, handed it back, and with an effort said nothing.

"Get anything out of it?"

"No."

"Didn't think you would. Really, nothing happened. The weather was horrible, we didn't find the caves, and there isn't anything more to say about it—except that Galpan still thinks we may find them when we go again next month."

"Look, dear, you were ten days in the jungle. Didn't you notice *anything* about George? What he said, how he looked, or anything?"

"No, I didn't, he just looked dirty to me. Why don't you come yourself next time, and find out what he says and does?"

"It's the only thing that will ever get me there again, I'll tell you that!"

"I suggest that you come with us next month. Will you?"

A groan.

"I suppose so."

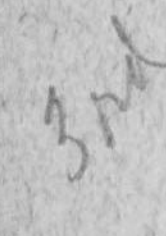

Thirteen men, a boy, and a woman who hates the jungle, stand, loll, squat, on the soft surface of leaves which spread over the hard, black mud like a brown carpet over waxed linoleum. The skins of the boy, two men, and woman are a sickly banana-yellow in the jungle light, and the rest are Dusun-and-Murut brown in shades of burnt sienna.

The elements have been at work, and as usual the rain falls. The dusk of noon suffuses the jungle in the half-light of a hidden world where we live in gloom, looking up at a roof of leaves, without seeing the sun. Outside the jungle, men drip with sweat; here we and the trees drip with rain.

"Shall I drink it out of the tin, Mum?" George suspends a condensed milk tin above his open mouth.

"Why not?"

The sweet, sticky milk goes down George's throat. "Ummm. Good!"

The brown-skins are eating cold rice, cooked the night before and carried with them to save time from building a fire, and Harry lights the Primus stove to make coffee. George sits cross-legged with the coolies, and between his knees is a coconut shell full of cold rice given him by Ungib, a Dusun, his pal, who squats beside him. Ungib at eighteen and George at eight see things alike, the same jokes amuse and the same pleasures delight. Ungib grins into his rice bowl as he nimbly rolls the rice into balls with his finger tips and shoves it into his mouth. George does the same.

"Ummm! This cold rice is good!"

"I'll remember to add cold rice to your diet when we get home," I promise. George is an epicure at home.

"I do like jungle travel, Ma. Don't you?"

"Only when it's over, and I write about how wonderful it is."

"Ready?" says Harry. "We can't waste time."

"O.K., Dad. Can I have some milk chocolate to eat on the way?"

"Here you are. Do your leech bites bother you?"

"No, but look at the blood!" George points proudly to dried streamers of blood which trail down from each leech wound to cake like red paint on his legs.

"I suppose you're a seasoned traveler now." I look gloomily at my own raw legs. "Did you burn the leeches yourself with a cigarette?"

"Sure, Mum. I borrowed a cigarette from Ungib."

Ungib grins at the sound of his name, scratches himself, spits, gets to his feet and withdraws slightly for purposes of urination, returns and pulls his pack on his back and his pack strap over his forehead, and waits, picking his nose, for the party to move. George stands beside him, having performed the same processes.

"Let's get going now, George. This is the last stop before we make camp for the night. Stick close behind me."

"O.K., Dad. And Ungib next to me. Come, Ungib."

Ungib stops picking his nose and falls in. The party moves.

In the old days it was I to whom Harry said, Stick close! I thought. The center of things shifts with the birth of a child, yet somehow one doesn't mind.

We had left Sandakan two days before by the *Elopura*, crossing the bay and traveling up the Kinabatangan as far as the landing at Lamag. Here we anchored, and the first excitement of the trip came when, with the final vibration of the launch and the quieting of the soupy water, we counted the crocodile heads in the river around us.

"Fifteen all at one time! That's a record, Harry!"

"I only saw six."

"There were at least twice that many when I counted."

"There always are."

"No! But honestly, Harry, there's no understating a crocodile, and you *can't* overstate him. Just one is so absolutely, positively abhorrent and horrible that being fifteen of them doesn't make it any worse. It's like the movies trying to convey horror—five times more awful than awful is still just awful. So I'm quite willing to reduce my fifteen crocodiles to six, to please you—or even one. *That* one, Harry! See!"

He saw. The snout was a streamlined ripple on the water, the blank eyes emerged open, then closed, and the crocodile became a floating log, then a sinking log as it submerged in silent threat.

"I suppose there's a standard of beauty amongst them, and perhaps the most hideous and leering one is the loveliest, in the crocodile world. Certainly they merge well with their surroundings, dripping with saliva and mud. It's the eye that frightens me. I never forgot the first crocodile I skinned with you years ago, and how his insides went on jerking long after he was dead. But I guess I don't even want to shoot a croc any more."

"Well, you don't have to—but you won't get any bath tonight!"

The next day the party is joined by ten Dusun carriers and Galpan, who has developed a further working theory as to where the Shaitan's caves are hidden, and he believes that five or six days' search will serve to locate the hidden hills. Food for ten days is now packed in carrying receptacles to be taken with us to the jungle.

At dawn the next morning as the sky lightens to gray and a steady rain falls, we draw away from the launch in small native dugouts, looking back to wave, then peering silently forward through the mist to the tree-walled jungle shore. Jungle travel at dawn is always a dismal adventure which requires fortitude more than daring and silence more than cheer, and not even George interrupts the sound of dripping paddles with his exuberant voice.

At the river's bank we form into single file with George and me in the middle and the carrying coolies last. As we proceed away from the river by Galpan's directions, the jungle proves only moderately heavy, but the land alternates between swamp and hillside and we are always either plodding through mud, or pulling up and down hills. It has been a good year for jungle fruit, illipi nuts, *meritam*, *lansat*, and *tampoi* are still fruiting, and game is evident. Pig wallows are frequent and muddy gray rumps slide out of sight into swamps, jibbering, gray river monkeys swing through the treetops, the cries of barking deer echo often in the distance, and elephant turds are underfoot to be stumbled over, but we move forward without stopping for game.

Light rains continue and every leaf quivers with a leech looping madly with ambition to attach himself to a passer-by. We have rubbed ourselves with leech repellent, a scented oil which protects while it adheres to the skin, but washes away after a couple of hours of rain and mud, and now the leeches are attaching themselves to exposed portions. But as our bodies weary, the annoyance of the leech tickle is swamped in fatigue, and I have to remind myself that night is the time to dread, when itching begins and scratching continues. The natives move through jungle without seeming to disturb a leaf, their eyes quick to note when a leech attaches, and they deal instant death by burning with a cigarette, or scraping them off with the jungle knife which is always in their hands.

As the rain grows heavier, so do our feet, the jungle damp creeps like a chill in the bones, and although we drip with sweat, we are cold. I have my mind categorically fixed on the evening drink, food, and bed, but George has his mind on Harry's rifle. He has survived the morning well, being perfect jungle size, about five feet four and the height of the average native. Tall travelers like myself catch their hair in trees and their feet in roots and bend double to stumble awkwardly through tunnels of vines cut by the natives to fit their own dimensions.

By three o'clock Harry is watching for a possible camp site, as in east coast jungle it is necessary to make camp by this hour if you hope to escape the heavier rains. If shelter is not established early, sleeping equipment will be soaked, campfires won't burn, the night will be misery, and the next day a weary one.

By three-thirty a site is chosen on a slight rise in the least heavy part of the jungle, after first making sure that no dead trees are near to fall in a storm. The coolies clear ground for camp, and Harry and George break branches and chop stumps for firewood. I bring out the gin bottle, and George refreshes himself otherwise.

"More chocolate please, Mum!"

"I thought I just gave you some."

"I gave it to Ungib."

I hand out a fresh bar of milk-with-nuts.

"Are you very tired?"

"Not tired at all. Isn't this chocolate good?" The chocolate mingles on George's face with mud, sweat and rain.

"Don't eat too much chocolate, or you'll spoil your appetite for supper."

"I couldn't spoil my appetite!"

"Hurry up with the firewood, or we'll never eat," interrupts Harry. "Where's your pal Ungib? He doesn't seem to be very energetic about making camp."

"He heard a deer call, and went to see. He's a wonderful shot, Dad."

Usually Harry travels with a light tent fly of sufficient size to cover himself and a companion, leaving the coolies to rely on *kajang* thatches, as is the native custom. But even a light tent is a heavy load after a wet night, and on this trip Harry has abandoned the tent theory and we all sleep under *kajang* thatching brought from the launch.

The thatches used are made from palm leaves sewn into three-by-five-foot strips with a fold in the center, and thirty *kajang* are enough to shelter all the party. The weight of the entire load is little greater than that of a canvas tent large enough to shelter two, after the tent is wet.

Now the men cut a number of saplings and lash these together with rattan strips to form a framework. The trees which have been left standing at convenient distances support the ridgepole, which is lashed to them at a distance of four feet from the ground. With the pole used as a crossbeam, the thatches are hung down much as canvas would be draped across the ridgepole of a tent, and extra thatches are shingled downward. This shelter is comparable to a low shed roof without sides; when finished, it is sufficient to break the rain but not luxurious enough to corrupt its occupants into late sleeping.

Now the roof is up and three small camp cots are placed at one end, with mosquito nets hung over them from the roof above. The remainder of the shelter will accommodate Galpan and the carriers, who will stretch out on their mats of split rattan, and scratch all night. The end near the fire is reserved for them as they do not use mosquito nets and the smudge will help dissipate the insects, although it will not stop the scratching.

The routine of camp-making requires about an hour, depending on how much jungle space there is to be cleared. The same length of time is also the minimum required to clear ground and erect a small tent sufficient only for our own needs.

The campfire has blazed and settled now to a well-controlled bed of coals, the saucepan of water is bubbling, the coffee boils, something which smells very good is sizzling over the coals and George Brown, in spirit, presides over the food.

It has been pointed out to me from the trip before that George Brown, a scientific camper, provided an excellent calorie menu worked out on a scientific basis for daily diet, and thus insured that no surplus food wasted the carrying power of the coolies. A discussion had preceded our packing.

"You always take too much, dear. Now this time let's only take what we need."

"I agree. But what do we need?"

"George Brown figures that bully beef with rice, apricots and cheese is a properly balanced meal."

"I never knew you to eat any of those things, except rice."

"Tasted jolly good the way George fixed them."

"Oh – well, if George can fix 'em, I can!"

Now the test comes.

"Hi, Ma, when do we eat?"

George's wet hair plasters on his forehead in sleek dabs, his damp shirt sticks to his ribs, his long, lean brown legs glisten, his gray-blue eyes squint with wood smoke, and his nostrils spread with the smell of food.

"Right now we eat."

I dish out George Brown's menu. Well, anyway, I do know how to cook rice. Here it is, cooked only as the Orient knows it, each grain separate and flaky and no soggy pudding effect. And over it a tin of bully beef with onions. Now comes the noise of the scraping of enamel plates.

"When the plates are clean, apricots and cheese are coming," I say. And as the customers eat the apricots and cheese without complaint, I assume that George Brown was right.

It is only six-thirty, but supper is over and Harry and I are in our cots ready for sleep, and it seems to me that this hour of peace makes it all worth while. It is so sensuously wonderful just to be lying there in a complete negation of all effort, not dragging my feet out of the mud, not keeping up, not smiling pleasantly, not doing my part, scarcely even existing. Surely, nothing can be as good as nothing, I tell myself!

But that's not the way George feels about things. Although the coolies have stretched on their mats for the night, smoking strong Dusun tobacco, sniffling, coughing, spitting, snoozing, George and Ungib squat by the bed of coals whispering.

"Come to bed, George."

"But Mum, I'm not tired, really! It's too early."

"Don't forget that you have to be out of bed at five tomorrow."

"I know. Dad – Dad . . . Can I go hunting with Ungib tonight? He is going to call a barking deer."

"He may call one – but what will he shoot it with?"

"A rifle – your rifle, Dad. That is . . . we thought we might borrow it. May we please?"

Harry groans. "I suppose so – but don't ruin it! And stay behind it, not in front!"

"Harry, do you think he ought to go? He's just a child – and Ungib's a moron!"

"Ungib knows hunting, if he is a moron. George'll be all right."

Sometime later as Harry is sleeping soundly and I am lying awake worrying I hear a squeaking sound in the distance; Ungib luring the deer, I decide. About the time I have made up my mind that George has been shot and the deer has escaped, something crashes into the *kajang* roof – the deer, or George? I wonder.

"George?"

"Ma? You awake?"

He paws his way under the dripping roof, crawls into the cot, sneezes, blows his nose.

"Are you catching cold, George?"

Negative grunt.

"Don't forget to tuck your mosquito net in, George."

"Unnnnh."

"Warm enough?"

"Unnnh."

"Hungry?"

No answer. George is asleep. I do not ask if they got the deer; if they had, I wouldn't have to ask.

Dawn. I am attending to my own dismal preparations for the day, and leaving George to his father. As far back as I can remember jungle travel, I recall these dawn preparations. First, the struggle to tear myself from the only comfortable spot on the trip, the blankets I sleep between. Not the struggle to awaken, because sleeping has been interrupted by scratching all night, as the warmth of the bedding makes the leech bites squirm. Then the pathetic pretense of starting the day clean, with face washing, tooth scrubbing, and the more protracted, maddening attempt to comb out and put up long, straight hair in semi-darkness, an attempt which lasts only during the first days of a trip, after which it is combed out and braided in two dark tails which dangle beside my high-cheekboned face.

Then the dab of rouge which turns purple when seen in the later daylight, and the smear of lipstick which makes a jungle-shadowed face with tilted eyes look like a mask — not a beautiful mask, but the one I face the world with, and a good hiding place. Then the blue shorts, shirt, and wool socks, sneakers and bandana on the hair.

Then the bed to make, folding the blankets, rolling the camp mattress, and stuffing them all in the bag. And then the tidying up, burning dirty Kleenex, cigarette butts, scraps of paper, placing dry shorts and shirt in my knapsack where I can get them as soon as we make camp at night, and collecting the other pair of sneakers from the fire where they have been drying, and slinging them in on top of the pack with the cigarettes, the leech repellent, the sketching block, and the toilet paper.

Now I can take time to look around and breathe deeply of damp, gray, early air, and feel grateful that another day is done, another one begun, I am that much nearer home, and still alive. In fact, in spite of complaints, more alive at this painful hour of 5:45 than I have been for some time.

"It's ready, Agnes, the life-giving fluid!"

"Coffee!"

One cup, two cups, three cups . . .

"Ah! Now the lifeblood starts to flow! But — not that I want to be critical at this juncture, because, even if it isn't coffee, it's done me a lot of good, but — what is this stuff, Harry?"

"I put eight tablespoons of coffee in the pot, and the rest is water from the jungle stream, the principal ingredient of which is mud. It's boiled to sterility, however."

"The epic of good earth. Well, very excellent mud, anyway.

I think I can live now. And the twirp? How does he find himself?"

But the twirp doesn't find himself at all, at dawn; he takes his sleeping seriously, and the one thing he doesn't approve of in jungle travel is early rising.

The *kajang* roof is bundled up by now, the beds are folded and in carrying cases, and it is just light enough to travel. The first day has left its mark without yet hardening the victims for the future, and the second day is bound to be the hardest.

The jungle is denser, the rain heavier, mud deeper, the hills more slippery, and feet grow heavier to lift hour by hour. Every leaf bears a leech longing to seek ingress by some sensitive spot, but each man goes doggedly along with the air of a job to be done, and I, without any air at all, spend considerable time in the mud. I see that Harry watches George a little anxiously, but George is O.K., now the dawn has passed.

"Are you all right, old man?"

"Yes, Dad. More chocolate, please!"

Harry reaches into the pack. "Not too tired?"

"I'm fine! This is fun, isn't it? Ungib says we're certain to get a deer tonight."

"Are you getting chilled, George?"

"No, I'm fine! I wish we could live like this always!"

Tonight we make camp earlier, and the same routine of putting up shelter proceeds, but hampered tonight by heavier rain. Meanwhile Ungib hears barking deer in the distance and gets George's ear, and George gets Harry's.

"My rifle? . . . My God, George, aren't you ever tired?"

"No, Dad—this was an easy day! So, please let us have the rifle? Ungib and I will get that deer tonight for sure. You'd better have a good hot fire ready to cook it on when we come back."

"You've been wet all day!" says mother. "If you had any sense you'd stay in camp and get dry. And if your father had any sense, he'd make you!"

"Why, I'm not wet, Mum!" He is as wet and sleek and shining as a young deer, and as much in his element.

"Why do you want to go out and kill things, anyway?"

"Oh . . ." This is not a new idea. "But we need the meat, Dad."

"We don't need it. We have rations."

"But the coolies want meat. Ungib says so. So please can we go, Dad?"

"The coolies always want meat—especially deer! Well, all right, go. I suppose it takes time to learn . . ."

"Learn what, Dad? To hunt?"

"Learn not to hunt!"

"Oh . . . Well . . . By, Dad. We'll get it this time!"

The shelter is up, the rice is cooked, the campfire burned to coals when we hear a deer call, followed by shots. Shortly after, the hunters arrive.

"We got it, Dad! We got it! Ungib called it by blowing on a leaf, and the deer thought it was another deer and came in our direction, and we shot it! Oh, look, Dad, look, Mum!"

We look, as George dumps on the ground before us a little barking deer, slender, satiny, small-boned with body stiff now and eyes staring in death. George stands triumphantly over it, young, sleek, streamlined and triumphantly alive.

"See, Mum!"

I turn away; he knows what I think.

"See, Dad!"

"Yes, you got it, George. You got your deer."

"Well, aren't you pleased about it, Dad?"

"Not very."

"But you used to hunt a lot yourself! Anyhow, *you* brought the gun!"

"I know, George. I brought the gun for emergency. I don't like killing things unnecessarily any more."

The little deer is quickly quartered, and the sweet meat, the equivalent of a filet steak, is placed in the stew pot in preference to my calorie menu; the rest goes to the coolies.

Now the stew is served and the meat is so tough it can scarcely be chewed. We make no comment.

"I say, Dad, this deer is good!" says George, chewing madly. "Lucky we got it, wasn't it?"

"Yes, and no." Harry feels his jaw tenderly. "What about a tin of bully beef, Ma? I'm hungry."

"Well – yes. Followed by apricots and cheese?"

"Excellent suggestion!"

"And save this for tomorrow?" asks George.

"Or perhaps you might give what's left to the men. After all, it's the first camp kill."

"O.K."

The coolies hang their portions over the campfire to smoke it through the night. Next morning they will cut it into small hunks to toss in the bottom of their packs where, in days to come, it will stink worse and worse, until it is, by their standards, edible.

As he cuddles into his sleeping bag George grumbles for the first time, "I wish we didn't have to get up so early tomorrow."

It is two nights and eight miles later. The campfire smudge hangs in the damp air, holding the light from the coals and illuminating the open space in the jungle hollowed out of trees. In this smoky, glow-filled, tree-walled room it is very cosy, no one minds the great wet splashes which shake down from the trees, and native skins turn to russet in the fire while scabs and sores are lost in night, until at the moment the whole of the trip seems like this, all comfortable and cosy with the soreness gone.

George has just cleaned his enamel plate of the calorie menu, and although it is scarcely necessary, has washed it in the rain. Now he drops back to the coolie's end of the shelter and squats with Ungib by the fire.

Ungib is eating with obvious relish, his jaws clicking and his diaphragm extending with hearty belches. The food is deer, rapidly softening to decomposition. George listens to Ungib as if to a musical refrain, and then says:

"Good, eh?"

"Good!" Ungib grins, smears his mouth with the back of his hand, and extends the hunk of meat to George. "Want?"

"Want!"

Ungib hacks a piece off with his jungle knife and passes it. George chews too.

"Good?"

"Good! When shall we hunt again?"

George's communication with Ungib is in Dusun and Malay, in which language Ungib's vocabulary is limited to the needs and pleasures of the body, and certain anatomical areas. It seems that four-letter thoughts are the same in all races, although the letters differ.

Another day comes, camp is made, and again George and Ungib go hunting. This day no shots are heard, but the two return jubilant in a short time.

"Mum, look what I got!" George holds up a tortoise a foot across, and gray with jungle mud, and Ungib displays a similar one.

"Aren't they fine? I'm going to keep them and take them home."

"What do you want them at home for? I can't imagine anything less appealing."

"I'm going to breed them and start a tortoise farm."

"What makes you think you have both sexes there?"

"Ungib says! He's an expert on tortoises. This is the female . . . see?"

Examination.

"Well, no, I don't, as a matter of fact!"

"Well – *that* means she's the female! Oh, you'll know I'm right when they start to produce babies!"

"Who's going to carry them home?"

"Ungib's going to make us a basket out of vines, and we'll carry them."

"We? That's nice for Ungib!"

"It's fun, isn't it, to bring something back alive and not shoot it, Mum?"

"You're getting the idea, eh? Now, George, you really must get to bed."

"O.K. I'm as good as in!"

And he's in.

"Mum, Galpan says that our God is really the same as his god, Allah. So perhaps I'll be a Muslim. It's a very good religion except for not eating pork."

Silence from me. The child should be asleep!

"Dad?"

"Ummmh."

"Dad, what is Ungib? I mean what god does he have?"

"He's a pagan, and he believes in a god called Kinaringan, and Kinaringan's wife, Munsummundok."

"Does he say prayers to them?"

"Not exactly, but he makes little offerings to them like a bit of cloth, or tobacco maybe, or anything the gods might like. Now go to sleep!"

Silence. Then, "Dad, don't you think those tortoises will be nice pets at home?"

"I think they are ideal traveling companions; they neither talk in bed, nor borrow my rifle! Go to sleep."

All this time we have been traveling the perimeter of a circle about the area where Galpan thinks the caves are located, but the limestone hill has not been found. The area has not been completely exhausted, and Galpan once more says that a week longer would make the search successful. But our calorie menus are consumed, the heavier rains are here, and if we do not return soon to the launch a search party will be sent.

It is the last night in the jungle. For the last time the *kajangs* have been laid, the cots placed, the nets hung, for the last time the coolies have stretched and scratched and smoked and coughed and laughed softly by the fire. For the last time we have cleaned our teeth in the drain and used the jungle as a latrine, squatting in the rain to hurry back to the fire wet and bitten by mosquitoes; and for the last time as we lie under shelter, the rain comes down, in the protective, curtaining, cosy fashion that rain has when you're out of it.

Home in a few nights, I tell myself. And am I glad? I'm supposed to be.

"Well, Mum, are you ever coming again?"

"Haven't made up my mind."

"She never is, but she always does," says Harry.

Cold cream – I'll have to use it every night when I get home, I am thinking – and it will take weeks to get my hands clean – not till a change of skin, I guess, and my hair is dank with sweat and dirt.

"Well, Mum? Coming?"

"No."

"But you might change your mind, Mum?"

"Easily."

"Good. Dad and I'll change it for you."

Later still comes George's voice through the drips and rain. "Well, Dad, we didn't find the caves. I guess the Shaitan kept his secret again."

"Yes, George – but maybe it's just as well. You remember what the price of finding the caves was? The sacrifice of the finder's son."

"Dad! You don't believe that, do you?"

"Well – out here in the jungle in the rain, things make sense that don't make sense at home."

III. Rulers of the River

OF Pengiran Digadong Samah, the fiery, shriveled little ruler of the Kinabatangan River in 1880, the sad and violent story has already been told of how he lost the Gomantong Bird's Nest Caves to Government and his life to the white man's guns. But with his death, his rule did not entirely pass from the long, slow, wallowing river that he had both scourged and loved, for he left there three daughters to shed tears by his hollow wooden burial coffin in the tree-veiled jungle cave. These daughters were Sinyora, Fatima, and Dagangan, and Dagangan shortly died. A compassionate grant was made to these daughters by Government, "sufficient for their needs until marriage," in recognition of Government's confiscation of the Pengiran's rich Gomantong Bird's Nest Caves.

After five years, Sinyora married and lost her allowance, then divorced, and demanded it back. This request was refused, and Sinyora has been working every angle since to get something out of the deal. Her son was appointed Government agent to supervise collections, thus exposing himself to possible perquisites of office, until he died. Meanwhile Sinyora and Fatima receive one half of one third of two per cent of one half of the gross profits for lifetime, if anyone can figure that out.

Sinyora and Fatima are sometimes guests in my home. In them I think I still see the old man; in their wiry, bent, brown bodies, shriveled beyond their years but vital and dominating; and in their quick, shifting, calculating minds I see the fearless old man, who, defiant and piratical in every bone, sang fiercely to the last, "I have always ruled the Kinabatangan River, no one shall take it from me!"

"Like father and mother to us, Tuan!" croons Sinyora to Harry. "Like grandfather and grandmother you are! And this child of yours is like the child of a holy man to us. To see him today is worth $500 gold to us. Truly, we prefer it to $500!" Sinyora advances to embrace George in her shrunken, amber hands, and gently smells him in the native fashion, while George backs hastily away.

"Make her leave me alone, Mum!"

"It's only because she's pleased to see you, George. Don't hurt her feelings."

Thus Sinyora, Fatima, Baud, Sinyora's daughter, and Norkia, a female relative indirectly connected with the bird's nest caves, invade the launch as we arrive at Bilit, home town of the caves' exploiters. Baud is dressed neatly in purple and blue hyacinth-flowered sarong and shabby, once white, silk blouse, and the three old ladies wear sarongs in burnt sienna patterns which blend with their skins and the rusty red sireh juice which stains their teeth, mouths, and lips. All have Chinese crash towels around their necks to wipe off sweat and blow their noses. The ladies have grouped themselves about us on the deck of the *Elopura*, squatting in an ostensibly admiring assembly which we know has more practical motives, especially as Sinyora's introductory speech has exceeded even the customary hyperbole.

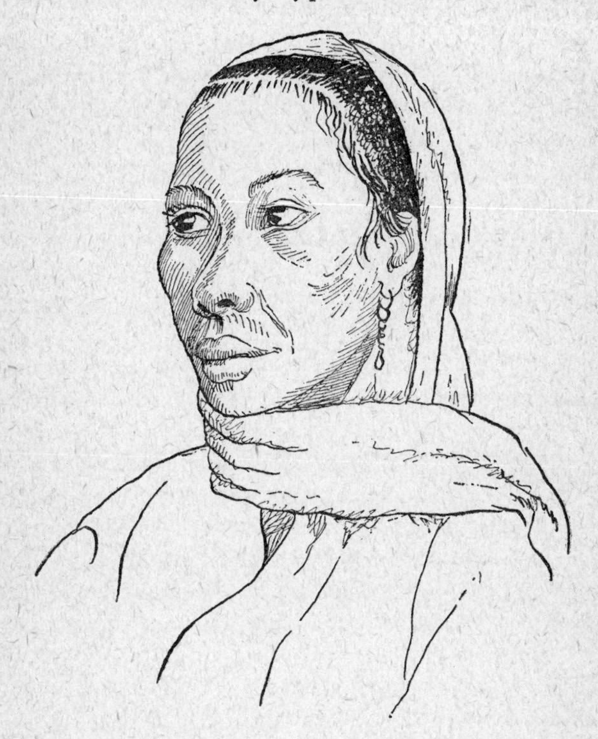

Sinyora now advances a market basket towards Harry and me, also a bundle wrapped in an old handkerchief, a covered tin saucepan, and a greasy packet wrapped in *keladi* leaves.

"We have brought a little food for the Tuan, the Small Tuan, and the Mem. It is little indeed for you, but for us it is the best we can obtain." Sinyora coughs modestly, dredges up a hunk of sputum from her larynx and ejects it towards the boat rail. "Now we will make the feast ready for you."

She and the other ladies open the bundles and cover the forward hatch with a brilliant assortment of varicolored cakes and sweets, with bacillus green, pyorrhea pink, and diarrhea brown predominating.

"For you!" Sinyora's gesture is both magnanimous and belittling, to cover herself from every angle.

"We thank you very much," Harry says cautiously, "but we have just had a very large meal and our appetities have not yet returned."

"Then you must take the food with you, and eat it when you are hungry." She settles herself on the deck now as if ready to give us her day, while all the ladies scrape their larynxes, collect sputum, and shoot for the side of the boat with indifferent aim.

"Old ladies, we are about to sail upriver for Lamag where we have business," says Harry, to discourage the attitude of relaxation.

"Yes, Tuan, certainly, Tuan. How happy we would be to accompany you – if there is enough space!"

"It is very bad luck, indeed, but there is not enough space," says Harry firmly.

"Bad luck indeed, Tuan!" Sinyora takes it philosophically as one whose mind is on bigger issues. "Tuan, before you go I would like to talk to you of this matter of the bird's nest caves. Now it is this way – " Once more the story unfolds, and once more concludes as usual – "So we would like to ask for a little advance from Government on the bird's nest produce this year."

"But you have had an advance."

"Yes, Tuan. Of course it is as you say, Tuan. But the advance was very small, and now it is gone – and now we owe the shop at Bilit – and it is a bad year – and – "

And so in the end another advance is made, which will be spent before the next meeting, when another will be requested. Now, their object achieved, the old ladies prepare to depart, but not before making another assault upon George, who retires below decks more disturbed by their embraces than by any possible jungle peril.

The ladies are safely away, the feast of food in chromatic colors is passed to the sailors on the launch – with the understanding, of course, that if we had not just finished a large meal we would have eaten it ourselves. As the engines throb again, George reappears.

"Are they gone? I wish she wouldn't try to smell me. She's got eyes like marble agates."

This is the country the old Pengiran ruled, the river he made his own, the jungle he filled with terror for white men, I had to remind myself, as I looked around me at the smiling, lamp-lit faces of our hosts at Lamag station. How different was this reception tonight from the Pengiran's day! Then, white men were met with knives and threats, tonight we were met with friendly greetings, festivity, and a dance in our honor; then we would have gone up the river with guns, now we went up it with medicines.

It is nighttime on the muddy river's bank at Lamag, and a hastily erected platform has been draped with the Union Jack and lit with a hissing petrol lamp from the house of the DADO, the Deputy Assistant District Officer. On this stand and about it the villagers and people from far up the river have assembled. Buludupies, Orang Sungei, Dusuns, Tengaras, Suluks, Murut policemen, and a few Chinese – all have come from far and near to take part in or watch the *dindang*, a local native Borneo dance, and the popular manner of celebrating every festivity. We, as a tribute to our dignity, are seated on the edge of the platform in old, rattan, bug-infested chairs, from the bites of whose inhabitants it will take us days to recover.

The music begins. It is made by striking small brass gongs which resemble saucepans sitting on strings, with pieces of soft wood, an instrument called a *guling tangan*. To its cadence is added the sonorous tones of native brass gongs, struck by hand, and the measured clack of handclapping which carries the rhythm of the dance. At first it strikes the observer as an unspectacular rhythm, but it is one which grows on you until finally you find yourself thumping out what at first you did not recognize as being rhythm.

The participants of the dance may be as few as one couple, or as many people as wish to dance. Tonight about thirty are dancing, all men, as the only women who dance are professional entertainers, and none of these are present. In the audience, mothers squat about, clapping, chewing, laughing, giving suck to babies, and smoking with their friends; coquettes adjust the scented flowers in well-oiled hair, slacking their sarongs to below their breasts when hot, sweeping them up again with a generous movement when need requires, while old ladies retire hastily to the outskirts of the throng to attend modestly to nature's needs under the canopy of the sarong, now conveniently held like a tent and used as a comfort station.

The pattern of the dance is a rhythmic shuffling back and forth, with the couples facing each other and singing topical *pantuns*, which are quatrains in Malay. The bodily movement of the dance takes place in the feet which shuffle, the ankles which twist, the shoulders which undulate smoothly, the wrists which writhe and wriggle, and the hands which trace, weave and knead the air in endless, flowering patterns. Almost no movement takes place in the torso, and the chest merely follows the behest of the shoulders twisting from side to side.

The art of this dance is to compose, supposedly on the spot, a really good quatrain of local current interest, with the audience itself as a subject, and the success of the dance lies in the quick response of the audience to the jokes and banter of the verse. A good *dindang* requires both quick-witted dancers and an agile-minded audience to follow and applaud.

Tonight is a good *dindang*, and the couples on the floor shuffle, sing, bait each other, and banter the audience, companionably including Harry and me. There is a verse to do with our arrival which they sing at us, standing before us and chanting in our faces, to cause much glee.

Now they shuffle over to George and sing to him, teasing, bantering, quipping, making play, and urging him to get out on the floor and dance with them, where already native children of infinitesimal size and pure nudity are participating in the swirling, excited edge of the dance. But George is painfully embarrassed; this is worse even than being smelled by Sinyora!

"Make play! Make play!" the dancers sing over him, breathing in his face.

George wriggles and squirms.

"George, won't you dance with them? You know the dance," I plead.

"Oh, no, Mum, I'd feel like a fool!"

"Make play! Make play! Come, make fun with us, dance with us!" Brown faces shine over him, white teeth gleam near, and hands stroke the air about his face.

George looks about for an exit; in front of him the laughing dancers leer, and behind him and all about the mass of onlookers applaud and clap and chorus rhythmically, "Dance with them! Dance with them! Dance with them!"

"Mum, make them stop! I don't want to dance with them!"

"Harry, George is getting awfully fussed. Can't you divert them from him?"

"Old Man! Old Man!" Harry calls to the *Orang Tua* who is host of the evening. "Old Man, what about giving us a good *main daling?* George has never seen a *main daling*. He would like to see one." *Daling* is a corruption of the English word "darling," a word brought to Borneo by Suluks from the Southern Philippine Islands, and the phrase means literally a Darling Dance.

"Darling Dance! Darling Dance! Si Jarchie wants a Darling Dance!" Old Man shouts in Malay, glowing with sweat and pleasure that they have found something that George does want.

"Darling Dance for Jarchie! . . . For Jarchie! For Jarchie! . . ." the word goes around. The gongs, pans and clapping stop, the dissonance dies, the dancers relax, and George settles back to stay again.

Now the Darling Dance expert is called out, a young Suluk of eighteen, his face all shining brown planes and wide nostrils, and his eyes snapping with vigor, expectation, and fun. He is a favorite, and the story he is going to tell is wildly anticipated by all, as is made plain by unrestrained excitement about us. Although a proper *main daling* requires two speakers, one to toss the story to the other, and take the answer back, tonight, as no equally expert partner can be found, the young Suluk undertakes to recite both parts himself.

Now the crowd gives rapt attention, interrupted only by involuntary sounds of coughing and spitting, and the boy begins. It is the story of a Japanese Commandant who in 1943 was journeying up the Kinabatangan with his soldiers to visit native villages and to put down those who did not obey. The Commandant makes triumphant military progress from station to station, but always unhappily and quite by accident encounters a new misfortune or disease at each stop along the way, until after developing yaws at Bilit, malaria at Lamag, dysentery at Pintassan, he is finally satisfactorily eaten by crocodiles at Pingas. The conclusion brings terrific applause from all, smiles and nodding of heads, and agreement by all that this is indeed a very proper ending. And it is whispered in my ear by the Old Man that there was an original to this story who did – ha, ha! – end up inside a crocodile at Pingas!

Thus the *dindang* ends, and we return to the launch, and bed. As I lie on the deck stretcher and wait for sleep, a thought comes to me. Seventy years ago when Pengiran Digadong Samah sang his death song, he commemorated the white man as his enemy. Tonight his people turn to us as friends, and commemorate the Japanese, a yellow man, as enemy.

"Sinyora and Baud came to see me today. They are coming up for tea with you at two this afternoon."

"Two! Heavens! Why didn't you tell them four, or four-thirty?"

"I did tell them four-thirty. But they'll still be here at two!"

"Damn! And they'll stay until dark! That means four hours of soft drinks and crooning. What do they want this time?"

"Money. I have not renewed Jikrun's contract to collect nests because he's so damned inefficient, and that means Jikrun will lose the perquisites he used to wangle. The old lady is determined to get the contract back for him, and keep it in the family."

At two-thirty a taxi arrived in front of the house, bearing Sinyora, sister Fatima, daughter Baud and her husband Jikrun, and five-year-old daughter Mina, three small boy cousins, a wooden box and a tin pan. From my bedroom upstairs I could see them dismount and come up the walk, cross the garden with admiring gestures towards flowers and house, and disappear into the open drawing room below. A moment later George popped upstairs.

"Mum! Folks to see you!"

"I'll be down soon. Ask them to sit down, and pass the cigarettes to them."

"Mum, they brought me a funny little animal like a squirrel. It's only a week old."

"That was in the box, eh? What a shame to take it from the mother. It will certainly die if it's only a week old!"

"No, Mum, Mat told me what to feed it."

"Who's Mat?"

"Oh, he's my new friend, the boy that brought it—he's an awful nice fellow. Hurry down, Mum, they want to see you."

As I went downstairs I saw George and three boys streaking across the lawn towards the bear's cage. When I entered the living room Sinyora, Fatima, Baud, and Jikrun were perched uncomfortably on the edge of modern furniture which had nothing in common with their own diminutive dimensions. Sinyora seemed to have lit uneasily on the divan which faces the bay and the green shore behind it, and here she fluttered like a bird, her feet unable to reach the floor and her back not touching the back rest, and only careful balancing kept her upright.

Jikrun was soberly covered in Chinese trousers and cheap cotton sweat shirt with a Muslim *songkok* on his head, but the ladies had on their best displays of henna-tinted sarongs and once-white blouses and sweat cloths about their creased and dingy necks. Small Mina wore a number of gold bangles and gold earrings, and a hideous purple cotton garment, machine stitched in European style, and no doubt purchased in market that morning for our benefit. When in gusts of embarrassment Mina twisted the skirt up to her chin, it displayed her naked navel and open plumbing to much advantage.

All popped to their feet when I entered, and gave me the

Muslim greeting of hand to forehead, eyes and heart as if wiping the face clean, and then both hands extended to stroke gently the hand of the greeted party. As I came to Baud, Jikrun pointed proudly to her swollen abdomen and said, "Six children, and one more inside!"

"Greetings, Baud. And so this is Mina!" I said, as an adult always says to the newly met child. "Hello, Mina." Mina sucks

her finger, leans back on her mother's stomach, tosses up her skirt, and squirms her naked torso.

Now Sinyora places in my hands a large object tied up in a dirty kerchief which proves to be a tin pan filled with turtle eggs acquired this morning from one of the turtle islands where the family has relatives.

"For you, Mem," she intones gently through her nose. "They make the body strong, and if a mama wants more babies, they make more babies."

"Thank you, Sinyora." I disregard the hint. "It is very good of you. Your heart is good."

Now we have coffee, made thick and sticky with sugar, and ginger beer and biscuits in faint hope that this may dispose of the party before Harry comes for tea. I call the boys from the garden for drinks. Small Mat, Usin and Arsat, all three between ten and twelve years, dressed in blue cotton shorts with *songkoks* greet me with polite ceremony in pleasant contrast to Mina's beady-eyed babyishness. More drinks and biscuits are passed. Everyone is careful not to eat or drink greedily, but with polite restraint, to show this is purely a social event rather than a necessary meal.

The visitors are more at ease now, and Sinyora and silent sister Fatima have rocked themselves back on their seats, crossed their legs, and tucked their feet under them. Sinyora gazes with interest about the room and out of the French windows to the blue bay, then she croons contentedly in beautifully spoken Malay.

"Mem, I feel happy to be with you. Your home is very beautiful and my heart is at home with you." She further settles herself on the seat of the divan and leaning against the back rest now she relaxes with a sigh, her rheumy eyes filled with ease and contentment.

Oh, Sinyora, I think, no one could have the heart to deny you your little pleasure – mercenary though your motives for this visit no doubt are!

"The Tuan has not yet come home, Mem? Then I will wait for the Tuan. Also I will be happy to watch the sunset here from your beautiful home."

And so we wait – for Harry, or the sunset, with interchanges of Malay and lemonade, while Mina bobbles and bounces about and successfully demolishes the plastic toys which George has given her at my request. George and the boys disappear with slingshots down the valley, and I know that my shouted command, "Don't shoot birds!" is not likely to be obeyed.

Harry arrives, and his face falls at the sight of the roomful – he had hoped against hope! Now we have tea in earnest, going to the veranda where the table is laid, and again the ladies mount the chairs like trained apes and cross their legs under them. Tea this time is tea, biscuits and cakes, with a separate table on the lawn for George and the boys. Meanwhile, Mina crawls all over her mother, stamping gaily on her abdomen and treading rudely on the unborn babe. As soon as food is brought she crams her fists full of everything within reach, and tries to push it all into her mouth at once, but is unable to succeed and sprinkles remnants over us all. The old ladies smile mildly and Jikrun wipes off crumbs and looks the other way. Now the tea is poured and Mina drops her cakes to pick up her teacup to which I have not yet added sugar and milk, fills her mouth with a huge swallow, and finding it isn't sweet spits it out on the floor. Everybody smiles politely – almost.

Now Sinyora is crooning to Harry, and business is as usual:

" – like mother, like father to us, Tuan! – my heart is at ease in your home. Indeed, when you and the Mem leave this country it is as if we have lost our best friends. You have always been a friend to my people, Tuan. For this reason I come to tell you about the trouble that exists up the river in the bird's nest caves. Now I will tell you – "

Meanwhile Mina has found the inner tube from George's bicycle tire and is blowing a mouthful of tinned biscuits through it into her mother's hair.

"And further, Tuan, let me tell you – "

Harry leaves the table long enough to turn on the radio to the approximate volume of Sinyora's voice, and then returns with his ear tuned to the radio, adopting the Oriental principle of evading the issue.

"But that is not all, Tuan, and now I will tell you – " intones Sinyora.

Mina fills her hands with what is left of the cakes and staggers off to the table on the lawn, where the boys are playing scissors-cut-paper. Here she collects the remainder of cakes which they amiably pass over to her, and starts throwing them into the flower bed.

"And so, Tuan, because of all these misfortunes which have come to us, we would like to ask you to make us a small advance – "

Harry leaves the table long enough to turn the radio up again.

" – a small advance, Tuan . . ." Sinyora's volume increases with the increasing radio volume, then suddenly she stops, sighs, picks up her sweat rag and blows her nose, wipes her wet old eyes, and looks out to the bay where the sun's rays are just coloring the sky and shadows fall across the bay, and lights begin to flicker in the busy town. She sighs again, and settles back—throwing herself on our mercy.

"The heart is at ease here," Sinyora has said. How mean to begrudge her her little day, I tell myself. She has the right to get what she can from us.

With the last light of day Harry delivers the family back to its sleek-lined, native boat, anchored in the town canal; here they will sleep the night before going back up the Kinabatangan. He returns to the house.

"Did you give her the advance?" I ask.

Harry turns on the radio. I know what that means; she got it.

"What a poisonous vixen Mina is! She could be awfully sweet, if they'd only take trouble with her. Why do the little girls behave so abominably when the little boys are so adorable?" I ruminate.

"The girls are brought up to be toys—to be played with—the boys are brought up to be men. That's one reason why civilization spreads slowly here. The women take no responsibility, and are far behind the men."

"What a morning! Jikrun and Baud brought Mina in almost dead, and I had the whole gang in the office in hysterics all morning."

"Mina? The poisonous female infant? What's the matter with her?"

"Don't know yet, but she's very sick. Jikrun brought her down river last night, and got a taxi to the office, and left her outside in it while they came for me. She was unconscious when I saw her. I told them to take her to the hospital, and paid the taxi there, and started them off, and the next thing they were all back again in the office. They said the dresser wouldn't take the child in because the doctor was away for the morning. So I put her in my car and went back to the hospital, and bawled hell out of them for not taking her, and insisted they give her a bed immediately – said we'd be responsible. By that time both Jikrun and Baud were kicking up a row about how they were afraid to leave her in the hospital."

"What did they bring her down for, if not to get her taken care of?"

"Medicine! They said they thought I'd give her some medicine and they'd paddle her back up the Kinabatangan again. They came all that way in a *prahu* with the kid lying in the bottom of the boat half dead, and they were quite prepared to go back the same way. God, what people! Baud's so pregnant I thought she'd have the baby in the office files at any moment."

"Did you get any idea what was the matter with Mina?"

"Everything, I reckon. I'm going up to the hospital now for a report."

At the crossroads which lead to the hospital there is an old stone trough once used for watering water buffaloes as they journeyed on the road, now used for sitting on, spitting into, and urinating over by little, bright-eyed schoolboys. Now as we drive to the hospital, this trough is converted into a monument of sorrow, with living statuary in attitudes of mourning. Here is Baud, squatting and scarcely able to be so for pregnancy, her sarong draped over her head and tears flowing; here is Jikrun standing beside her looking useless, mournful and loving; here are Mat and Usin and Arsat with brown eyes roving, half-sad, half-excited, and here are the minimum of ten gentlemen followers without which a respectable Muslim will not leave home, all in attitudes of expectant mourning.

"My God! Mina must be dead!"

All except Baud spring to their feet and surround our small car in mournful attitudes as we stop.

"What is it, Jikrun? Is Mina worse?"

"We do not know, Tuan."

"What are you crying about then?"

"Mina's mama says Mina will die in the hospital!" explains Jikrun.

"She'll damn well die if you *don't* leave her in the hospital!"

"Yes, Tuan. But the mama knows best for the child, and the

mama says Mina will die if we leave her there. My wife has had six children, and she knows."

"Six? Where are they now?"

"Five died, Tuan. Only Mina is alive."

"Your wife has had six children and five of them died – so the mama probably doesn't know what is best! You tell Baud that she is to leave Mina in hospital or Mina will die too. I am going to hospital now to talk with the doctor. Meet me there and I'll tell you what he says."

We find Mina in bed in a little cot with a Chinese nurse beside her and the doctor waiting with a penicillin injection. I place the little red plastic dolly I have brought beside her on the pillow, and I see that her small brown face is purple with fever, and her scalp covered with scabies.

"Pneumonia, malaria, dysentery, hookworm and roundworms," says the doctor. "And I think her recovery is very doubtful."

"And her father and mother are waiting out there to snatch her away!" groans Harry.

"She will certainly die if she is moved."

"Harry, I'm frightened. It's going to be awful if we make them leave her here, and she still dies. They'll blame it on us and the hospital."

"Doctor, would it be possible for the mother to have a cot to sleep on here beside the child?" asks Harry. "Then she may be content to keep her here. The mother's about to have another baby at any moment, and the best place for her is hospital."

The doctor considers a moment. "Well, we usually try to get rid of the relatives, especially with these native women. They're dirty, un-co-operative and ignorant, and just make things harder for the nurses. But in this case, I'm willing for the mother to have a cot and stay with the child, as she is pregnant. We may get the delivery of the infant that way, also."

We go outside the ward and find Jikrun, Baud and followers, tears wiped away for the moment, standing in a respectful group awaiting news. Harry repeats the doctor's verdict: the child's only hope is to stay in hospital, the mother is to stay with her.

"She can have the baby in the hospital," says Harry, "and

then perhaps you'll have *two* children out of six – a boy this time, perhaps."

Jikrun looks doubtful, and then translates Harry's Malay into Dusun for Baud's ears. Baud begins to wail again and the sarong comes up over her face.

"She says she is afraid to stay in the hospital," Jikrun says. "She wants to take Mina home."

"Hell! Tell her she can't take Mina home, and she has to stay in the hospital. I have made arrangements with the doctor."

"Yes, Tuan."

Jikrun translates and the wailing increases. "She says she is afraid to have the baby in the hospital. She wants to go back up the river where the old ladies know how to help her have the baby."

"Jikrun, tell her – Oh hell, what's the use! Jikrun, put her in that ward and make her stay! And listen, if you take Mina away from the hospital I'll see that you never get another advance from Government, or another cent out of me."

"Yes, Tuan." This argument is practical.

"And Jikrun, after you get her into hospital, bring the boys and your friends to my house for coffee and biscuits."

The next morning we go to hospital to see what the report of Mina is. Jikrun meets us gloomily in front of the ward.

"Mina is not better. I wait all night here by the hospital to watch."

"That wasn't necessary. The doctor and nurse will take care of her. What about your wife? Is she in there with Mina?"

"My wife left this morning to go back up the Kinabatangan to have her baby. Already she had pains. My friends took her in the boat."

"You mean she left this hospital where she could have the baby with a doctor and nurse to help her, and went back to a dirty hut in the jungle to a lot of dirty old women with dirty hands to have a baby that will probably get sick and die?" roars Harry.

"Tuan, I could not stop her. It is the mama who knows best about babies! She was afraid to have baby in the hospital with doctor. She went back to the old ladies who know how. The mama has already had six children, and she knows—"

"The women! You can't beat 'em!" groans Harry.

We go in to the doctor who says he thinks there may be a chance for recovery, if the child is not disturbed. We ask to be

called immediately if a crisis occurs in her condition, or if Jikrun tries to remove her.

"Jikrun will probably be all right now that the woman's out of the way," Harry says.

The next day Mina was the same, which at this stage meant she was better. She was battling her diseases with more stamina than was usual in natives. But Jikrun was worse—he had made up his mind that the child was going to die, therefore she must be taken out of the hospital before she died in order to have the Muslim priest say prayers and perform the rituals which would ensure her going to Paradise when she died.

"If you take that child out of hospital, I'll see to it that you and your people never get another penny from Government!" threatened Harry, illegally.

For a week Mina struggled with death. Her head was shaved, and nothing was left of her hair for the Angel Gabriel to jerk her up to heaven by, but the longer she struggled the further away she drew from her approach to heaven. The doctor and nurses were fighting for her now in tireless, impersonal struggle which money alone could not have bought. To them and to us Mina had become a test case; she was no longer one child whose life might be saved, she was the entire population of native children all over our uncivilized country who could be helped and served by Mina's survival, because that survival might spread faith in our ways. If Mina lived, the hospital had saved her, and the ways of the white man were wise; but if she died, in native hearts, we had killed her. It was a terrible responsibility.

"Well, I don't give much for our reputation if she dies," said Harry. "I guess we'd better leave town."

"She's not going to die, Harry. She can't die. This is too important."

Ten days later we knew that she wouldn't die – not this time, at least. The hospital, the doctor, the nurses, and Western medicine had won. One small, brown, scabby Dusun child would live. I could not have thanked God more.

It was arranged that Mina was to stay in the hospital for a month longer at least. Jikrun, more than content now to leave her to the hospital and us, had gone back up the river to his wife and the son who had since been born. Harry and I saw Mina regularly at the hospital, where her hair began to grow, her scalp healed of scabies, her thin cheeks plumpened, her eyes brightened, her manners became attractive and gentle and she asked for milk instead of tea. Her bed was surrounded by bright-colored toys that nurses and friends brought to her, and Mina was the pride of the ward.

Five weeks later Jikrun came down from the river to fetch Mina home, and with Mina in his arms he came to the house to say good-by. Mina now looked at her father as at a foreigner, and smiled at us with friendliness. Jikrun regarded Mina's round head, just sprouting new, stiff black hair, her fresh cotton Sandakan garments, and her armload of cheap, bright toys with rather subdued approval.

"She is well now, Tuan."

"Quite well, Jikrun. But if she gets sick again, bring her back. Bring the baby next time – a son, isn't it? – and let the doctor look him over, too."

Jikrun looked away for a minute before he spoke softly, looking at us over Mina's head, "Tuan, my son is dead."

I knew then that such statements no longer surprised me – but they would always shock me. It was useless to ask what the baby died of, or why. We already knew – ignorance, superstition and dirt.

Harry looked off at the trees, across at the bay, down on the town, up at the sky, and then back to Jikrun, or rather, beyond him.

"Well, Jikrun – " he began.

Oh, don't say it! I begged in my mind. You can't tell a man that he killed his son!

"Well, Jikrun – well, Jikrun – "

But Harry hadn't the words, any more than I. We three sat silent, while Mina smiled.

How many years, and lives, will it take? I asked myself.

And I could only answer – until women, men and ignorance cease to fill the same bed.

IV. Turtle Islands

HAVING traveled uneasily all night in the little forty-foot *Elopura* we anchored off the coast of Taganac Island at dawn, feeling and looking more like beachcombers than representatives of the British Government attending an international ceremony. We had spent the night on deck on stretchers in spite of a rolling sea and spray, rather than use bunks in the odoriferous cabin below.

Now, anchored in a heavy swell off the island of our destination, we could see the Philippine Islands' presidential yacht, *Anemone*, bearing the other participants of the ceremony, just coming into view on the horizon, and we could no longer put off going below to dress. Here in the tiny combined cabin, galley and w.c. the air was close and heavy with the odors of bilge water, cockroaches, damp clothing and the patent pump toilet which regurgitated its contents endlessly instead of sucking it down. As the water tanks were leaking no water could be spared for bathing, and I struggled hastily into my shorts unwashed, and got on deck again just in time to avoid being ill.

The occasion of our trip was to witness the transfer of administration of the Turtle Islands, Philippine Island possessions, from British administration to administration by the new Republic of the Philippines. The East Coast Resident of North Borneo, Nick Combe, and Harry were attending as representatives of our government, while Diana, Nick's wife, and I were guests.

In 1930, by the Line of Demarcation then drawn, the Turtle Islands had been officially acknowledged to belong to the Philippine Islands, although the islands themselves were still administered by the British because they were closer to North Borneo than to the Philippines. British administration was continued by agreement with the United States Government in the Philippines until the independence of the Philippine Islands in 1946 and the formation of the new Republic. At this time the young Republic stated its desire to resume administration of the islands. It was in accordance with the terms of the 1930 agreement that administration could be resumed after a year's notice by the Government of the Philippines, and this notice was given in 1947, and the transfer verbally arranged. Now on this June day a year later, the actual ceremony of transfer was to take place at Taganac Island, the principal island of the Turtle group.

Some Manila newspapers had already featured stories which represented the transfer of administration as being a matter of actual acquisition of territory to the new Republic. Stories to the effect that "the disintegration of the British Empire was being precipitated by the transfer of the Turtle Islands," and that "on the coming auspicious day the Union Jack will be hauled down and the flag of the new Republic will be victoriously raised in its place over the Turtle Islands!" gave a dramatic picture which disregarded the fact that the Union Jack had never flown over these islands which always had been Filipino territory, which was a most important fact from the British viewpoint. With the newspaper stories in mind we had been advised that if any misrepresentation of the facts occurred at the ceremony we should protest it, and we had agreed among ourselves to walk out of the ceremony if this happened.

Now lying on the deck of the launch in the cool of coming day we watched the rapid approach of the *Anemone*, a rakish battleship, compared to the little *Elopura*. We saw her steam in, and anchor further offshore than we, and lie there impressively motionless despite the heavy swell, a long, slate-gray reminder of newly expressed Filipino dignity.

Through binoculars we could watch with interest while she lowered a large motor lifeboat into the sea, then dropped a dinghy overboard beside it, wrong side up. This misadventure cheered us, and seemed to make up a bit for the inferior size of the *Elopura*. The dinghy was soon righted and figures swarmed up and down myriad ropes, while signals of sorts and varieties such as we had never before seen flashed madly up and down.

As we watched, it became obvious that the heavy sea was as much as the large lifeboat could cope with, and we began to think we could never make shore in our own leaky rowboat. Nick decided to approach the *Anemone* for information about the ceremonial plans, and at the same time to mention that we feared we might not be able to land in our own boat.

The *Elopura* headed for the lee side of the *Anemone*, but as we approached the captain of the *Anemone* signaled for us to go to windward, where for some unaccountable reason they had let down their gangway. Arriving at the weather side we bumped up and down against the *Anemone* while their sailors and ours struggled to align the two ships long enough for Nick and Harry to climb on board. Finally the two managed a jump to the gangway, and before they were halfway up they were the target for Filipino photographers. Once on deck, they were swamped in a white sea of silk-suited, smartly groomed Filipino diplomats in patent-leather shoes, whose sartorial elegance made Nick and Harry look rudely Anglo-Saxon in shorts and open shirts.

Diana and I on the deck of the *Elopura*, also in shorts and shirts, were unready for public life, but as we watched the press reception given our husbands, we unwittingly caught the eye of Dr. Diosdado Macapagal, who had visited Sandakan six months before to discuss today's ceremony, and whom we had met. Recognizing us, like poor relations in the squalor of our small, wet boat, Dr. Macapagal hospitably called down to us to come on board – the last thing we wanted to do then. We visioned ourselves on the windswept gangway in shorts, a spectacle for photographers to be commemorated at our worst to the elegance-loving Filipino public. We hastily indicated No, by gestures which Dr. Macapagal graciously acknowledged, and then he and a crowd of delegates, the gentlemen of the press, and our husbands, retired from sight inside the foredeck.

Gazing interestedly at the throngs which lined the rails of the *Anemone* we saw to our surprise a large number of young women and girls, most of them smartly dressed in pastel-colored linen slacks and thin silk shirts which clung in the breeze to their dainty, well-formed figures. Less surprisingly, we saw a large number of neatly uniformed Philippine Island Constabulary, also an assortment of what we assumed to be ex-guerilla Brass Hats with pistols and chests covered with medals, and two men who looked like giants among the dapper Filipinos, and were obviously important. Those two wore impressive looking but unlike uniforms, and we guessed them to represent Army and Navy, and later learned one was a colonel, the other an admiral.

Half an hour later when Nick and Harry galloped down the gangway and hopped back on the *Elopura* they were much mellowed in spirit due to excellent beer, and gave us a cheerful picture. The ceremony was to take place at 9:30 A.M. on Taganac Island itself, and the Admiral had volunteered to be responsible for getting us ashore.

Meanwhile we were pulling away from the side of the *Anemone* for the sake of privacy, and the *Elopura* was rolling worse than ever. I went below to put on my ceremonial robes, and cold sweat and nausea swept through me as I entered the cabin and breathed the fetid air. Had I cared less for my country's reputation, or for my own pride, I would have gone ashore in blue shorts and red shirt, with my hair in two braids just as I stood. But diplomatic respectability triumphed and I combed, braided and pinned up my annoyingly straight hair, put on make-up and a white linen dress and high-heeled sandals, fighting down vertigo and waves of green heat as I worked. Diana, who is quite unmoved by heavy swells, having stoked a boat as a WAVE in the war, and is beautiful anyway, looked as lovely as if stepping from her boudoir, and perfectly composed.

I was the last one dressed, and was just jabbing at a button on my shoulder when Harry shouted down, "They're here!" I looked at myself in the glass, pale green under cyclamen rouge like pistachio ice cream with strawberry sauce, and thought angrily, What a hell of a diplomatic addition I'll be!

Harry called again, "Hurry! Everybody's waiting for you!"

I ran up the ladder from the cabin hoping death would come soon. There was no one in sight. Harry's voice came again, this time from below the rail—"Hurry! We're waiting!" I ran towards the rail on the side from which his voice came, and with complete indifference to destination I launched myself over the side.

Fortunately or otherwise, I landed right side up in a motorboat which was parked there, the Admiral's own. Here the rest of the party was already established in spotless, starched white, all standing clinging together in the center of the boat, determined not to sit down as the bottom was already awash. The craft which was manned by small, knotty Suluk sailors now progressed towards the shore, meeting each wave with a friendless smack and shudder, while we balanced our bodies against a combination of the wind, spray, gravity, and the sturdy torso of young Sayid Ali, the handsome Suluk District Officer from Taganac Island, who had been commissioned to deliver us.

As the motorboat approached the surf line a lifeboat banged merrily into us, and we were gestured to transfer to it. Now on the crest, now in the trough of the waves, we proceeded to leap from gunwale to gunwale, from the shoulder of sailor to sailor, until we were all in the rowboat, which was then propelled as near shore as the depth of the boat allowed, when we again performed the boat-changing trick, this time into a flat-bottomed craft. In this we rode the surf successfully into the shore, where the boat was hauled out of the incoming waves by sailors who waited dripping on the beach to receive us. As the waves receded we took turns jumping from the bow of the boat to the wet sand

and the waiting arms of a sailor, who then raced us up the beach ahead of the next wave. I have never anticipated a safe arrival with less confidence, or cared less.

By now fresh air and excitement were steadying my stomach, and I began to respond to the vivid beauty of the island and the shore about me, a Sulu Sea picture whose extravagant color was beyond compare. The frothy turquoise waves poured in and out along the silver shore line, beyond the waves the deeper water melted into cobalt blue, and beyond again clear aquamarine sea stretched out to meet indigo depths where the launch was anchored, depths which melted on the horizon into a less blue sky.

It was a coral world; the submerged catacombs of coral were responsible for the pigmentlike richness of color and crystal clarity of the water, and the blazing whiteness of the shore. Here throughout generations and generations of progeny the local coral families had built themselves up, layer upon layer on their own sarcophagi, living and dying for one achievement only, to form these jagged layers of coral which now came out of the sea in guise of the Turtle Islands.

These islands harbor the homes of a few native Suluks and Bajaus, but are better known for being the lying-in home of huge turtles who come out of the azure waters at prescribed intervals to hollow nests in the moonlit sand and deposit myriad eggs which look like ping-pong balls, taste of fish, and are very rich in protein. Taganac Island, upon which we now stood, was the largest of the group, just a crescent of reef and white sand tufted with green coconut palms, with an unexpected hill in the center. The island boasted nothing more than a few native shacks, a Chinese shop, the District Officer's house, and was without landing facilities.

Having landed us safely, the same routine was then followed to bring the entire Filipino delegation, visitors, press and twenty rattan chairs for the V.I.P.s from the *Anemone*. This business took an hour and a half. All necessary parties being now ashore we assembled in the coconut grove a hundred yards from the beach and were introduced to the plenipotentiaries of the delegation, and the Dayang Del Guardia.

The Dayang, although herself of royal Suluk blood and born on an island of the Suluk group, had married an officer in the Filipino Army many years before, which liaison had slightly tainted her glory in the fanatic eyes of the Suluks. Even today, this mother of thirteen living children was an extremely handsome woman and it was obvious that motherhood had agreed with her. She still had the vital quality and radiant magnetism which one connects with sensually alive women, but which seldom survives continued pregnancies.

She was dressed in a magnificent dark red satin tunic heavily embroidered in gold, with emerald-green satin Suluk trousers, and a yellow silk sarong embroidered with turquoise and green flowers, and her breast was studded with gold brooches. Her fluffy black hair was wound in a low knot on her neck, and her pleasantly Mongoloid features were animated in conversation.

Her husband, thirteen children and unnumbered grandchildren all lived together in the family home in Jolo, she told me. One of the grandchildren was ill there now, and the Dayang was impatient to hurry back and care for him, and expressed little excitement over the Filipino ceremonies which were keeping her away. She said that her husband had fought in the Philippine Army in the last war until its surrender, when he was taken prisoner, later escaped, and then fought on as a guerilla, until the peace. The Dayang spoke English extremely well, with better use of idiom than the average, and a quick understanding of double meanings, and she laughed and joked informally with us.

Standing with her was the wife of the acting Governor of Sulu, a very beautiful, pure Suluk woman, tall and slender with delicate bones pleasantly softened by sufficient padding, and a clear, creamy skin. Languid and graceful in her movements, she had a full-lipped, drooping mouth, wide flat cheekbones, a noble forehead and sloe-black eyes which could not hide their challenge. Her straight black hair was pinned loosely back from her forehead, and fell softly over her shoulders without artificial wave. Her slender, shapely hands moved gracefully but without coquetry to touch hair, silky skin, and almond eyelids, as she smoked.

She wore the Suluk costume with very wide trousers made of

sheer pale blue crepe silk flowered with mauve orchids and green leaves, and her loose blouse was of sheer cotton in pastel blue. Being neither royal nor rich she wore few ornaments, and had neither gold buttons nor gold embroidery on her costume. She was infinitely cool and flowerlike and young, and looked intelligent. As she spoke Suluk only, I could not understand her conversation, but her manner had neither coquettishness nor calculated sophistication, and she was dignified, composed, and youthful without showing immaturity.

With her was the young wife of Sayid Ali, the District Officer, also a Suluk, who had the same pure type of southeast Asian beauty. She was dressed in Suluk costume, with pale yellow-flowered silk trousers, and an unpretentious cotton blouse of turquoise blue which became her creamy skin and dark loose hair. These two young wives stayed together, talking and laughing very quietly, smoking languidly, and later, when the rest of us drank beer, drinking water only for they were Muslims.

After introductions and gossip we settled ourselves comfortably thinking that the main event was about to begin, when suddenly the Suluk onlookers from neighboring islands, who had formed a curious ring about us, turned at a cry towards the beach. Then, melting from us, they rushed breathlessly towards the surf and an incoming boat which was beaching. There on the wet sand, with their feet in the lapping waves, they gathered in a great, gaping, admiring throng, bowing and even weeping as they waited to welcome the commanding female figure which stood like a figurehead in the bow of the incoming boat.

The boat grounded on the beach, and its brilliantly dressed occupant leaped with agility onto the wet sand, then as the wave receded the waiting mob flung itself on her in such a scene as I had never before witnessed. As her colorful figure pressed through the welcoming mass the people threw themselves before her, grasped at her silken garments and snatched her slender hands to cover them with kisses and tears — for this was the Suluk Princess, Dayang-Dayang Tarhata Kiram, returning to her people. That she was sovereign here on Sulu soil by acclaim of her subjects, if not by Filipino law, was obvious.

To my surprise the Princess seemed unmoved and almost scornful in her manner, passing through her peasantry with more apparent concern for keeping her yellow satin trousers dainty and her slender hands unsmirched, than for the feelings of her subjects. The Suluks, however, seemed content that such was the proper royal attitude, and they wiped their eyes and their tears and followed contentedly after her as she picked her dainty, high-heeled way through the driftwood on the sand to the fringe of shade under the coconut trees where we sat.

Now it was our turn to be introduced to the Princess, whose intelligent, wide-awake eyes in a handsome face were quickly responsive to each introduction. Her hair, like the Dayang's, was a soft, fluffy black mass twisted in a knot on her neck. Her face, as well as classic Suluk features and regular beauty, had another outstanding quality, a look of open and questing interest and challenge – a look which would sometimes for no apparent reason be replaced by a secretive screen which closed away her responsive personality as completely as if she had drawn a curtain against Peeping Toms.

The Princess spoke excellent English with an American accent, which she explained was acquired at University of Illinois in the United States. The Governor of Sulu presented us to her, and Harry reminded her that he had met her once almost twenty-five years ago, when as a Forestry undergraduate he had stood on the steps of the library of the Berkeley campus in California. Tarhata looked at him with a quick grin – then she let the curtain drop across her face, and murmured vaguely, with an extremely royal air, "Dear, dear, that is *too* long ago! You must be wrong!" Then up zipped the curtain while Tarhata took a peek – then, as if seeing him for the first time, she said firmly, "Young man, *I* do not admit to being more than forty, and on my best days, thirty-five!"

The Governor of Sulu, who was listening to the interchange, laughed and said to Harry, "You know that the Princess is now a widow?"

"Yes," interjected Tarhata quickly, "a widow! But negotiable!"

The Princess, I remembered, had been married to a Suluk, Datu Tahil, leader of a group of rebels who had never ceased to fight the sovereignty of the Filipinos over them. Tahil had spent his life leading rebellions until he was finally captured, and in the end he died officially of "blood poisoning," a phrase which was interpreted by some to be literal.

It would be difficult to guess the real age of the Princess, as her high-pressure charm, animated face, and youthful figure gave her the semblance of youth. As she conversed with us and with Dayang Del Guardia, her cousin by blood, her conversation was uninhibited, a mixture of calculated sophistication and coquettishness, and both ladies had a sense of humor which might be socially alarming.

Princess Tarhata explained that she had been appointed by the Philippine Islands Government as "Deputy Governor" of the Turtle Islands, an appointment which, her tone suggested, was a sop to the Suluks. Her attitude towards the day's ceremony was one of detachment and amused tolerance, which seemed to say, "Well, I know it's only a political junket, but what better can one expect!" Dayang Del Guardia's attitude was more guarded, tempered perhaps by having a Filipino husband. Both ladies cordially invited us to visit them in Jolo, assuring us they would show us everything worth seeing, which we believed.

Now the masters of ceremony had collected their speeches, glasses of water, and rattan chairs, and we were beckoned to follow them deeper into the coconut grove. Here in welcome shade, for the sun was now blazing on the shore, we mounted a speaker's stand erected for the occasion. Twenty of us sat on the platform and faced a standing audience composed of natives, the Philippine Islands Constabulary, the imported mourners and rooters from Manila, and the gentlemen of the press with their girl friends.

These were the girls we had seen by the rail of the boat in shorts and slacks, with hair cosmetically sealed with permanent waves, and it seemed to me now, looking more closely, that the Western sports costumes did not do justice to their ultrafeminine appeal. In contrast to these modern girls, the two young Suluk women dressed after the fashions of their own country and conducting themselves by their own standards seemed attractively at ease in their background, while the modern girls seemed to fit neither into the Western world they were assailing nor the Eastern one they were eschewing.

Just as we settled down to listen to the ceremony the practical thought came to me that if occasion arose for us to leave hastily, we might walk out of the ceremony, but we could not leave the island nor return to the launch, without the Admiral's co-operation.

The program began with a musical overture by the Filipino Constabulary Band, followed by an address by Mr. Jesus Serrano. Mr. Serrano meticulously referred to the transfer as "representing a triumph of diplomacy of the President of the Philippine Islands — a triumph made possible through two conditions, the magnanimity and good sportsmanship of the British Empire, and the diplomacy of the Philippine Islands!" We breathed easier.

"This transfer is a reaffirmation of the spiritual ties between two great mother countries, the United States and Great Britain, and their offspring, our young new Republic of the Philippines. The transfer of today reaffirms the triumph of democracy, and reaffirms on both sides the belief in the principles of democracy which these mother countries have inculcated in us, and which we have adopted.

"We give thanks to the King of England for his magnanimity and good sportsmanship, and especially we welcome warmly all who have come today to represent him, and give especial gratitude and thanks to the delegates who have attended this ceremony, despite difficulties, inconvenience and discomforts!"

As he sat down, the Filipino delegate next to me whispered anxiously, "There was no offense in that, was there?" From which I judged that the speakers were as anxious as we were.

Now Nick, as the representative of the British Government, gave a short address of "Delivery of Administration," in a factual, untheatrical, very English voice, which was in contrast to the oratorical style which was as natural to the Filipino speakers as this was to him. Nick repeated the story of the Line of Demarcation in 1930 and reminded his listeners that the Philippine Islands, then under the United States, had themselves agreed that Great Britain should administer the islands; that by the terms of the 1930 agreement, a transfer of administration could take place at a year's notice, and that in 1947 this notice was given. The transfer now taking place was one of administration only, as the Turtle

Islands had never flown a British emblem. His remarks were greeted with amicable nods of agreement.

Now our friend, Dr. Diosdado Macapagal, accepting the transfer on behalf of the Republic of the Philippines, made a fiery and earnest speech which he closed with the following words— "However, it is only natural that we have today a feeling of exultation and happiness at this extension of our Government so early in the life of our new Republic. We take this as a symbol of new growth, strength, and vitality of our Republic. This is an extension of moral imperialism only, the only imperialism to which we aspire, for we are true disciples of our mother countries who have taught us their democracy. This extension of our Government is a portent of the place the Philippine Islands will take in the future drama of the spreading of the democratic principles which we have inherited from Great Britain and the United States of America."

Dr. Macapagal then stepped forward and raised the flag of the Republic of the Philippines, in time to the slow measure of the Filipino national anthem. As the melody trembled uncertainly on the air there were tears in the speaker's eyes and in those of many about us, and even the Dayangs took this seriously. As I felt my own eyes grow wet in sympathy, I asked myself rather resentfully why the Filipino national anthem, poorly played, should do this to me? It seemed to me that the answer was that a national anthem brings to the people of its homeland the vision of home and family which makes that land so dear. And because love of homeland is common to every human being, such love ceases to be nationalistic, and becomes instead a common bond between the peoples of all nations.

In the midst of my thoughts, Princess Tarhata Kiram, seated near me, rose to her feet, deposited her red bead bag and flowered hanky in Dayang Del Guardia's lap, and stepped daintily down from the speaker's stand and trotted forward to a five-foot, flag-veiled monument which had for some time mystified me.

Here she took the stance of one who is about to do something important, adjusted her hair and bangles, and gathered up an end of drapery which dangled from the tablet. First she twitched it casually, then impatiently, then as if gathering all her strength she flipped back the bunting and revealed a cement tablet engraved in romanized Tagalog, which told the story of the day's historic occasion.

The band, which had lost place in the ceremony, was now goaded into playing, "Philippines, I love my Philippines!" while the audience sang through the first two lines with gusto, after which memories waned and the song ended with diminishing volume which marks second verses of national anthems everywhere.

The Admiral now chivalrously offered to transport us out to the *Anemone* where we were to be guests for lunch. Successfully arrived at the *Anemone,* we and the delegates drank beer together, laughed at each other's jokes, and consumed a large banquet which ended with huge, sunset-colored Philippine Island mangoes which dripped juice all over us. Immediately the young Suluk wives disappeared, the two Dayangs looked impatient, and it became obvious the party was over.

As we drew away from the *Anemone's* side in the Admiral's boat, headed for the *Elopura,* the last thing we saw was the ship's rail lined by delegates, constabulary, press, dainty girls and Dayangs, all with smiling, friendly faces waving graceful hands in warm good-by.

In inconspicuous fashion the little *Elopura* hauled up her rusty anchor chain, lashed down her torn curtains, started her worn-out engines, and steamed off into an oncoming storm. The sea was rough, and soon rain came, but as we huddled under coats and ground sheets on deck in old clothes there was a wonderful feeling of relaxation. We arrived in Sandakan that night congratulating ourselves upon the success of our mission.

The next morning at six o'clock Nick rang Harry, and said, "Turn your wireless to Manila!"

We did, and heard: "The British flag yesterday came down on one of the last far-flung outposts of the British Empire. The flag of the Republic of the Philippines was gallantly raised in its place, marking a triumph of diplomacy and territorial gains for the new Republic!"

PART FIVE

Lightning in a Luminous Sky

Lightning in a luminous sky,
Thunder impregnate with rain,
Signs of storm to come.

—*From a Malay Proverb*

I. My Enemy

I HAVE recently received a letter which ends like this:

> How the publication of your new work is progressing?
> You will understand that my cherished ambition is to translate one of your recent works one of these days.
> Please give my best regards to your husband and children.
> Yours faithfully,
> TAKUO MATSUI

In January of 1943 a very small, very old coal-burning steamer was traveling down the west coast of North Borneo from Sandakan to Kuching, Sarawak. On board were a number of Japanese troops and a few officers, as well as forty-seven miserable women and eleven seasick, half-starved children, prisoners of the

Japanese. George, not three years old then, and I were among these prisoners on our way to a new prison camp.

This journey lasted for ten days, and if there was anything it lacked of hell, I did not know it then, although later experience taught me. We had been imprisoned almost a year on the small island of Berhala off the coast of North Borneo, and we were being moved from this island camp by boat; we left there on Monday noon after a meal of rice and weeds, and the next food we received on our journey was Thursday at 5 P.M., when we ate rice and rotting fish cooked by ourselves on the ship's boilers. Our drinking water came from the boilers, and there were no provisions for sanitation on the trip. We were crowded together on an open deck with no protection from tropical sun or deluging rain, equatorial winds, or driving salt spray. We crouched upright against each other in misery and filth, without sufficient space to lie down either by day or by night.

The few Japanese officers on board were quartered in the one small cabin, and their entertainment was to come out on the deck and gloat over us at their ease and pleasure. The soldiers were stretched out in comparative comfort on the protected part of the same deck as we.

The boat traveled without lights at night, and carried neither life belts nor lifeboats. By day she anchored in ground swells awaiting secret signals, or sneaked stealthily into small ports, where we watched hungrily while the Japanese soldiers bought fish and eggs from the peddlers on the wharf. Seeing this, our children begged unavailingly for food of the same sort.

Our own diet of rotting fish stank worse each day. The children would cry for food, eat it and then vomit, and then cry again with the ache of their starving insides. By night they wept from exhaustion, with no space to sleep; and they wept because we, their mothers, were frightened, even while we said to them, "Do not be afraid!"

By day I struggled and swore, by night I prayed. I could not meet this alone – and I had to. After a year of war this was the worst. All through the first year I had fought with myself to remember that in war all men suffered and I was no worse off than others, the women of the enemy suffered too; telling myself that I must keep an unprejudiced mind, I must not hate.

But on this journey I looked all about me for help, and finding no help in God or man I steeled my weakness with hate, for now I faced life without mercy. I knew myself grown cold and hard, and I resolved that from now on there should be no human softness left in me for anything. I had but one thing to live for now, my child – and I had learned how to fight for him.

Midway on the journey I was crawling to the rail one day to empty George's pot when I heard one of the Japanese soldiers calling softly, "Mrs. Keef! Mrs. Keef! Can I help you?"

I hesitated, telling myself this was some new, cruel joke. But the soldier continued to speak very softly. "Mrs. Keef, I read your book *Land Below the Wind*, translated to Japanese. I like what you say about Japanese people. I sorry to see you like this. I wish to help you. You tell me – I help."

In order not to attract attention I continued to the rail and finished my job, then as I crawled back I whispered, "Ask the officer for food for our children!"

The soldier looked at me in distress and alarm, and said, shaking his head quickly, "No can! No can!"

I knew I had asked him for a dangerous thing. Japanese soldiers do not show pity to fallen foes. Soldiers are in the business of killing, and anything they give you less than death is a boon. But, I was fighting for my child. My heart was hard. I did not care what happened to this soldier, if I got food.

"Ask for food!" I urged. "If you wish to help me, ask for food!"

The soldier looked at me. He was a brave man. "I try," he said.

That night very secretly in the dark, for he did not dare to be seen talking to me again, he followed me when I went to the boiler for water.

"I very sorry. Officer say no give food, this food plenty good enough! But I give you this myself to help you. I very sorry for you and baby. Please not to talk to me again. I am afraid." He placed in my hand a wadded piece of paper, and slunk away.

As I took the secret paper I could imagine the scene with the Japanese officer hissing and spitting. "Hungry? Paaaahh! Hungry?

Sodeska! Hungry? Good enough for them. They're not so proud now! Hungry? So are my wife and children in Japan. So are yours, if you have any! Hungry? These people are alive, aren't they? And lucky to be! Hungry? Good. Leave them be, leave them alone, don't go near them . . . you . . . you . . .!"

Silently and secretly I crawled closer to the boiler light, and uncreased the wadded paper and looked inside. There was a ten-dollar Borneo bill, and this note printed in capitals:

> I present to you $10 which is my salary. That is a few money. I am regretable not to be able to give you enough money because I am only soldier. Please do not fear. Take this money. I do not need money, because I may die in battle and have no wife, no child, no father, only mother.
>
> A JAPANESE SOLDIER

I crept back to my space on the deck. I sat there in the hot wind in the blackness with my son's small, warm body limp from sleep in my arms, while I reminded myself that I was hard, very hard, and all human feeling had left me! Then, with George's heart beating against mine and his soft hair blowing in my eyes and his soft little hands half open against my heart in sleep, I cried.

The tears that fell that night were not for self-pity, nor even for gratitude, nor were they for myself alone, nor for George. They were tears which came from my heart for all sons and all mothers in every land who are born into this world in love and human imperfection, only to learn to kill and to hate. These tears fell because even a soldier was kind, and it is the will of man to be kind – yet this soldier, and man, must kill.

I knew then that there were just two things which could break a heart; one is the terrible harshness of man, the other is his transfiguring mercy.

Now secretly in the dark, by feel, I wrote a note to the soldier on a torn scrap of paper.

> I have been learning to hate all Japanese because of the way they treat us, but now I see that you are kind. I know that you are good. I will never forget your kindness. I pray that you will live to return to your home. God bless you.

The money I hid in my shoe and in due time the ten dollars bought contraband food for George, and in time both money and food were gone. But the memory of the kindness stayed with me through three more long years of captivity, years when there was little else to prove the mercy of man, in either ourselves or the enemy.

That was my first meeting with Takuo Matsui, Japanese soldier.

After the war was over we returned to Borneo to a destroyed home and city, in a ravaged land. The energy of every human being was now employed in reconstruction.

In early 1949 I received a letter from Tokyo:

> DEAR MRS. AGNES KEITH,
>
> I read in newspaper that you and son George and husband are safe from war, and you have written a new work, *Three Came Home*. I am Japanese soldier Takuo Matsui who go with you on that, for you, so very terrible and accursed journey of storms, hunger and disgrace on boat from Sandakan to Sarawak. You and baby are without food and I make you then present of ten yen. Always I cherish as momento the letter you write to me for thanks. I make a photograph of letter and send to you now.
>
> When I read of your new novel I remember your talk with me on deck in January 1943. Then you said that when war ended you would write about the extraordinary experiences that you had and the cruel treatment of Japanese army. I find in *Three Came Home* how hard you tried to keep a record of the war which, if found, meant death penalty for you by Japanese army, and I cannot help but admire and be surprised at your enthusiasm and aspiration for literature at risk of your life.
>
> When I meet you on boat I am forlorn soldier, now I am married with one wife, one baby one year old. I work again for the brewery my former employer.
>
> There is such lack of housing here I hope in vain to build for myself at least a small shed.
>
> But I was writing about myself too long. How is your baby? Please remember me,
>
> TAKUO MATSUI

Enclosed was a photograph of the note I had written him on a torn scrap of paper, dated January 17, 1943, in appreciation of the kind deed of a Japanese soldier.

I replied to this letter saying that I was happy to know he was alive and safe, and that I had never forgotten his kindness to me, and that George and I had now returned to Borneo to join my husband.

Several months later I received another letter.

Dear Mrs. Agnes Newton Keith,

I was very glad to hear from you after six long years, especially to know that you and son George are in good spirit and leading a happy life again in Sandakan.

I remember vividly the daily life in your country, where there is no change of seasons throughout the year and people in thin shirts and short pants work under a strong sun wiping off their perspiration.

I have also heard that the streets in Sandakan were reduced to ashes during the latter days of the war. I imagine a great many people suffered the calamities.

I feel very sorry that the Japanese Army, while occupying your country, troubled you and your people so much. As one of those who actually passed through the war, I can realize from the bottom of my heart how a cursed thing the war is! How many people there were with their houses burnt, properties destroyed, husbands, wives and children lost, and with nothing to eat and wear!

After seeing you to Kuching in 1943, I immediately went to Singapore where I stayed for about two months. Then I went over to Siam, from where I further went to Burma on foot, proceeding through jungles with heavy burdens on my shoulders. It was so hard a work that even now I shudder at the thought of it. Making narrow escape more than several times on the way, thank God, I could survive all those difficulties.

In the middle of 1944, I was back again in Borneo and remained at Jesselton until the end of the war. I could come back to Japan in 1946 and am glad to inform you that I am now leading a peaceful life.

I feel as if it were by Providence that I can again talk to you, though by means of a letter.

Around October 10 Mr. Sessue Hayakawa, who played the part of the Colonel as a main actor in the movie *Three Came Home*, returned here from Hollywood. I heard him saying that he could make a very fine picture favorable even to the eyes of the Japanese. I am also thankful to you. The picture will probably be imported into Japan early next year, and not only I but also all the movie-fans are anxiously waiting for it.

Please understand my good-will to you. Please give my best regards to your husband and son George. Hoping you are in good health.

I am, truly yours,

TAKUO MATSUI

Christmas 1949 was coming. I had sold *Three Came Home* to the Book-of-the-Month Club and the movies, and for the first time since the war, instead of being objects of charity ourselves, we had something to give to others.

I had followed in periodicals the sudden religious conversion of Japan and its swift and worthy reform. I knew that the Oriental Santa Clauses on Tokyo's newly Christianized but frozen streets would sponsor gifts for sale once more this Christmas, but that the Japanese would have no money to buy them. The Ginza was brightly illuminated again, and the windows would be gay with glittering displays of gifts, but the poor were still poor. Many an ex-soldier, Buddhist or Shinto once, now conveniently converted Christian, would ask himself as he wandered there in the cold, what it was all about—was Santa Claus the Number One Christian?

I wrote to a friend in Seattle and asked her to purchase several suitable CARE packages on my behalf for Japan, as at this time CARE was the only agency for delivery of gifts in Japan. I especially wished these packages to be delivered in time for Christmas as I knew by experience that Christmas is the saddest of all times in which to be sad and poor.

In February I received a letter from Tokyo again.

DEAR MRS. A. KEITH AND GEORGE.

Nothing was more surprised to me than your gifts arriving. I shared your gifts with my friends. They admired this friendship originating from my trivial favor to you in the war, and your inordinate kindness. I served them with coffee and they said I was a fortunate fellow. Most of all we liked the coffee, sugar, soap, towels and white cotton cloth and wool stuffs for the baby. The gifts have cured me of the fatigues after hard work at office. I was deeply touched by your kindness. These gifts will delight my family for some time to come.

For your kindness I wish to help you also. May I help you to sell your stories in Japan? My friends will read them.

Yours faithfully . . .

I replied to this letter saying that I already had a contract for stories as yet unwritten, and my primary difficulty was writing them.

Then another letter came, with, amongst other comments, the following paragraph:

I would like to be author also, and publish my writings in United States. Can you help me to sell them please?

With this note sounding between author and author, my conviction was cemented that everyone wants to write. I answered my friend that I would be glad to send his stories to my publisher, if he would send them to me.

Another letter:

Thank you, but my stories not yet written.

I would like to give you as present some bottles of beer brewed by our company's brewery, but I am anxious whether that might trouble you in case import duty levied.

In case duty does not give you trouble, I should like to send them by vessel, freight payable at destination. Please inform me whether you will accept them.

We informed him, and some time later the beer arrived. We were living in our new house, built on the foundations of the old one which had been burned to the ground by the Japanese with all our possessions. Our windows again looked out over the town of Sandakan, slowly rebuilding, but still a monument to war's desolation and man's destruction.

It was a hot, bright, violent day and the sheets of reflected light from the waters of the bay struck up into my eyes and reminded me suddenly of something – it was just such a bright, blinding day when under Japanese guard we had been marched from this site to prison camp; it was such a day when men had been spat upon, beaten, shot, tortured; it was such a day . . .

We opened two bottles of Japanese beer very thoughtfully, and drank to a Japanese friend.

II. Everybody Has to Have a Friend

Perhaps the same principle that determines which comes first, the egg or the chicken, would work to determine whether Russia is using China, or China is using Russia," I worried, as I looked at the open letter in my hand.

"I'd rather ask a Ouija board myself – it's more reliable," says Harry helpfully. "What brings this problem on us tonight?"

"This letter of Jeannette's. It upsets my ideology, and reminds me that the situation is not so simple as our propaganda makes it out to be. Her attitude to the Communists' regime undoubtedly represents that of most of young China and, somehow or other, that regime has given them national spirit for the first time since I've known any young Chinese, and you can't ignore that. From their point of view, they are using Russia. From our point of view, they are being made fools of by Russia. And yet I'll bet on the individual Chinese, any day, against the individual Russian – and *nobody* makes a fool of him!"

"I won't bet on either of them," says Harry cautiously. "Where is Jeannette now, and what's in her letter? Last I heard of her, she had a job with ECA in China and liked American GI's better than British boys because they were 'easier to get acquainted with'!"

"She's in Shanghai, and the letter is dated just after the fall of Shanghai to the Communists, and it has taken all those months to reach here. I'll read it to you, it's a good letter and gives her side intelligently, but you'll probably be shouting No! No! all the way through. She sent this snapshot of herself. Isn't she lovely now?"

"Phew! She certainly grew up to be a good-looking gal!"

The girl in the photograph is in Chinese dress, and tall with the well-proportioned, graceful height of the northern Chinese and the long, shapely leg which makes the slit Shanghai gown so becoming to them. Her very Oriental eyes show a sparkle of quick humor, even in a photograph, and her skin looks smooth and shining, her hair waves with a new permanent, and her quickly smiling, generous mouth has a stronger set to it than I have seen there before. She looks now like a person who has convictions — and from her letter, she has.

We first knew her before the war in Sandakan as a girl and near neighbor, the offspring of a Chinese father and a European mother. Here we watched her with sympathy, affection, and unease as she grew through a gently awkward adolescence in which she eschewed her Asiatic ties, yet found no satisfactory substitute for them. When I would ask her, as I sometimes did, why she tried to ignore her Chinese blood, she would shrug her shoulders and not know the answer. But I thought I knew why; in the young Chinese then there was no national pride — there was nothing to rival the blind legend of racial supremacy which the white man had created for himself in the Orient.

Jeannette had inherited Kuomintang political convictions from her father, and Western prejudices from her mother, she was educated in both the East and the West, she had lived in Europe and the Orient, and as she grew up she had to choose which race she would cling to. She chose the white race, the race of, as she saw them, the rulers. She dressed in European clothes, she spoke in American and British idiom, she laughed at Western humor, and wept for Western reasons. As a too slender, too pallid, delicate, diffident child, she had to force herself to self-conscious public gaieties, and longed for Western boys to go about with. When she went out with the Chinese lads in town she would describe them to me later, and wrinkle her nose as she said, "Oh, well, you know how these Chinese are!" But the young woman who writes me today is no longer a Eurasian girl assailing the Western world – she is a woman proudly Chinese.

Jeannette writes:

Dear Agnes:

First I must warn you not to jump to conclusions and start thinking that we are behind the "bamboo curtain" and all such bosh on which American politicians and journalists dwell with such delight.

Not being totally Chinese, I must say that I too sometimes feel it is hard to understand the Chinese, though it is easier for me to do so than for a Westerner. But the real trouble with most people is that they do not even bother to *try* to understand the Chinese, because it is more restful to just dismiss us from their minds.

Due to the development of the situation I was terminated last November when ECA completely liquidated its operations – at that time it was only a regional office as the head office had moved to Canton prior to the liberation, then to Hong Kong, where a few people are maybe thinking now to pour more supplies down the rat hole. After two months' idleness, I was lucky enough to secure a job where I am kept extremely busy. Although the salary is not at all brilliant and quite a change from my former positions it is better than nothing, at this time when so many are unemployed, and by Chinese standards it is considered very good.

The few months preceding the liberation of Shanghai were so confused that I hope never to see such times again. The KMT once again showed its inability to cope with a situation which it had created with its own hands, because it had sunk so low that it just couldn't rise for any kind of effort. The monetary situation was absolutely terrible, with the black market reigning supreme and price fluctuations so violent, that if one did not dispose of one's money immediately, it lost as much as 50 per cent of its value within a few hours. When our salary was due, we tried to get it as fast as possible, as a delay of 10 or 20 minutes meant a big loss. There were Chinese silver dollars in circulation, and peddlers at every corner selling and buying them, and the tinkling of coins as they rang them became a familiar and irritating sound, with prices being upped all the time and white-collar employees and others were wondering whether to buy Chinese or U.S. dollars, and where not to get cheated. Pay day was not workday for any of us, but a series of speculative suggestions, and when one thinks back it was all very funny – but at the time it was more tragic!

Though it was a foregone conclusion that Shanghai would fall to the Communists, we did not think it would happen so fast, at least, not when the KMT was boasting of its impregnable defenses and warning the population to stock in six months' supplies. One of the fortifications built around the city was alternately called "great wall of Shanghai," or "toothpick defense," and consisted merely of a wooden barrier. No doubt, someone managed to get quite a bit into his pockets on that project!

"Graft in China didn't begin with the KMT!" interrupts Harry practically.

"And graft isn't confined to China," I amend. "What about defense project scandals in the U. S. A.? What about making money on munitions?"

The battle for Shanghai was quickly decided. On the morning of May 25th and KMT had a "victory parade" in town to celebrate the "huge victories" they had gained! At two P.M. the same afternoon they were retreating, and the People's Liberation Army came in around 10 P.M., and we were awakened by the sound of running feet in our street and discovered the KMT soldiers were running full speed toward the Bund with all their gear. When we got up the next morning, the city had been liberated – all very peacefully except for a little resistance in some districts, which was quickly put down.

"I'll bet it was! She doesn't go into detail about just how they put it down," murmurs Harry.

> The first surprise in Shanghai was the good discipline of the PLA soldiers — we had become so accustomed to the behavior of the KMT soldiers who were always disorderly, and more a public menace than a protection; they would throw grenades in theaters and cinemas because they couldn't get in free of charge, and beat up or shoot bus or tram conductors who would ask them for tickets, ad infinitum. On the contrary, an event never before witnessed in China, the PLA man is polite, pays for everything he buys, and is well disciplined. Yet he does not have a beautiful uniform, and many of them wear plain Chinese shoes. It is argued that the reason for it is because he knows *why* he is fighting, and I believe this is true.

"He *thinks* he knows why he is fighting," corrects Harry, "because the Communists have good propaganda! They promise Asia what Asia needs — a living and land. But it is yet to be shown that Communism gives these things."

> The attitude of the people [I continue] towards the People's government is varied, as can be expected — I frequent both sides and am totally neutral.

"Obviously!" says Harry.

> Moreover I never worked for the former government, but I lost my job because the policy has changed, so I believe I should be impartial in my opinions. I believe that the New China government will do something for the country: they are all full of good intentions, and they have already shown their willingness to reconstruct and rehabilitate the land. But of course before everything is set right it will take time, money, patience and fortitude, and many people get discouraged.
>
> For instance, people thought that the new government would do miracles and that as soon as they arrived, everything would be fine, and they were consequently disappointed. However, the government had to cope with such a messy heritage that it has taken time to disentangle problems. Shanghai runs much better now than before, the trains at

least are running on schedule all over the country. One can travel in thirty-six hours most comfortably to Peking as in prewar times.

"One can," agrees Harry, "if one is Chinese. But one cannot travel at all to Peking if one is British or American!"

Laws are enforced and all people have to obey them and that's what gets the goat of so many, especially foreigners. Foreigners had been accustomed to consider China a colony, and their attitude was that of a superior race.

"She has a point there," agrees Harry.

They had many privileges, and even after V–J Day, many a foreigner would get away with a lot of things just because he was a foreigner. Now, it's different, and tears are shed and lamentations heard over "the good old days" – Yeah, they are gone forever and forever, and all the better!

"Well, I don't blame her for feeling that 'the good old days' from our point of view were not good days from theirs," I admit.

No one regrets the KMT, they did too much harm to all. If they had not ruled as they did, the Chinese people would not have thrown them out – the Chinese may be easy-going, but there is a limit to everything, so the KMT have only themselves to blame for what happened. Madame's speech before her departure to Taiwan was certainly a tear-jerker! – if one doesn't know her, and her gang! You get a pain in the neck when her gang talks of "democracy" and "freedom," beautiful words with which to catch the Americans, but only words without meaning.

"There is terrible truth in that, Harry. For the Chinese people in general, democracy and freedom have been words without meaning. They have no experience to relate such definitions to. When you talk about food and land for everybody, then they know what you mean."

Madame Chiang, her husband, and her family sucked China to the lifeblood, and now they can't get used to the idea that their days are over, and they can't add more millions to their pile.

"No one deals as badly with an Asiatic as another Asiatic!" murmurs Harry.

The KMT showed what they meant by "democracy" and "freedom" when they shot and tortured thousands of Formosans in 1947 when the latter revolted against the government's get-rich-quick policy and carpetbaggers – the Formosans even regretted the Japs whom they hated so much. The KMT has shown its true face by inviting Jap soldiers and pilots to come and fight and bomb the Chinese people they claim to love so much; they have shown their cowardice by retreating "strategically" from every city without putting up any defense, but by coming back later to bomb and strafe the civilian population. Chiang said he would commit suicide if he was not back in Shanghai within four months after liberation. We are still waiting to hear of his death.

The vacillations of the American government toward China are incomprehensible to most Chinese. There is no beating around the bush that the KMT has ceased to control China and that therefore it has absolutely no claim to represent the Chinese people.

"That's the real point. Whether we like it or not, the Chinese government *is* the Communists, and unless we deal with that government how can we deal with the Chinese people?"

The KMT is just holding on to Formosa because it happens to be an island, yet when the civil war started they were numerically superior, had planes and the latest American arms, whereas the PLA were certainly not so well off and had no Soviet support, then. Now the People's government talks a lot about Soviets, the study of Russian is the fashion, Soviet methods take first place, but actually most people are inert to such propaganda (as they were inert to American propaganda, too).

"As they are inert, period!" suggests Harry.

"Now wait, Harry, here's the point. Listen – "

When you ask a Commie why he chose Russia, he says:

> "In life you have to have a friend" – which is very true. And of course they do not want to have anything to do with the Yanks who helped the KMT so much – the Yanks who bet on the wrong horse this time.

"Oh, how did we get maneuvered into this position, Harry? We Americans have always prided ourselves on being good friends to the Chinese. I've been proud of the fact that Chinese often welcomed me because I was American. That Ah San said to me, 'Americans very good people, very kind people!' It is terrible that they have lost that belief in us. And I agree with Jeannette that help to the KMT now is more 'money down a rat hole.' But help to Jeannette's 'Commies' is feeding vitamins to the rat himself, so long as the Commies run with Russia. In life you have to have a friend – but a friend you can't trust is no good."

"China never trusts anyone very far, anyway. Let's hear the rest of the letter."

> The PLA brought folk dances and songs with them – short, easy songs, which everyone hums or sings, and easy dances, representing harvest and other agricultural events, and these are always featured when there are parades or festivals. Also drum dances which are very colorful and graceful.
>
> There is no censorship of any kind – press agencies were suppressed because they belonged to countries which had not recognized the government.

"What is that, if not suppression?" wonders Harry.

> However, the English paper continues to publish all the news (without mentioning the agency's name) from the world, and we can listen to any shortwave stations. The local stations continue to feature dance music and "Happy Birthday to You" happens to be a favorite. Foreign magazines come in when there is a ship. The blockade was economically a big shock, but we hope with the eventual recognition by all countries that it will be entirely eliminated, and right now most goods come through Tientsin or Tsingtao, and of course luxury goods are forbidden. Cinemas still show American films, but they are getting quite old as there has been a quota for some time, and very few new pictures

come in. Dancing halls are still open, but people not being able to make as much money as before, do not patronize them so well.

1950–51 will most probably be a difficult year for China, as announced by Mr. Mao, but if it can lead the way to recovery, it has to be gone through. Bonds are being launched to stabilize the financial situation and the people are enthusiastic about them. The budget for the year provides 23 per cent for military expenses, whereas the KMT spent 75 per cent.

"I'll bet you any money that the Communists triple that 23 per cent budget in actual expenditure!" wagers Harry.

The monetary situation is comparatively stable, but some inflation is inevitable. Salaries are based on certain units which in turn are based on four essential commodities, so that people do not lose anything if the currency depreciates. The possession of foreign currencies is theoretically illegal, but people are allowed to change it at the People's Bank at a very good official rate, thus eliminating entirely the black market.

To begin with there were quite a few difficulties between labor and management, but with time and understanding, these have been ironed out. There were also a few incidents involving foreigners, but these were brought about by themselves who find it difficult to tear away from their superior attitude, and who are readily "insulted." For instance, for years many foreigners had not paid any taxes, either for their houses or lands, and when the government started to enforce taxes and collect taxes in arrears, how the foreigners howled! But if they were at home they would have to pay many more taxes. It's a fact that in France you are taxed for your piano, your dog, your cat, your blinds, and anything the assessor can lay hands on.

Well, I guess I have bored you enough with my summary of the political situation — but I do feel that people abroad should know what is happening in New China. Too many people are prejudiced because of the word "Communist" and imagine all sorts of terrible happenings. Or, they just aren't interested in China — it's too far away. I guess this can't be helped, and it's always news about China that interests *me* first, I admit.

All the best to you, and much affection—

JEANNETTE

I turn to Harry with a feeling of complete frustration. "What she says is no doubt true, the facts are there. She is an intelligent young woman, and that is the way it all looks to her. If so, it's frightening, Harry! Everybody has to have a friend—but just how and why did we fail to be that friend?"

"Because we didn't promise the right things," says Harry soberly. "It's as Jeannette said, democracy and freedom half the world away have no meaning to people who have never known them—people who are schooled to the bondage of want."

I met old man Lo the next day, the paterfamilias of at least a hundred local Los, the best Chinese in our country. The old man was standing in front of the Dispensary looking very pictorial in a long, cream-colored, gabardine Chinese gown, quite the best-dressed man in sight, with a large black cotton umbrella poised thoughtfully above his fine, well-shaped, long head, his inborn air of dignity giving him the appearance of having a secret mission of great importance to accomplish. I asked him what his errand was, and he replied with a look of Confucian wisdom on his face that he was deciding what brand of tinned milk to buy! After exchanging comments on tinned stuffs, our children, and the weather, I asked him what impressions he had received on his recent visit to China, about the Communist regime.

"Very energetic!" Mr. Lo said promptly. "Very busy, very hard workers, and at first, very good! The People's Army comes into a village, the soldiers have ragged uniforms, but very fine discipline, and behave very politely and are honest, and always careful to pay for what they take. Then everybody very much impressed, and say Very good! Very good! And Communists say, Business as usual!

"Soon a levy is made on all shops and businesses, and a heavy tax is collected from shopkeepers, either in money, or in donations of necessary foods and materials. Then the shopkeepers say,

We cannot do this! But the Communists say, You must do it because you have shops and materials, and you must share. The shopkeepers say, If I give you my materials I cannot do business, then I do not have a shop, then I myself need help. Then *I* go broke! So he goes broke! And then business is not as usual." Old man Lo laughed heartily, as the Asiatic so often does to hide a mirthless emotion.

"But China is a country with more people who have nothing to lose and something to gain," he continued, "than people who have plenty to lose. So more people will welcome Communists, than are afraid of Communists coming, for fear they lose something."

It sounded very reasonable to me. "What about the KMT?" I asked. "Did they help business? Or did they hinder?"

Mr. Lo looked both wise and cautious. "Well, the Kuomintang did not help business, but they left shops and business alone."

"But under the old system," I persisted, "didn't you have to pay assessments and private contributions to government officials, to keep your business going?"

"Y-e-e-e-s, but we learn how, now. After we know the system, we make our money in spite of it." The old man laughed heartily again, and added, "This Communism all right for young men who have nothing. Not good for old men like me who are too old to learn new ways—and find new masters."

I left him standing in the sun under the umbrella still earnestly deciding whether to take Klim or Nestlé's.

When Harry came home at noon I said, "Why don't you get some dependable, sensible man of property like Mr. Lo to talk to these young Chinese here who rush about so anxiously waiting to get a chance to wave the Red Flag? He might put some practical common-sense ideas into their heads."

"Old man Lo's worked hard all his life," Harry answered, "and accumulated money and possessions in spite of the abuses of his own government. But there isn't a single young Chinese in Sandakan today who would listen to what the old man says. Any more than they'd listen to me! The day of the old men, and the white man, is past in the East."

III. Bitter Tears to Shed

THE Singapore broadcast brought the first bitter news. Harry had gone to Jesselton the week before, and I was sitting alone in the hot, damp dusk of our living room waiting for George to finish his bath and come down in pajamas to tell me good night, when the terrible words crackled out over the radio. I leaned forward and held my breath as the story came; I wanted to call out to them to repeat it – it must be a mistake – it was too dreadful to be true! Too dreadful that this had happened in Sarawak, the next youngest colony to ours and geographically adjoining us on the island of Borneo. But at the very same time that I was telling myself it was impossible that this thing had happened, it also seemed to me it was impossible that it had not happened before . . .

It was the month known in other countries by snow and ice, by tinsel-trimmed pine trees with gilded angels, by children's laughter and carols sung, by holiday greetings, and the story of Christ. But here on the equator a hundred miles from the ex-white Rajah's ex-palace, up the Rejang River in the town of

Sibu, Sarawak, on the island of Borneo, the month of December is known for other things. Here it is known for its violent, shifting Asiatic monsoons, for the rapid growth of mold and fungus, for its busy, hungry mosquitoes, and for the long, long rains which make any sunny day seem a holiday.

And today is a sunny day, and also a holiday. This sun is most fortunate for by virtue of its muggy warmth all these banners of welcome lettered brightly in *Jawi*, in Chinese characters and in English script will not be draggled, as they would be by rain, the paint will not fade from the Welcome arch, and the silk jackets of the Malay youngsters in giddy colors, turquoise, purple, Mexican pink, blue, and green, will not grow limp and sad, and all the best batik sarongs, all the neat cotton Chinese tunics and clean cotton pants of the greeting throng, will not be ruined by it. Even the Dyak costumes which are not subject to ruin by rain being only long, colored loincloths for the loins and tattoos for the chest, are gayer in the sun, and the day is good.

It is into this pleasant gathering, on this sunny day in December 1949, that a tall, impressive figure with military bearing and smooth, sunburned face steps from a river steamer. This is the British Colonial Governor, Duncan George Stewart, just nineteen days old in his job, who comes today as the King's representative to accept greetings from the King's new subjects, in the newly made British Colony of Sarawak, until last year an independent state and Rajahdom.

The green banks of the river are lined with excited people from Sibu's three racial groups, Dyaks, Malays and Chinese. The immediate vicinity where the Governor is to land is reserved for especially privileged representatives only, and here stand the Police Guard of Honor, the leaders of the community from all races, and long rows of shiny-faced school children and teachers in best bib and tucker. Between them and the honored visitor is the arch of triumph through which he is to enter, with the happy words, "Welcome, H. E. the Governor!"

Duncan Stewart stands very straight as he greets them, with his shining starched white uniform buttoned to the chin by glittering brass buttons, his ceremonial sword at his side with its long sharp blade sheathed in its scabbard. His gubernatorial helmet supports with pride the great, white silken plume, emblem of office and honor, which cascades luxuriously over it, shading his face from the sun, but even so it is seen that here is a face filled with great good will and deep earnestness, that here is a man who today is more than himself, and more than a man – for today he is His Excellency the Governor, well-beloved representative of His Majesty the King.

In this very same fashion, on many days in many years before, in histrionic costume and with ceremony, with good will and hope, with ambition and temerity, with faith and prayer, have many British Governors for many years begun illustrious careers.

Now the Governor takes the salute, standing at attention through "God Save the King"; now he steps forward through the welcome arch. He is smiling as he passes through the rows of admiring children, smiling not as a politician for the votes he may get, but as a man who has children of his own and takes pleasure in the bright looks of all children. And small, brown faces grin back at him, shy small Fatimas and Habibs dodge back and forth behind bolder ones to peek again, and dark Dyak children stare bravely and frankly up, while small Chinese lads gaze unblinkingly at this ceremonial magnificence. The Governor has already made friends.

The thing which now happens does not fit into this picture of a sunny day gay with the spirit of welcome and a ceremony well planned. For now the image of good will blurs as if with a different picture imposed on it in a completely disparate theme – and from amongst the smiling, friendly school children a young Malay boy pushes hastily forward. Nervously, with agitation, he steps quickly up to the Governor and bends confidently towards him as if to offer an obeisance, or deliver a gift with his own brown hands.

The Governor bends graciously towards the young Malay to accept whatever he offers – and with this contact of man and boy the picture of good will changes, for something furtive, treacherous, terrible passes between these two – and suddenly the Governor's head droops forward, the white plume hangs down, and he claps his hand to his stomach.

Now there is confusion, and everything, everyone, has gone

slightly wrong, though nobody knows yet what or why, and through all these assembled people passes the sudden, terrible, emotional knowledge that trouble has come. Still, only the boy and the Governor know what the trouble is.

People close in, still acting without knowing what to do, or why, and grab at the boy, who has fallen at the Governor's feet, drag back another Malay boy who is struggling to reach him, and look towards the staggering Governor for a clue. But the Governor has straightened now and stands calm again, and only his white gloved hand pressing tightly against his tunic over his abdomen shows anything wrong.

He takes a few steps forward in line of direction of the stand where he is to speak, and the crowd sighs in momentary relief from its tension, and cheers and applauds him again. The Governor smiles with quiet dignity to acknowledge their cries, but his hand is still tight across his stomach, held like a clamped shield against his stomach, and there is something very frightening there hidden behind the chalky, immaculate, gubernatorial glove. Now and now only is seen what the glove hides, as blood, dark and arterial red, comes oozing through the chalk-white fingers. Now and now only is known the secret which passed to the Governor from the dark-faced boy.

Now this is the picture which must remain forever to tell of one terrible thing, the picture that Sibu must be known for. Forgotten are its handsome, lazy, log-packed river and shady shores, its prosperous spicy pepper vines, its green-scummed swamps, its flower-scented nights, its children and women and men of good will. All now are stained by this innocent blood of a fine man killed ruthlessly, murderously, without meaning or value, the second Governor of Sarawak, slain.

All the world knows that a week later Duncan George Stewart died from the wounds of a Malay dagger driven through his stomach and intestines. The world knows that with his death a good man was lost to fame, a blameless woman became a widow, and three children were left without a father. The world knows that Duncan George Stewart was guiltless of any crime, of anything to justify his murder, unless accepting the responsibility of government has become a crime.

An impressive funeral was held in Singapore, to which city the dying Governor had been flown for medical care. Great men there bowed at his pall, and gold braid followed his bier, but

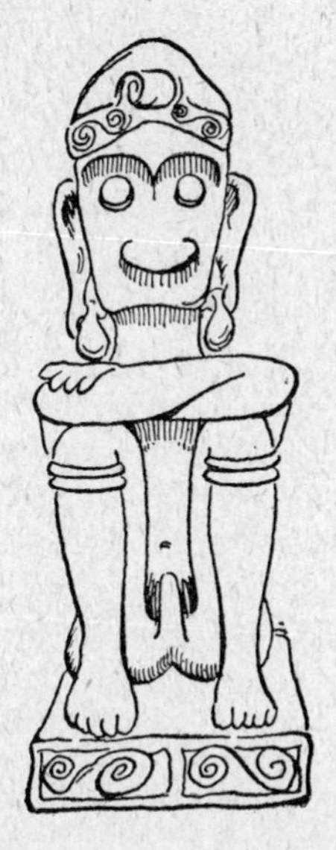

neither floral greetings from famous people, nor tears dropped over a flag-spread coffin, nor letters of sympathy from Their Majesties, can give back to Duncan Stewart the priceless possession of life. No inquiries or examinations, no sentence of guilt, passed on men or ideas, can make his heart beat again, or make his eyes smile in welcome for his children and wife, or for subject peoples or peers. For this fine man, all is finished.

His life was his own to dispose of. He did his duty while he lived, he accepted responsibility with high courage, he was not afraid of living, and when he died he died bravely, with valor beyond any phrase. No man can do more. Perhaps he would have chosen thus.

But for those who are left behind, this is not enough. We need this man and others like him. We need those who are today doing what Duncan Stewart did, and who still smile, still hope, still strive to accept with virtue and dignity the responsibilities of government in foreign lands. For them, there is yet time.

The world knows this man was made a martyr to something. But to what? It is not *who* killed Duncan Stewart, but why? Is the murder of this guiltless man a mere coincidence timed inopportunely with the disturbed East? Is it merely an accident, that a new Colonial Governor happened to connect with a murderer's knife? Or is this murder one of many symptoms of Asiatic feeling against the government in Asia of Europeans? Is it a symptom of the approach of an irresistible end?

It is the answers to these questions which must be determined from the trials of the self-confessed Malay murderers, Rosli *bin* Dobie, and his accomplice, Moshidi *bin* Sidek, and by the inquiries into the political movement called for convenience' sake after its thirteen members, the Thirteen Essential Ingredients, and the trial of its thirteen members. It is noticeable that none of these accused men were natives of the state of Sarawak; they were Malays.

The Thirteen Essential Ingredients is described by its members as being a secret political movement, with the object of terminating the cession of Sarawak to the British Crown. This organization was alleged by the two Malay boys to have inspired, sponsored, and demanded for its own purpose, the death of the Governor.

Rosli *bin* Dobie, nineteen years old, who struck the fatal blow, was a pupil-teacher in the Malay school at the time, and a pupil still in the Methodist school. After trial he was judged guilty of murder, sentenced to death, and hanged. Moshidi *bin* Sidek, who plotted with him, was also judged guilty of murder and hanged. Both claimed in their trials that they were driven to perform the deed by leaders of the political movement, the Thirteen Essential Ingredients.

Rosli told his story thus – "I was told by Awang Rambli, the leader of the Thirteen Essential Ingredients, to murder the Governor. I did not wish to do this, and at first I argued against committing the murder, saying – I am afraid!

"To this Rambli answered – If you live in this world, you must look out for a name for yourself! You cannot be well known unless you make that name for yourself –

"But still I was afraid, and again I talked against doing it. And then finally Rambli said – If you do not kill the Governor

YOUNG MALAY

you have no love for your country – and as Rambli was my friend and told me to do it, I was ashamed not to do it. So I did it."

Rosli named the following reasons as explanations of the demand of the party for the murder of the Governor, saying that these reasons were given to him by the leaders of the party. First, the party wished for the freedom of Sarawak. Second, the party claimed that it had never been the wish of the once independent state of Sarawak and Rajahdom of the Brooke family to be ceded to the Crown as a Colony. Third, the party believed that all attempts to free Sarawak were being obstructed by the

Governor's refusal to allow the former Rajah Muda, Anthony Brooke, to re-enter Sarawak. Fourth, for three years the party had protested passively and by legal means but without success against the cession of Sarawak. Fifth, the party believed that the people of Sarawak "were being summonsed and jailed because they could not pay taxes imposed by the British Government."

From this mumbo jumbo, which held just enough reason to give appearance of truth to the lies, there formed in fanatic minds the motive to murder.

The following things can be reasoned from the above statements – First that if the murder was a blow struck to reinstate the British Brooke family in Sarawak, then it was not a blow struck against *British* rule. That if it was a blow struck to reinstate the white Brookes as rulers it was not a blow struck against the *white* race. That, third, if it was a political blow struck against an Empire for acquiring a Colony, then it was a blow struck in default of the fact that the Colony had itself voted to cede to the Empire, but at the same time, a blow prompted by perverted emotions aroused by the deed of cession. If so, then this murder was a symptom of the temper of a time which makes such emotions for such a cause seem plausible to men.

Whatever its motive, this crime with all its horror was in reality a blow against Sarawak, whose decent people are shamed by its violence and suffer by its guilt without being guilty. There is no one who condemns the deed more truly than do Sarawak's peaceful people, and it has proved to be a blow against the anticession movement, rather than one to assist it.

Yet these are only results of the blow, and the vital question still stands – Was this murder of an innocent man the irresponsible, emotionally crazed deed of amok, the strain of which outbreak runs periodically throughout all of Asia's history? Or was it a political murder, conceived of by irresponsible individuals, but shaped, given apparent reason to, and brought to fruition by political motives which arise from a great force existing all about us in the East in crucial form today – the demand for Asiatic rule for Asiatics?

If so, then the answer to such violence is not simply to expose or exterminate organizations which work towards this objective, for such organizations are only symptoms of the vital thing. The vital thing is the mighty, irrepressible, emotional determination for self-rule by Asiatics. This determination is constantly showing itself in brutal outbreaks which come horrifyingly to bloody heads and festering sores which are only the surface demonstration of the internal condition. The sores may be lanced, or burst by themselves, and thus afford temporary ease, but the emotional force which causes them will not have been changed.

When the members of the Thirteen Essential Ingredients were questioned as abettors in the crime committed, a diary was produced belonging to one of them. In this diary was found a list of people. This list included the names of many of the highest and most respected men in British Far Eastern Government. This list was admitted by the members to be a list of men discussed, or proposed, for early assassination.

The diary owner was asked to explain why he was considering these people for assassination. He gave as his reasoned response the following statement: "I wrote those names when I was in a bad state of mind!"

A bad state of mind, which is so bad that to remedy itself it feels justified in and takes steps towards promoting the murder of men of outstanding integrity, honesty, and unselfish dealing, is more than a bad temper. It is a state of emotions and mind which is too psychopathic to be disregarded, and one not to be remedied by treatment for tantrum or tummy-ache.

A bad state of mind is a name for what takes place in a man's mind when he experiences a strong emotional urge for an end he believes legitimate, and at the same time finds himself without legitimate means of achieving the end. To such a state, there are three possible answers: one, to exterminate the minds in which the desire exists; two, to eliminate the desire from the minds; three, to concede to the desire.

By our own creed, and all the oaths that we have sworn at others for ruthless methods, we are forbidden to give the first answer, extermination. By our claims to educate subject peoples for self-government, we are morally forbidden to give the second answer, even *if* it were within our power to eliminate the desire for self-rule from the heart of men. Yet to give the third answer, self-rule for inexperienced peoples, when their primary need is still food and housing, is economically dangerous. And to give self-rule to any group not yet able to keep its own independence and maintain self-rule exposes it to certain exploitation by less well-meaning masters than ourselves.

So nothing is done. If nothing is better than anything, then we are right. If anything is better than a grievance which leads to "a bad state of mind" out of which comes murder, then we are wrong.

And meanwhile matters do not stand still. Out of a bad state of mind comes soon disregard of methods, and then follows quickly the end justifying every means. And then comes the long line of martyrs, the crepe-adorned, flower-strewn death-pale faces of conscientious men who followed their duty, only to be slain by other men, dark-browed, fanatic-hearted, bloody-handed men driven by a mad force madly – but to accomplish a not-mad end – self-rule.

Is this to be the white man's finish in the East? Is the thankless, thorny martyr's crown on the white man's brow, and the murderer's blood guilt on the brow of the brown man, to be our contribution to Asia's evolution? When all that divides us, white man from brown, is that thin, fine layer of pigmented skin, when we are all born to love and hate and die in the same incredibly beautiful, terrible way – what is there that stands between us?

This is the story that began that night as I sat alone in the hot damp dusk in Sandakan. It seemed then I could scarcely wait for Harry to return; it seemed I was afraid. Not afraid of anything that might happen to him, or to me, or to any of our goods, or to any of our friends. Not afraid of any event. But afraid of the terrible, mad emotion of the hatred of men for men.

IV. This Happy Land

TODAY, four commercial airplanes arrive and depart weekly from Sandakan's jungle-hedged, wind-swept landing strip, once the burial site of two thousand war dead, now the hub of thirty thousand living. With rapid transportation and quick communications the face of Borneo life changes, and we see these changes: we are no longer an isolated community in an artless land. With a five-day air trip functioning from London, we have become the favorite oasis for world experts and United Nations Committees, who need miss only two nights between planes while they complete detailed, expert surveys of North Borneo. Then, jotting it on their cuffs as they wave good-by, with generous descriptive adjectives bouncing off their tongues, they are sure to include in their reports these phrases—"This harmonious country! This happy land!"

The old residents of North Borneo are becoming a little self-conscious about a halcyon condition of living which elicits so much comment by travelers from afar. It is almost too obvious that North Borneo *is* an unusual state in the Far East; we hold our breaths and ask, For how long?

The fact is that this primitive land which five years ago was as drenched by blood as by sun, under the rule of Asia for the Asiatics, is now a happy, prospering country.

This condition is due primarily to the existence of a government which guarantees security and safety to men and women of every color, while they pursue the fundamental business of living. Whether it is the Chinese in his shop, the Indian or Arab in the bazaar, the native in the interior village, the Murut in his long house, or the white man in his home, the inhabitant of North Borneo is free to devote his energies to making a living — not to fighting off desperadoes to save his life, not to shooting it out on the doorstep to protect his home, not to struggling against a tyrannical government to keep his plot of land. The government which maintains security happens to be British; whether it could be North Bornean, or Asian, and do the same thing, is still to be proved.

The achievements here since the Civil Administration resumed authority in 1946, starting from worse than nothing, are unpretentious, but sound. Although the condition without which we could not have prosperity is security, the factors directly causing prosperity are Chinese and British business initiative and capital which have been attracted to Borneo because of its peaceful conditions.

The most important feature of "this happy land" now is that no one is hungry. In 1946 people dropped in the streets, dying of starvation, and people of the villages were carried in to hospital to die of malnutrition. Today the population in general is well fed and well clothed. Rice is still a shortage and native planting must be perpetually forced by the Government, but rice acreage has increased, and substitute crops are more willingly accepted. Native fishing boats again make the Sulu Sea a romantic, rainbow-sailed picture, and add fish to local diet, while Chinese junks bringing deep sea fish and adventure in equal parts come and go from our harbors. A new fisheries department seeks by modernizing fishing methods to make large-scale fishing an economic livelihood, in spite of the higher prices paid for labor in the rubber industry, which tempt former fishermen away. The

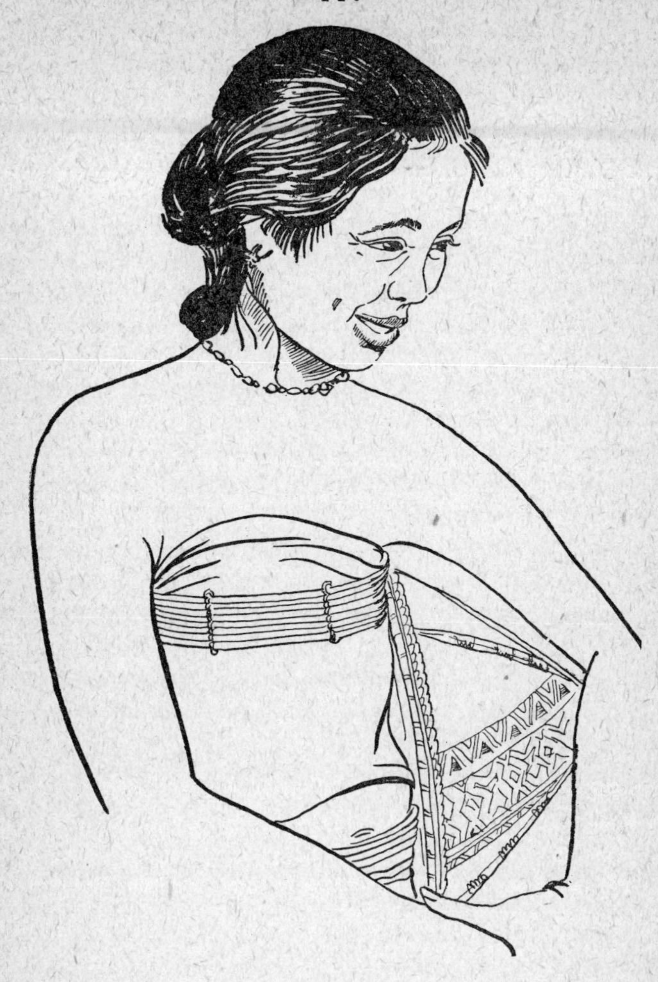

department also promotes husbandry of fishing resources.

Cloth of all kinds, cotton, rayon, silk, may be purchased locally in coast towns, and small Chinese shops are made hideous with children's and men's grotesque, Chinese-manufactured, European-style garments hanging and twisting in the warm breezes, for sale ridiculously cheap. These have largely replaced the more attractive native garb for our male population in the towns. Although these garish Western costumes are a nightmare to look at, they provide a cheap covering, and fortunately for beauty's sake, women still cannot buy Western ready-to-wear off the hook.

Concurrent with increased communications with the outer world, three Chinese-run bookstores have appeared in Sandakan, whose names tell of widening horizons here, the "Educational," the "Cultural," and the "Fundamental"! These stands furnish magazines, papers and schoolbooks in English, Chinese, Romanized Malay, and Arabic, and cheap editions of cheaper English novels.

A cold-storage service from Singapore and Australia now sells beef and lamb, and frozen pork at a cheaper price than is paid for local market pig – but still higher than we can afford – and brings lettuce, celery and turkeys to us at proper seasons so one may ape Christmas banqueting in spite of limpness and sweat. I have never before eaten so well in Borneo – but none of it equals for taste a chop grilled by myself in North America on a cold, crisp evening.

Permanent housing moves at a snail's pace in replacing temporary buildings, but at least there are no families in the clock tower, as the ruins have been removed. The usual so-called "shanty town" which springs up after a city fire, built of blackened remnants of noninflammable materials, has been done away with, and the occupants have moved into semipermanent frame structures with palm-leaf roofs, built over the sea. Row on row of palm-leaf houses still picturesquely adorn the hillsides of Sandakan and Jesselton, many built with fully plumbed depths with shining w.c.'s in them; the houses may blow away but the w.c.'s remain. Still, until it blows off, there is a roof for every head.

Bombed and machine-gunned roads have been resurfaced, and a new, rough-hewn road has been cut a hundred miles over the hills from the capital into a one-time isolated district. One may now step into a jeep from a doorstep in Jesselton and drive to the doorstep of the rest house in the Bajau village of Kota Belud with no worse injuries than a bruised behind from bouncing over the bumps.

For the first time, telephone communication connects Sandakan and Jesselton, and there is no escape from the worthy advices of the Secretariat. Mail still goes by ship along the coast, or by plane, as no jungle road has yet been attempted to connect these cities.

Bus lines flourish with vehicles made out of old jeeps, and taxis are acquired cheaply from Europeans going on leave. Private cars are the rule for Europeans and many Chinese of property.

The wages of coolies are more than five times what they were before the war, and so is the cost of living. White-collar wages have doubled, but administrative salaries are only very slightly increased, and the cost of living for Europeans is materially more than what most of us make.

A permanent hospital is to be built in Sandakan in 1951. Local malaria has decreased, and the state of general malnutrition with which the entire populace suffered after the war is lessening. A European doctor has at last gone far up the Kinabatangan with drugs and medical advice.

The rubber industry is booming, tobacco pays, timber is in a reinvestment stage, and hemp for Manila rope, copra for coconut oil, and cutch from mangrove bark for use as a dye and for tanning leather are important to the country's economy again.

In addition to a few new Empire ships which occasion much admiration when they arrive in port, anything that floats is still used for shipping – and occasionally something that doesn't float.

The town of Sandakan is now electrically lighted and the power extends fourteen miles along the jungle road, further than before the war. In several other Borneo towns one may also search for centipedes, snakes and scorpions by electric light instead of petrol lamps. The railway from Jesselton to the interior district functions now with rail coaches instead of postwar jeeps, and a real hotel, the first ever in Borneo, has just been built in Sandakan by Malayan Airways, and takes the place of old government cockroach hideaways known as rest houses.

In Forestry diction the term "shifting cultivation" is a synonym for slow suicide, and this agricultural method of delayed self-destruction has long been tenaciously practiced by the native hill people of North Borneo. This is the lazy man's way of feeding himself easily, this year, next year, but in the long run, never again, by destroying the source from which his food comes. The hill villager chooses a spot in virgin forest to settle because of good humus and soil, he clears the forest and plants hill rice and lives on his crops for two or three years until the soil is exhausted. Then he abandons his clearing, moves his village, fells another bit of forest, and plants rice again. Meanwhile his abandoned clearing, without the protection of planting to prevent erosion, washes down the hillside, through the valleys and into the sea, and it is many generations before the village site becomes anything but waste land.

As the native must grow rice to live, the answer to his problem is twofold, to educate him in scientific farming, and-or persuade him to use valley land and become a permanent cultivator of wet rice. Both these methods have been employed by government, and are beginning to show some results.

In order to protect the forests, concessions to timber companies for logging rights are carefully scrutinized with reference to a long-term policy of reforestation. Improvement felling areas, for forest conservation after areas have been logged, have increased by 50 per cent in the last few years.

North Borneo is still, however, bankrupt, which seems an anomaly for a prospering country. But this newest colony has not yet paid back its purchase price for joining the British Empire, and technically its expenses must be reduced until we are out of the red. Meanwhile U.S. capital, which is being withdrawn from the Philippine Islands because of currency controls there and lack of security, is turning its course towards Borneo, which if it were any country except British Borneo would no doubt flirt ardently with the prospect. But, being British, we just may permit them to invest their dollars, if they are good.

I am often asked by outsiders what the feeling is here between Asiatics and Europeans, and my answer is that this differs with individuals. I have one friend who says, "They hate, despise, and resent us, in Asia or out of it!" Another one tells me, "Where they eat they love!" Somebody else says, "The Chinese are traders, and *they'll* never let national spirit interfere with their trade!" And another says, "The Asiatic loves no one but himself." From all of which I conclude that the Asiatic is like the European — his feelings are not to be compressed into a single phrase.

I return to my friend who tells me that Asiatics "hate, resent, and despise us," and ask him, "How do you know this?"

He answers, "I feel it!"

Hate is a quality to be felt, rather than reasoned, and this man feels it. I do not feel it; I feel mutual interest between Asiatics and myself, frequently sympathy, often admiration, but also, sadly, at times misunderstanding. But I think the judgment of "experts" given us in their phrase, "this happy land," could not have been so persistently applied here were mistrust, antagonism, and hate predominant.

One may wonder whether the natives of North Borneo are any happier, or better off today for some of these metropolitan changes, and it would be difficult to say. However, I do not think that is now the vital question. In a world where the struggle is crucial for very existence, the state of North Borneo gives a

living to and houses in peace and security 335,000 persons who have to exist someplace, Asiatics who in all of Asia have no place like this. This is worth while.

This is the picture of North Borneo after five years of laborious, penurious, painful reconstruction, working against the lethargy

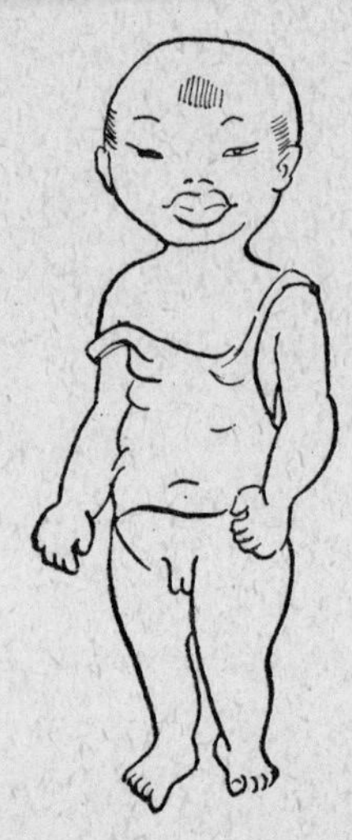

of perpetual heat and the inertia of empty stomachs. That Harry has been a part of this effort, I am proud.

Gung Ho grows wondrously, and is still a model of health and happiness except when his mother pinches his neck black and blue or burns him with her cigarette to cure a cold by the old Chinese treatment of counterirritation. He also is now Elder Brother, with the arrival of a new boy baby. Ah San, the perfect Borneo cook, shakes his head again as he whips the frosting for the cake which Misiter will not eat, and mutters pessimistically, "Too much trouble, more baby! Too much trouble! Too much money!"

Ah Min, who was sixteen years old three years ago, is at least forty now, and respectable, hysterical, forceful, lovable, and a fury. She is still great friends with Ah Kau, who remains the same, except that we have discovered that the always smoothly braided, long, black-ink pigtail which Harry and I gloried in as a reminder of old China had been cut off during the war for convenience' sake, and although we glory in it still, it is tied on every morning after a night spent coiled on her table in independent repose. Of course it was George who revealed this.

We hear frequently of Arusap now. He is becoming a big man in his own district, and he remembers to good purpose his schooling in agriculture and rice cultivation, and is inculcating the white man's teaching in his brother Muruts. (Note to Agnes – be sure to bring back something from leave to contribute to Arusap Junior.)

Osman, who housed us once on the Kinabatangan in a storm, is paying back bit by bit the money Harry advanced to him for his fine to keep him out of jail, and to prove him an honest man – if only to himself. Kamsia and Norudin still belong to the Forest Department; Norudin draws a salary for one job and does ten, and Kamsia draws a salary from her husband's pocket on pay day, as she married a native forest guard, to everybody's relief. The Gill boys lead the local Red Cross and Boy Scout movements, and they with George's help make jungle films pay in this jungle town.

As we are going on leave soon, we had to dispose of Heba, the bear with the Walt Disney face, and he has just gone away in a large cage, with thirty tins of milk and thirty *katis* of rice, a month's supply, to be shipped by steamer to the zoo in Sidney. He left screaming, cursing his fate, and weeping with fright, and he will be the last bear, if I can help it, to go from Borneo to a zoo. Why should a bear go to a zoo? He doesn't want to see people; let people who want to see bears come here.

We have sent Mr. Mink-monk, the happy macaque, to a good home with Borneo newly-weds; the bride says she wants something to pet, and to be company for her. Something is askew with this sentiment from newly-weds, but Mr. Mink-monk profits by it. After the third goldfish bowl broke, the surviving goldfish were given away, and are now wearing out their extended, nearly sightless, telescope eyes by bumping them against the maddening circumference of other glass worlds.

The white doves have left the dovecote now, and belong exclusively to the furthest, highest, most shimmering and silvery albizzia tree in the wildest part of the valley, and spend little time on the ground, and the monitor lizard hunts elsewhere. Perhaps he keeps company with the disappearing mud turtles, who after reportedly copulating in a carefully guarded love nest on the lawn, disappeared from sight presumably to have their young, and have never been seen since, thereby closing down George's turtle farm. The last white mouse finally died, and nobody cared; in fact it relieved my conscience to have that sad commentary on man's treadmill actions removed from my sight.

Sinyora, Baud, Jikrun, and little Mina came in to see us last week. After the inevitable "tea," I waited for a touch of some sort. Instead Sinyora says, "We hear you are going on holiday soon, Mem."

"Yes, we will be away ten months."

"I am sorry, Mem. My heart is sick!" She rocks herself gently, her wrinkled brown feet tucked under her, her big toes caressing the woven seat cover.

"Do not be heartsick, Sinyora. We will return."

"But ten months is the same as a year, Mem, and a year is the same as always. And when you go there is no one to take care of our welfare, Mem." She coughs, spits, wipes her seamy face on the sweat rag, and repeats, "No one to take care of we people, Mem. You and the Tuan are like father and mother to us. We are very sad that you go."

I know it's the same old tune, but my eyes begin to grow wet; Harry's just grow glassy.

"And so we are very sad!" A deep chorus of sighs from Sinyora, Baud, Jikrun.

Then Sinyora becomes more practical. "And who will take the Tuan's place here?"

"Mr. Brown will take over."

"And will Tuan Brown live in this house?"

"Yes, Sinyora." I see the Brown family in line for some nice tea parties.

"Tuan Brown. Yes." Sinyora ruminates, sitting silently and estimating her chances for the future. Baud, obviously pregnant again, moves uneasily in her chair, while Mina, who has new sores on her scalp, is once more a baffling combine of forwardness and temerity. Dressed in a turkey-red and Mexican-pink checked cotton frock, she rolls her wet marble eyes from face to face, and picks at her flat little nose. A mordant silence settles. Then Jikrun speaks.

"Will the little Tuan ever come back to this country?"

"He must go to school, Jikrun. Perhaps, if all is well, we will bring him back for one vacation," I say, trying not to face the fact myself of George's departure.

"Yes, perhaps he can come back," Jikrun nods. "But of course he must go to school, and become a very clever man like his father!"

"Yes! Yes! Like his father!" we all agree, while Harry's glassy look almost cracks.

"And where is the little Tuan? We would like to tell him good-by," suggests Sinyora.

"I am sorry, but George went fishing with Surjit Singh Gill."

Sinyora shakes her head sadly. "Then we will not see him again!"

This is providential from George's point of view.

"I will tell George that you wished to say good-by," I promise.

"I'll drive you down to the town," offers Harry hopefully. "Is your *prahu* tied up at the wharf?"

"Our boat is tied near the house of a relative, Tuan, at the village of Red Earth," says Jikrun.

"I'll take you there," says Harry determinedly.

The four guests rise slowly to their feet, shake off crumbs, pluck at sarongs, Sinyora twists up her tumbling knot of gray hair again and anchors it with a skewerlike hairpin, Mina adjusts her glaring cotton gown which during this visit has unprecedentedly remained below her navel, and Baud adjusts Number Eight safely inside.

But Sinyora lingers, looking at me and mouthing her gums as if searching for words, while she touches my hand and repeats, "There will be no one to take care of us now, Mem!"

"Oh, Sinyora, there are plenty of others. Tuan Governor himself is very interested."

"Tuan Governor." Sinyora's voice is blank. "But who will talk with we people? Who will we people go to when there is trouble?" I see in Sinyora's bleary eyes more than the film of old age and past memories, I see the same moisture I feel in my own.

Who will we people go to when there is trouble? Sinyora has said. And isn't that the answer to why Harry and I have been happy in this country? Because its people have come to us; because we could try to give back something for the fullness of life we have found here. The nuisance and responsibility have been far outweighed for us by the satisfaction of having something to give.

"Never mind, Sinyora, other men will help you," I comfort.

But Sinyora has the persistent pessimism of the aged. "No

one to care for us," she mutters sadly, as we exchange the Muslim good-by, each in turn touching his forehead, eyes and heart, then each other's hands.

"Peace go with you, Mem! Peace go with you, Tuan!"

"And peace remain!"

The words are direct, beautiful, sincere, full of meaning; this is the farewell of friends.

With many backward glances, with last-minute waves and salutes, with heavy sighing which changes to restrained giggling as they all crowd into the tiny motorcar, then to sighing again as they look back at me and the clean, new, ivory and green house, the descendants of Pengiran Digadong Samah, who died defying the white men, depart from our home.

Half an hour later Harry returns. "Did you notice anything wrong with that visit?" he asks.

"Yes. Nobody asked for an advance!"

V. Thunder

SIBUAN is so small a coral reef island in the Sulu Sea that it gives no sense of reality. Even the exquisite, absinthe, Venetian-glass waves crash and splinter on clear wind-smoothed white sand with such crystalline effect that I nearly expect to find shattered glass fragments lying at my feet. Instead, the warm, wet sand absorbs, and sucks down ceaselessly, tepid layers of liquid, salty sea.

When I stand on the shore and look through soughing coconut trees to the blue sea beyond the further shore, only the sea, glassy waves, screaming, white-bellied sea birds, swaying, tufted coconut trees, exist; the island itself is a chimera, a myth. And yet I am standing on it.

Here the world lies before me in sheets of riotous ocean color, chartreuse in the shallows, then turquoise, aquamarine, Prussian blue, and out in the depths, deep indigo. In my faded yellow bathing suit, I enter the warm water and swim slowly out a hundred yards to the very edge of a subterranean precipice, where the coral reef falls off into the deeps, a drop plainly marked by the water's sudden, rich blueness, and a strange, strong, underwater pull. At one moment I am looking down through water at my red-painted toenails which almost touch the bottom as I tread; at the next moment, if I drift with the pull of the current, I will be treading water which extends below me for many fathoms. Here is the line of demarcation between safety and danger, for the deep water is the home of sharks, always ready to be tempted upwards by a floating form.

As I flutter my hands against the pull of the deeps, I can see clearly below my toenails to the bottom of the sand, where there is an exquisite miniature coral village, a whole world just larger than I can put my arms around. The industrious settlement is filled with busy little fish in every shade of pigment-pure blueness—turquoise, ultramarine, cobalt, sapphire, royal, periwinkle, and pale, cerulean blue. Others have rich, black stripes, some are brilliant chrome yellow, some are startling black and white, and all stay within a one-foot radius of the perimeter of their village, while they dart busily in and out of its interstices, its domed doorways and Gothic windows, telling each other, no doubt, as we do, to hurry, hurry, hurry!

The metropolitan life of fish is fascinating, but even more so is the drag of the deep, as I paddle nearer to the bottomless blue cliff and feel the pull of water. I am no longer drifting now, but being towed beyond the danger line, and soon I look down into murky, opaque blue liquid which swallows up my gaze in nothingness, and its very lack of visibility is frightening; here is the unknown, below me lie fathoms of water, undisturbed except for sharks. Thinking this, I almost feel the rasp of abrasive fins, and suddenly I panic, and start swimming strongly against the downward, outward pull. Swimming on my side, I look back apprehensively until I regain the royal-blue depths, then aquamarine, then green. And now in shallow, lime-green liquid, I dawdle again, looking lazily down at red toenails, faded bathing suit, cream sand, seen through a broken mirror of water; knowing at this moment that life is not often like this. Here one has only the elements to fear, other places one has man.

Midnight two months later we landed at San Pedro, California, for home leave. Our arrival was accidentally concurrent with the opening of the film version of *Three Came Home* in Hollywood, and George's first trip was down Hollywood Boulevard to the theater. Here he stood and stared at the oversize stills of

Three Came Home for some time, and then refused to go inside and see the film.

"Just Daddy hugging up Mum!" he said in disgust.

We found a new world to him and to us, reconstructed in luxury and lavishness; we had left here in the postwar shortages in 1947, and now there seemed to be too much of everything. We traveled to Canada by train, not plane, because George was a Hopalong Cassidy cowboy fan now, and wanted to see the cowboys riding the range. We crossed the mountain divide early in the morning and Harry and I saw with joy, snow on the ground! We waked George to see it, he complainingly opened one eye, peered sleepily out of the window, saw there were no cowboys, cactus, nor steers, and said "What about it!" and went back to sleep.

". . . two gray flannel school suits, and an extra pair of shorts," I counted. "Four pairs of underpants, four vests, one blue football jersey, one pair football shoes, one pair football stockings, one white tennis shorts, one white wool jersey . . . and three dozen Cash's name tapes. Oh – and two school ties!" These items are packed into a new school trunk in Victoria, B.C., where we are spending home leave. "Luggage to be delivered at school not later than Tuesday before term opens. Boarders will please arrive the same day." I close the trunk.

Six weeks later George, the barbarian from Borneo, returns from his first Canadian boarding school for his first week end at home. He is immaculate in gray flannel shorts, gray wool stockings banded with navy and white, navy reefer, navy cap with school badge, and navy and white school tie, when we call for him at school. He looks enormous in woolen clothes, greets his father as Sir, shakes my hand with dignity and reserve, and hisses anxiously at me, "Don't kiss me!" On the way home we chat as follows.

"How are you, dear?"

"Fine, thank you," in modified tones not familiar to me.

"Do you like school?"

"Yes, thank you."

"Do you have nice meals?"

"Yes, thank you."

"Do you like the boys?"

"Yes, thank you."

"Do you like the masters?"

"Yes, thank you."

"Do you like the studies?"

"Yes, tha – ! No! Mum, of course I don't like studies!"

Arrived at home, George dodges hastily inside, turns on the radio, lets out a cowboy whoop, and the house shakes with the galloping of imaginary horses – Roy Rogers rides once more! I hurry to the kitchen to cook his favorite meal, relieved to hear noise again.

"George, dear!" I call from the kitchen. "Do hang up your school clothes nicely so they will be tidy for when you go back on Monday. I'm sure you hang up your clothes at school!"

I visit the bedroom; George is lying on the floor reading a comic, in his old torn blue jeans, with a faded T shirt and scuffed black boots. His new school clothes are in a heap on the floor.

"George! What about your clothes?"

"Aw, Mum, you hang 'em up for me. I have to hang 'em up at school!"

"I know. That's the whole idea. You're supposed to be learning to take care of yourself," I protest mildly, hanging up the garments.

"Oh, Mum!" A hug persuades me that it is really a pleasure to hang them up for him – especially as I have so little time longer to do it!

At supper George outdoes himself in food consumption, and afterwards I suggest, "And now, dear, *do* tell us a little more about school. What are you studying, and who teaches you?"

George expands gradually. "Well, Mr. Grey teaches us literature and writing and sums, and he's a fine athlete and a fruitarian and very nice, the most popular master, and if you get him talking he'll tell you all about all sorts of interesting things and forget to make you do the sums. And there's Captain Garry, he teaches algebra and tells funny stories and he likes boys a lot they say. He gives us sweets, and he has high blood pressure."

"What about the Headmaster? Does Mr. Jimpson teach too?"

"Mr. Jimpson? Jimmie, you mean – Oh, no, he just canes."

"Well, to be exact," I ask, "just how many boys have been caned since you've been there this term?"

"Plenty, Mum! Plenty! Till the blood runs!"

"Did you see the blood running?"

"Not exactly – but that's what the Old Boys say! That's what a Headmaster's job is – to cane, you know!"

"Oh – What else do they do besides cane at school?"

"Play football. Mr. Arnold – Arnie, we call him – coaches football. Mr. Stevenson teaches music and art. And then the Matron, she's nice, she lets us talk at night sometimes – then she tells us to go to sleep or she'll tell Jimmie! And she sews buttons on our pants."

"And who runs the school – while the Head's caning?"

"Oh, *Mrs.* Jimpson *runs* the school, of course! That's what *she's* for!"

"And do you like it, dear? Are you happy?"

"Oh, sure, sure! School's O.K. I like it fine – except for the lessons!"

For George is sadly behind by Canadian standards, where a child of ten is assumed to have had four years of regular schooling. Again I ask myself, Did George need a school more than he needed his parents? I still don't know; the future product must prove it. But I know his parents needed him.

We had hoped that the war might be over before we started East again, but we never really thought it would. The Korean situation was only another symptom of a critical condition, not a new disease.

So when Harry called to me from the radio, "MacArthur says the troops will be home for Christmas!" it seemed like a wonderful Christmas present, and the tight bands of anxiety clamped around my chest began to ease.

"Thank God, that problem's settled! Selfishly speaking, at least. It seems to me that I can't bear to go East again and leave George behind – but it makes it a lot easier if we know we don't have to go back into the teeth of a spreading war," I said.

But a few days later the headlines read, "190,000 Communists on Manchurian Border. Mass Attack expected on U.N. troops," and I thought to myself, It couldn't be much worse!

But it could be – for us. The next morning Harry received a cable asking him to fly back to Borneo immediately for an urgent conference, missing Christmas at home with George, and leaving me to settle business matters, and follow.

I began this book with "Rendezvous," the meeting of two who love and their resolve not to be parted; I close it with parting, as Harry leaves today by plane for Borneo via Hong Kong.

He has a job to finish; the very soul of that job is conservation of forests, one of the most important of the earth's resources, and of man's sources for food. The successful execution of his job may be one step forward in eliminating the causes for which men fight.

Before Harry goes, I am complaining and unheroic. I tell him it is beyond the call of duty to fight three wars, the first at the age of fifteen; I plead with him to resign his job and stay at home in North America where he and I and George can be together. It is not that I expect to avoid danger by staying out of the East, but that whatever happens, I would like to face it all three together. Leaving again in the face of war is too alarmingly like what we did in 1939; I ask myself if we are going through the motions blindly, helplessly, without reason or motive, in a dream?

But Harry goes – as I knew he would do from the time the cable came. And I will follow, as I knew I would do.

Today at the airport when Harry leaves, there is a dreadful moment as he walks away from us. George puts his arm around *me* this time, tall, blue-coated, gray-flannel-trousered George with his school tie twisted under his chin, George with his oval face growing angular now, nearly a man at ten; George, my son, puts his arm about me and comforts me – "Don't cry, Mum, Dad doesn't want you to be unhappy!"

No, he doesn't want me to be unhappy; but happiness ceases to have much part in life when one becomes an adult. Or perhaps the sources of happiness change. I know why Harry went; there is only one way the individual can show his belief in the dignity and value of human life and this is to act to the end on the assumption that his own job matters.

It is the night before Christmas, and I am listening to the radio and polishing George's football boots with dubbin, the Old British Standby for Leather, and listening for news of a plane traveling from Vancouver, B.C., to Hong Kong; listening, but hoping not to hear, for no news is good news. And I am remembering last Christmas Eve.

There is a plain on the west coast of North Borneo which lies below lazy, absinthe-colored hills and looks up to the towering, blue rock crags of Kinabalu, the highest mountain in the Far East, and has for its other boundary the clear, swiftly flowing Kadamaian River with its dark, casuarina tree fringe. This pleasant plain is the site of the village of Kota Belud; or as Harry names it, the favorite native anthropological reserve of North Borneo. A year ago Harry, George and I spent Christmas there.

Kota Belud is an idyllic native Bajau village with inhabitants of much vaunted simplicity, virtue and prowess, who happily co-operate to give the white visitor what he comes for – a picture of native Borneo village life as it seldom is – but could be. This village is rightly the pride of British administrators, almost a Utopia, and as such it is carefully protected from the corruption of modern ways. Desirable visitors with pink cards only are admitted by pass to the district, and white women's morals and the length of their shorts are equally carefully scrutinized in order not to corrupt the simple savage. Kota Belud is an example of life under a benevolent feudal system in which Poppa knows best. And as long as Poppa does know best and no nasty other influence creeps in, this setup is ideal. Perhaps this is the criticism – it is ideal, not real.

It is very comfortable in this little room in Canada this Christmas Eve with the wind howling outside, and a fire burning on the hearth; sitting contentedly thus I sorrow at the situation hanging over us which may rob me of this happiness and comfort, by another war. And I know that I and my country are ready to do anything to avoid this loss – anything, except sacrifice the form of government under which we have acquired these comforts. And, as I sit in comfort tonight, so also do the majority of the people of this continent.

But in Asia it is different. There the majority of people do not have comfortable homes, glowing hearth fires, happiness and material contentment, and they never have had. Their living, or their dying, means little by Asiatic values. But democracies do not have masses of people who do not matter, masses to be sacrificed safely to the enemy as cannon fodder; the password of democracy is that every man matters.

We say that the Chinese in Korea are mixing into our fight; the Communist leader of China says they are volunteers helping fellow Communists; but to the masses in China, they are Asiatic forces pushing the white man out of Asia where he doesn't belong.

As I sit here tonight I am making out a shopping list of things not to forget to take back to Borneo with me. Ah San wants an American wrist watch. Ah Kau wants black wool material for warm Chinese trousers to wear when she finally packs up her snapshots of George, her old Christmas cards, and worn cotton clothing in an expandable suitcase and retires to Canton, China, a rich woman by peasant standards. Ah Min asked for a black patent-leather pocketbook, and Gung Ho hasn't asked, but I know what he wants – a mechanized red dump truck like the one we bought for Petie Grant in Victoria who is Gung Ho's age. The Gill boys will like U.S. comics full of genuine American gunmen and desperadoes from the West, Angela needs a sequined evening bag to brighten the dull years ahead, and I will take George's abandoned Hopalong Cassidy hat and boots for the son of Arusap, to adorn him as befits a headman's son!

Now I am no longer unhappy to go. Locked in the dread of parting, I lost for a moment my view of the world, but now I am well content that I will soon travel towards the setting sun. No man is great enough to afford to ignore half his world, or to try to lock himself within his own hemisphere. Now is the significant time in the history of the East, now is the reverse of Marco Polo, as the Orient penetrates the Occident.

These are the stories of my friends, people whose ways have meaning for me, whose lives prove a theme to me – that human blood is a greater tie between people than the same color of skins.

Everybody has to have a friend, Jeannette has said. As human beings and as friends, we are needed by the East now, just as we need the East, and the time of need is never ending. Our relations must be based on this need, and on mutual trust arrived at through understanding; you cannot talk to a starving man, you cannot reason in an unknown tongue, you cannot pray to a God you know not of.

All the affection and love I have for these strange people and places, for these curious, exciting other races, does not suffice me today for practical help. It is just a sad understanding, a helpless reaching out in friendliness towards other human beings who as individuals reach back with friendliness to me – but as races stand with their backs against the wall, shouting – KILL!

We are being caught by the need to hate, just as they are caught, too. Our only escape is to remember that the individual is good, the man next door is kind, the girl beside you in the street is human – and so is the individual half the world away. Ah Min is loving, Ah Kau is gentle, Angela is loyal, José Agama is brave, Surjit Singh has brotherly love, Ah San is honest, Sinyora, Baud, Jikrun, are warmhearted and kind, and Mina is a child like our George, and needs help.

The white man returns – as man, to remain.

Christmas Eve, 1950
VICTORIA, BRITISH COLUMBIA